Oh My Goddess!

ああっ女神さまっ

22

STORY AND ART BY
Kosuke Fujishima

TRANSLATION BY
Dana Lewis AND Lea Hernandez

LETTERING AND TOUCH-UP BY
Susie Lee AND Betty Dong
WITH Tom2K

DARK HORSE MANGA

CHAPTER 136

Let's Make A Deal

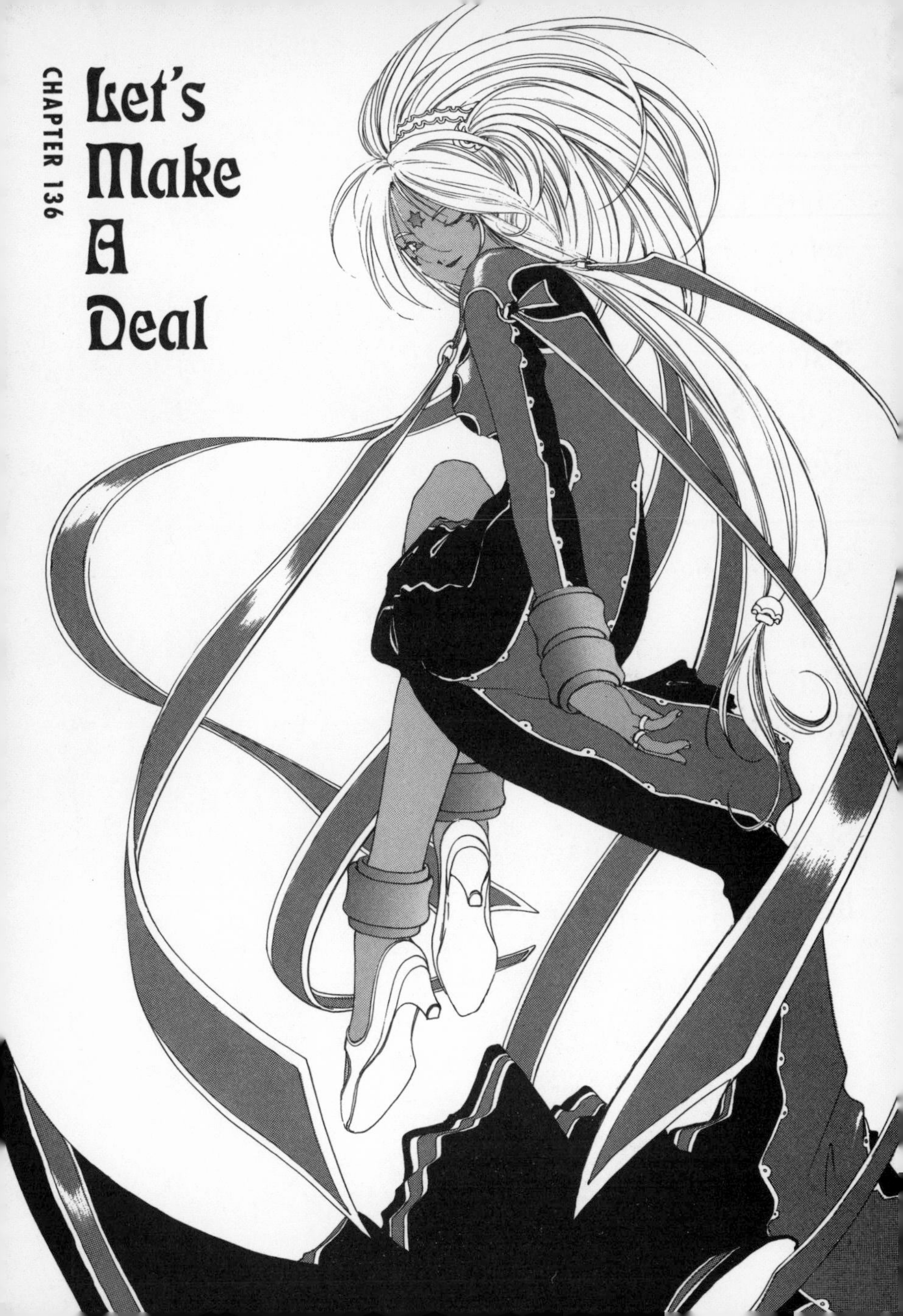

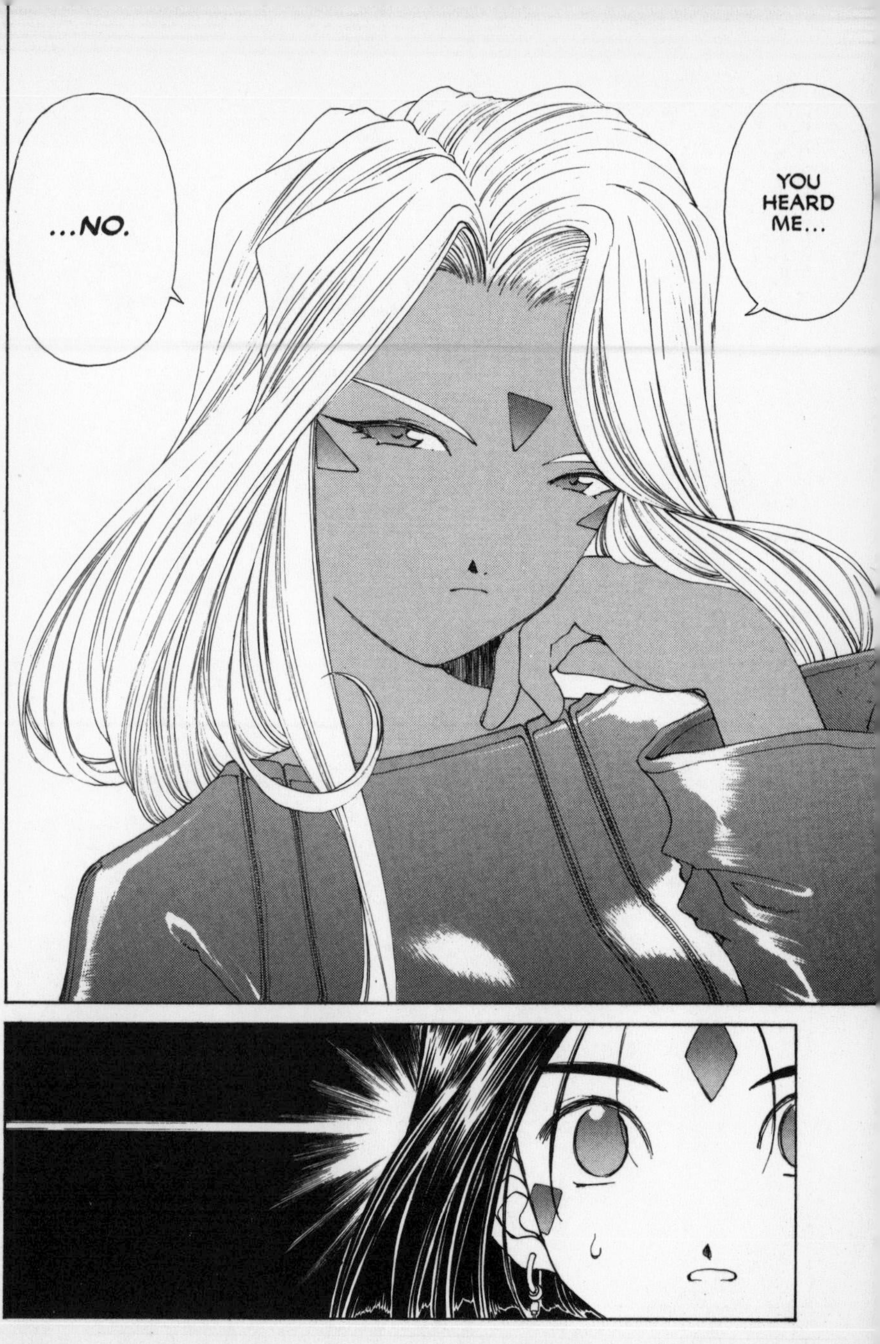
YOU HEARD ME...
...NO.

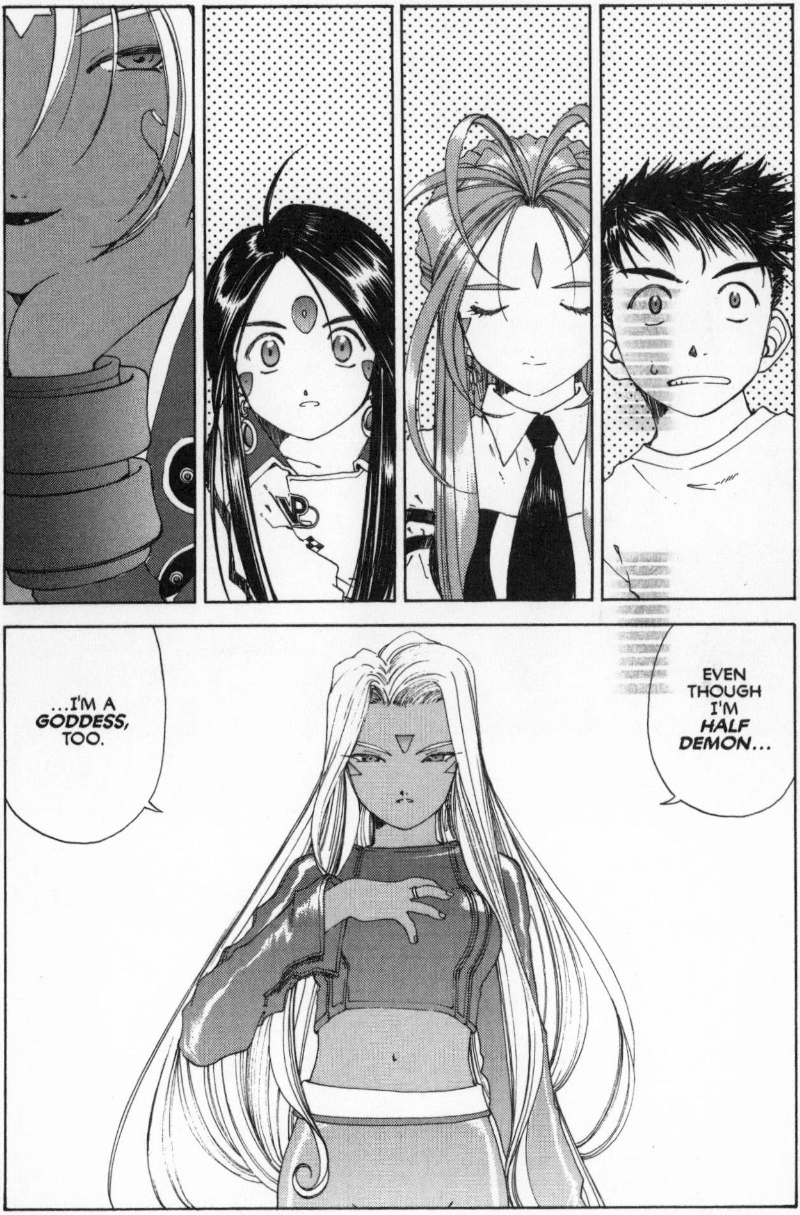
EVEN THOUGH I'M *HALF DEMON*...
...I'M A *GODDESS*, TOO.

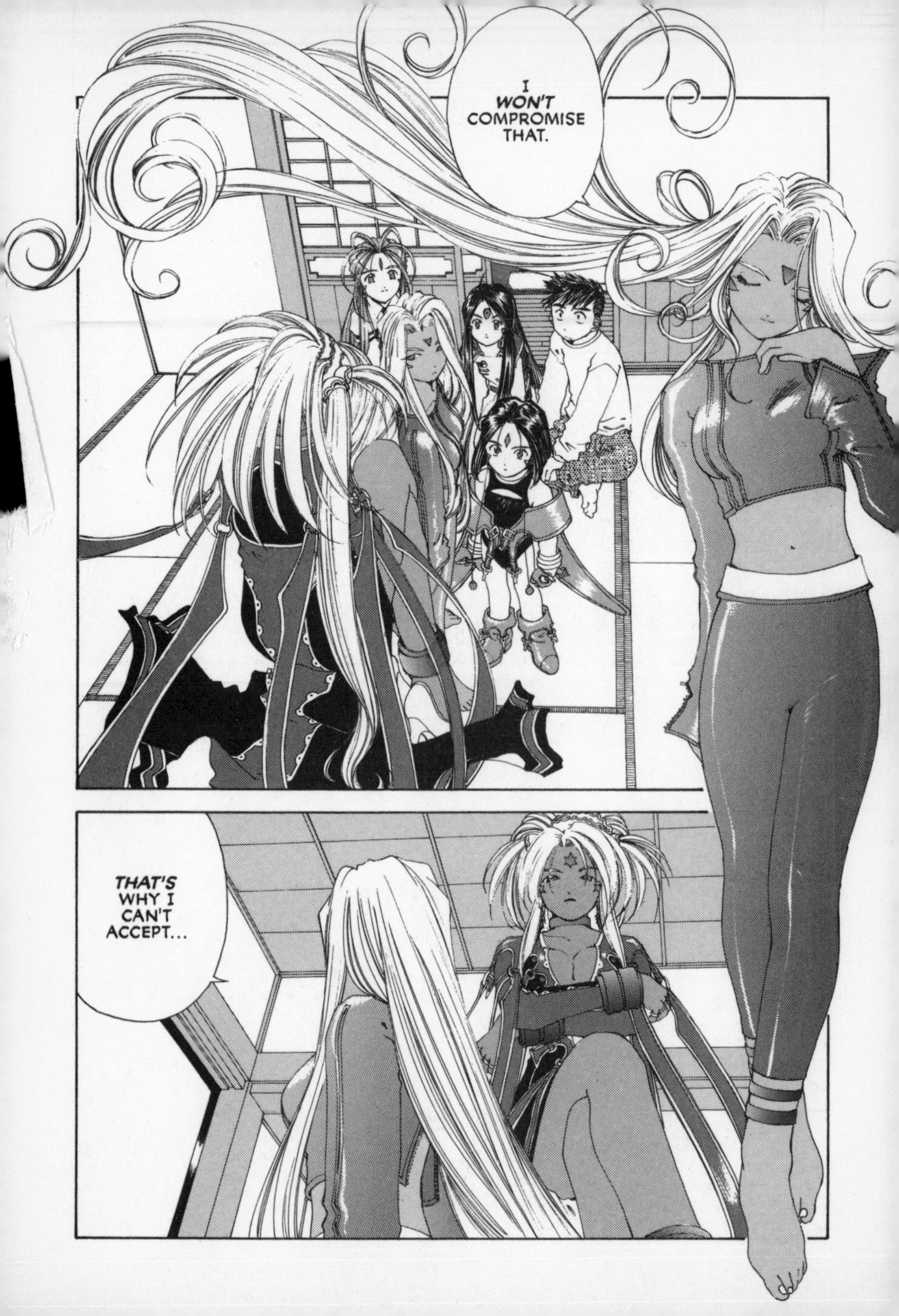
I *WON'T* COMPROMISE THAT.
THAT'S WHY I CAN'T ACCEPT...

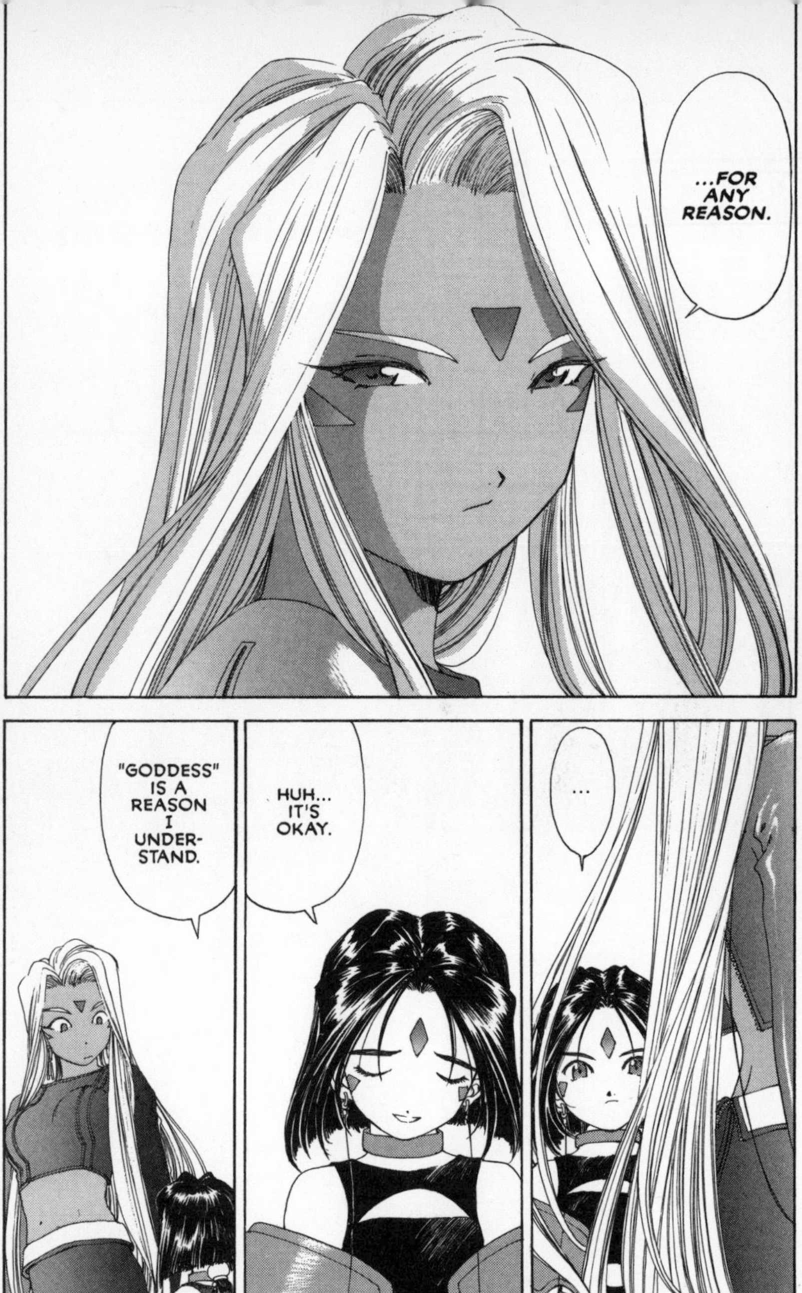
...FOR ANY REASON.
...
HUH... IT'S OKAY.
"GODDESS" IS A REASON I UNDER-STAND.

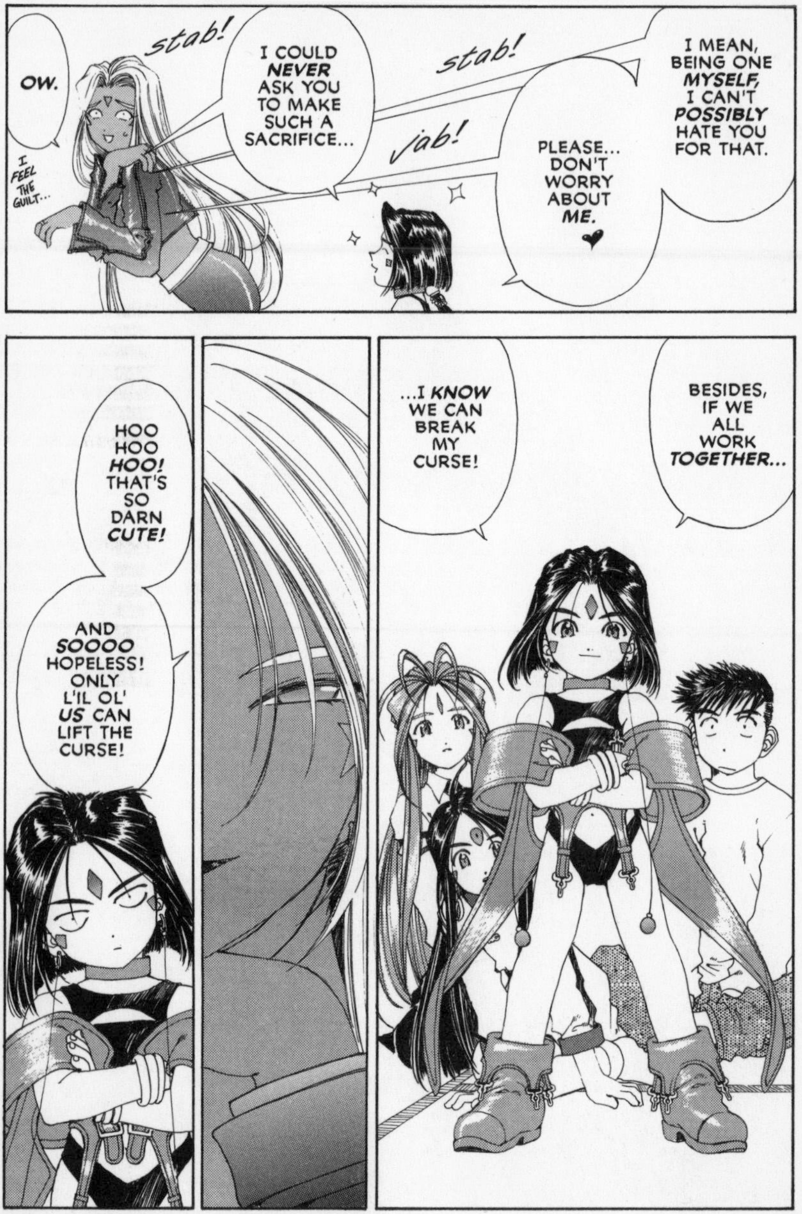
I MEAN, BEING ONE MYSELF, I CAN'T POSSIBLY HATE YOU FOR THAT.
PLEASE... DON'T WORRY ABOUT ME.
stab!
jab!
I COULD NEVER ASK YOU TO MAKE SUCH A SACRIFICE...
stab!
OW.
I FEEL THE GUILT...
BESIDES, IF WE ALL WORK TOGETHER...
...I KNOW WE CAN BREAK MY CURSE!
HOO HOO HOO! THAT'S SO DARN CUTE!
AND SOOOO HOPELESS! ONLY L'IL OL' US CAN LIFT THE CURSE!

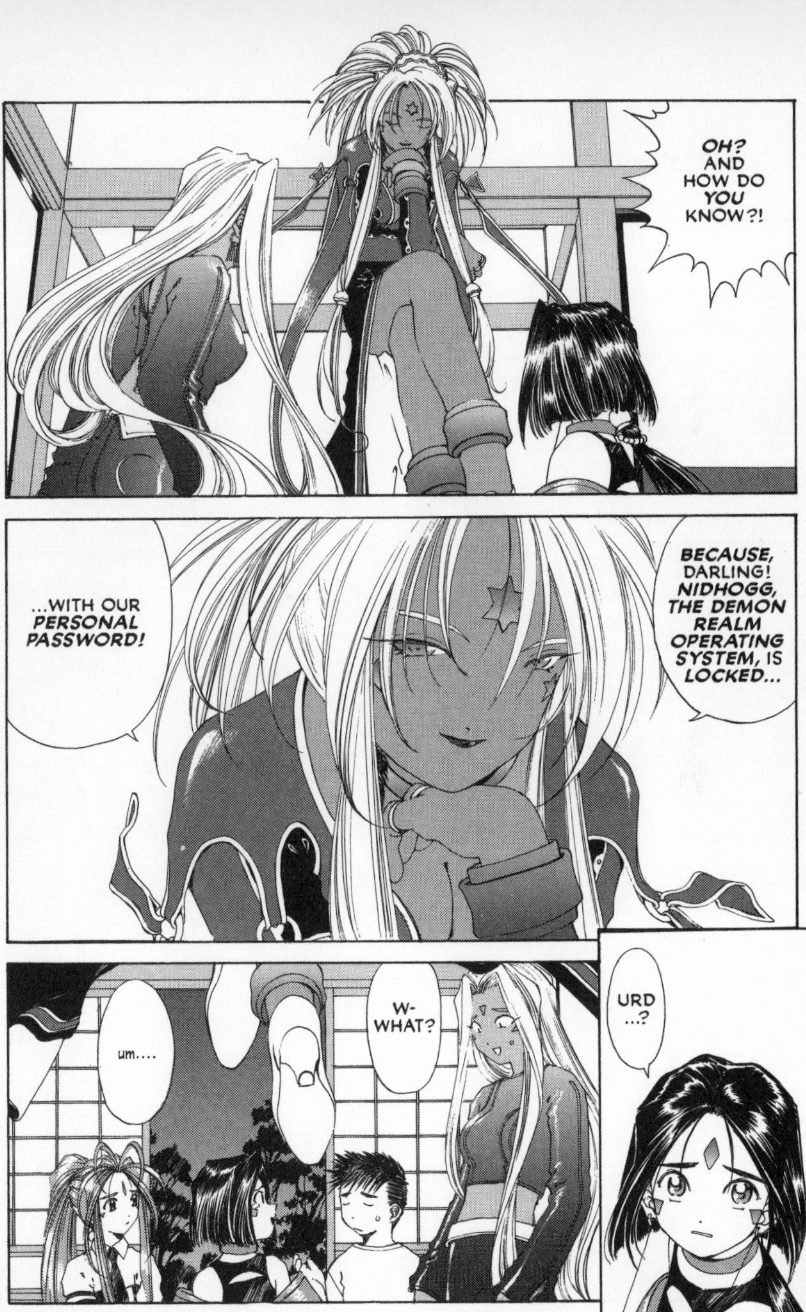
OH? AND HOW DO YOU KNOW?!
BECAUSE, DARLING! NIDHOGG, THE DEMON REALM OPERATING SYSTEM, IS LOCKED...
...WITH OUR PERSONAL PASSWORD!
URD ...?
W-WHAT?
um....

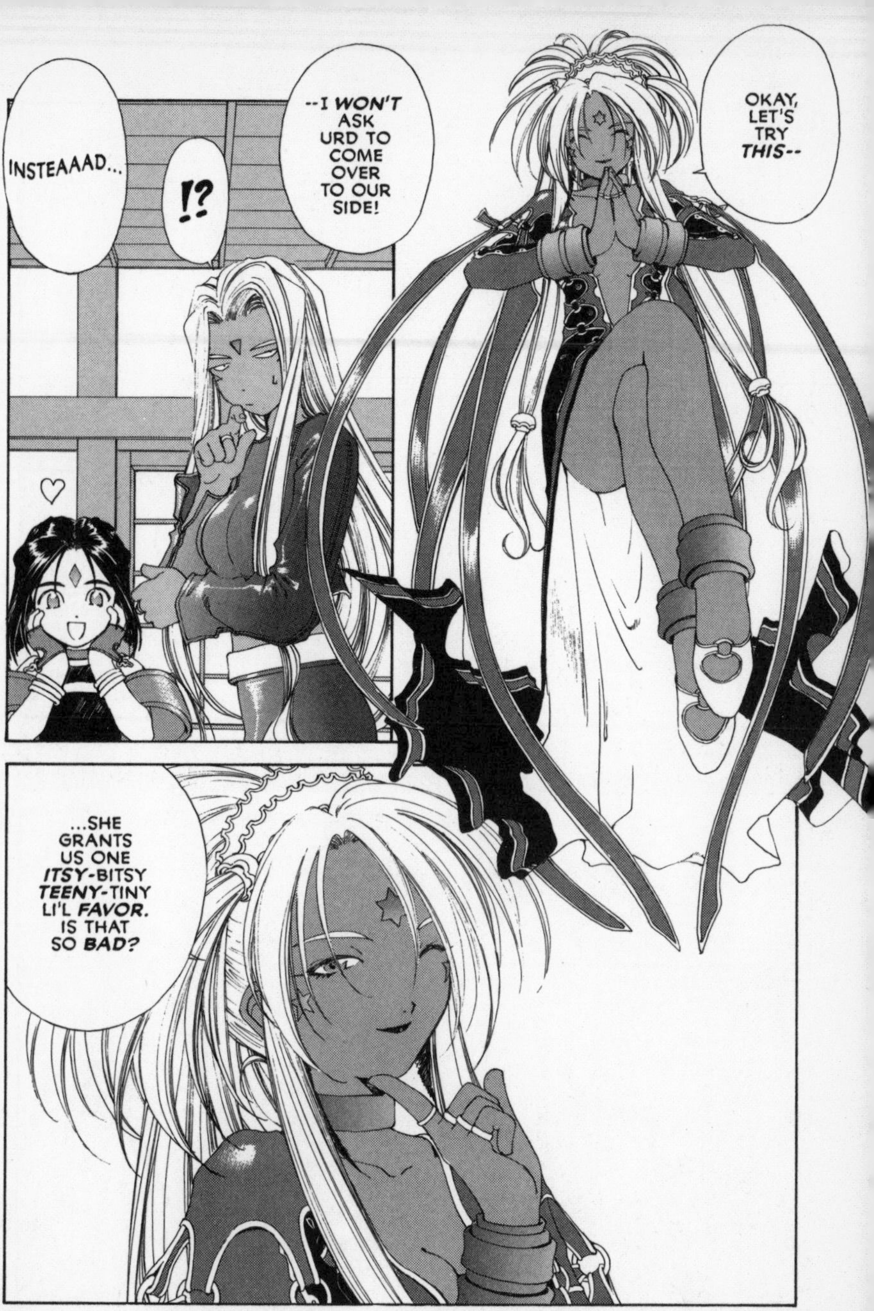
OKAY, LET'S TRY *THIS*--
--I *WON'T* ASK URD TO COME OVER TO OUR SIDE!
!?
INSTEAAAD...
...SHE GRANTS US ONE *ITSY*-BITSY *TEENY*-TINY LI'L *FAVOR*. IS THAT SO *BAD?*

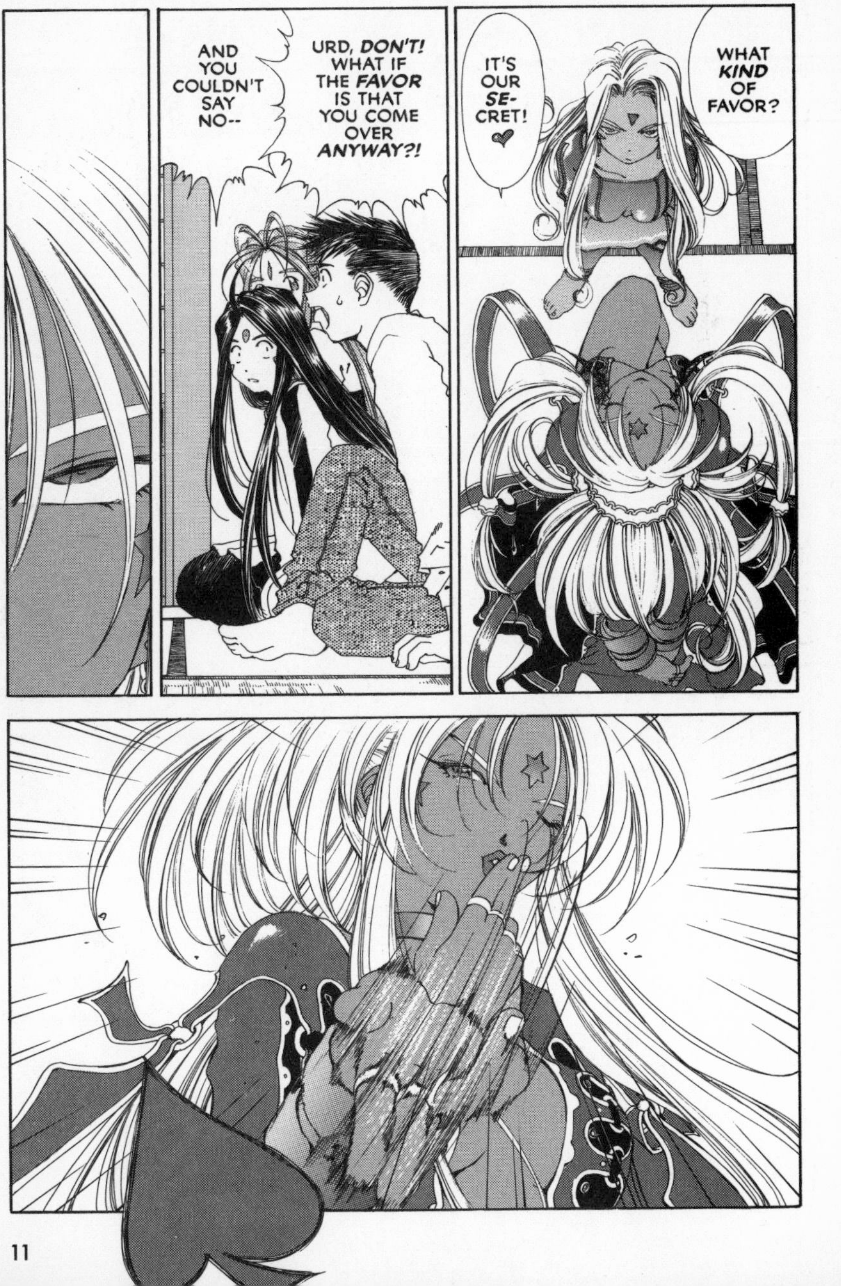
WHAT KIND OF FAVOR?
IT'S OUR SE-CRET! ❤
URD, DON'T! WHAT IF THE FAVOR IS THAT YOU COME OVER ANYWAY?!
AND YOU COULDN'T SAY NO--

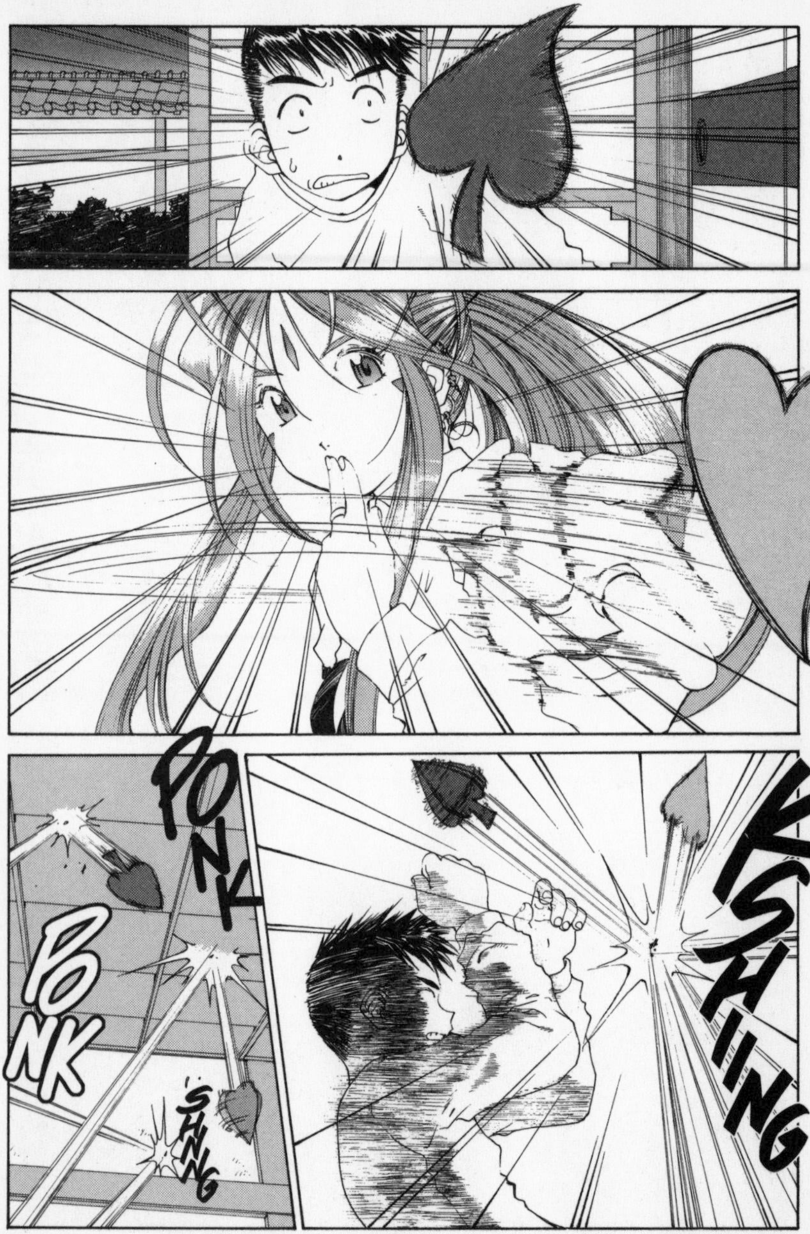
K'SHING
PONK
PONK
'SHNNG

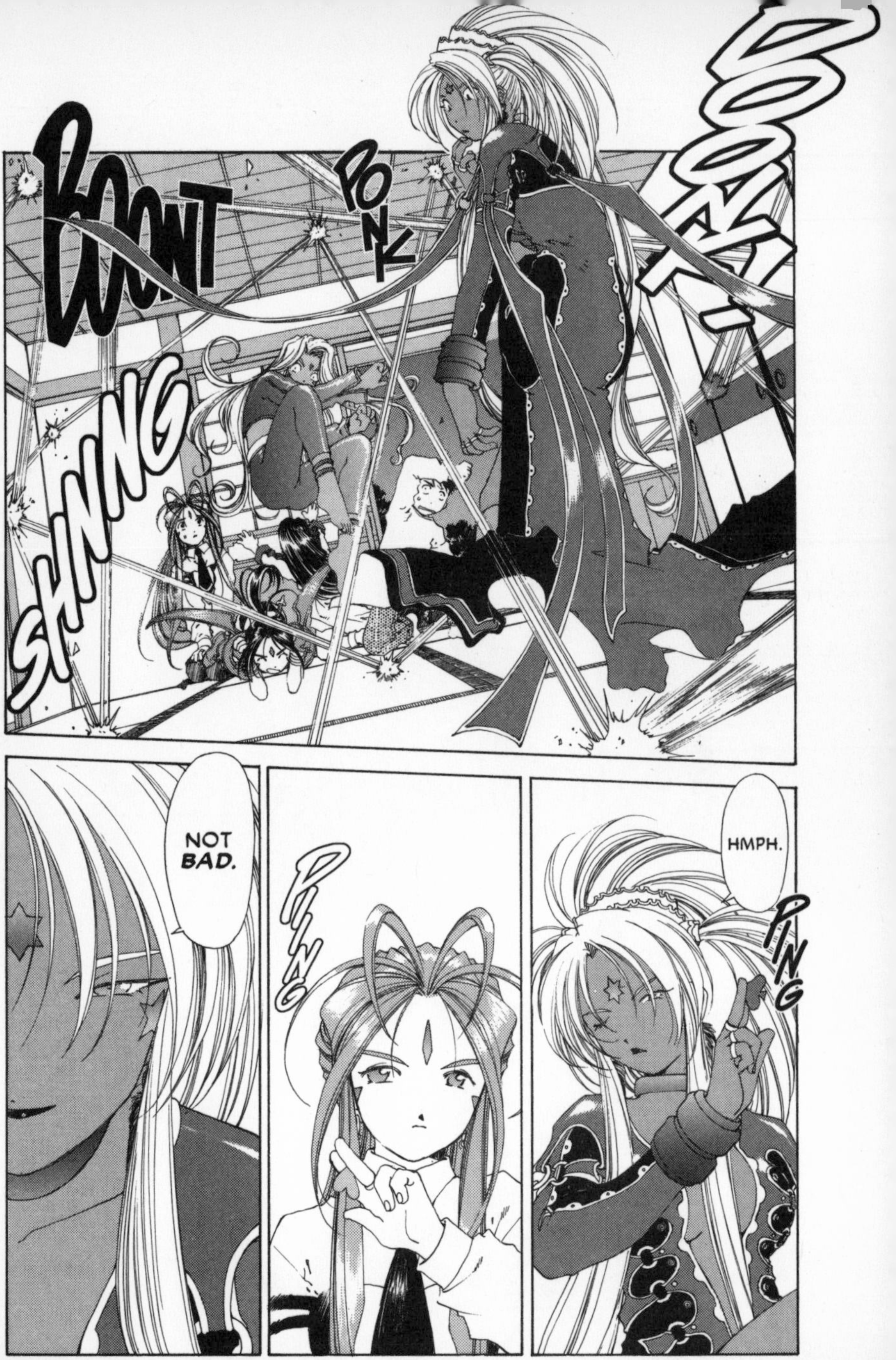
BOONT
PONK
SHINING
HMPH.
PING
PING
NOT BAD.

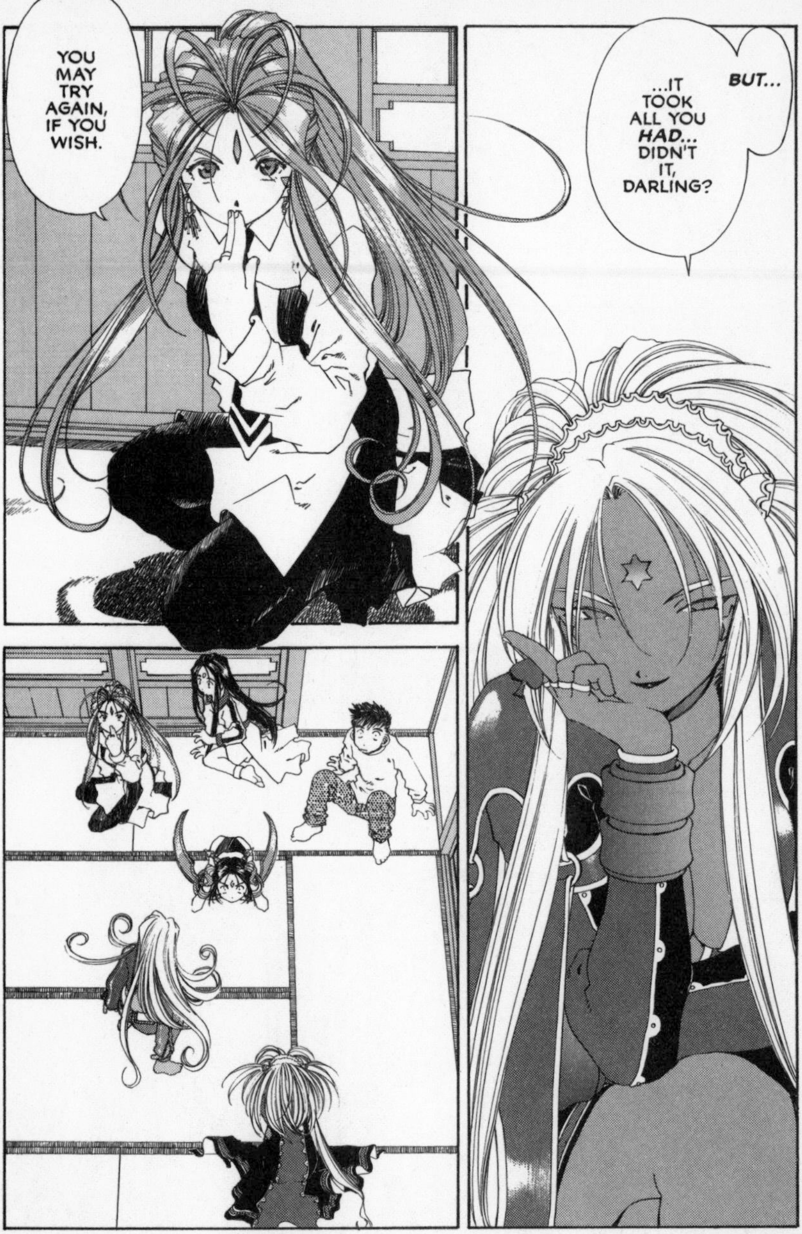
BUT...
...IT TOOK ALL YOU *HAD*... DIDN'T IT, DARLING?
YOU MAY TRY AGAIN, IF YOU WISH.

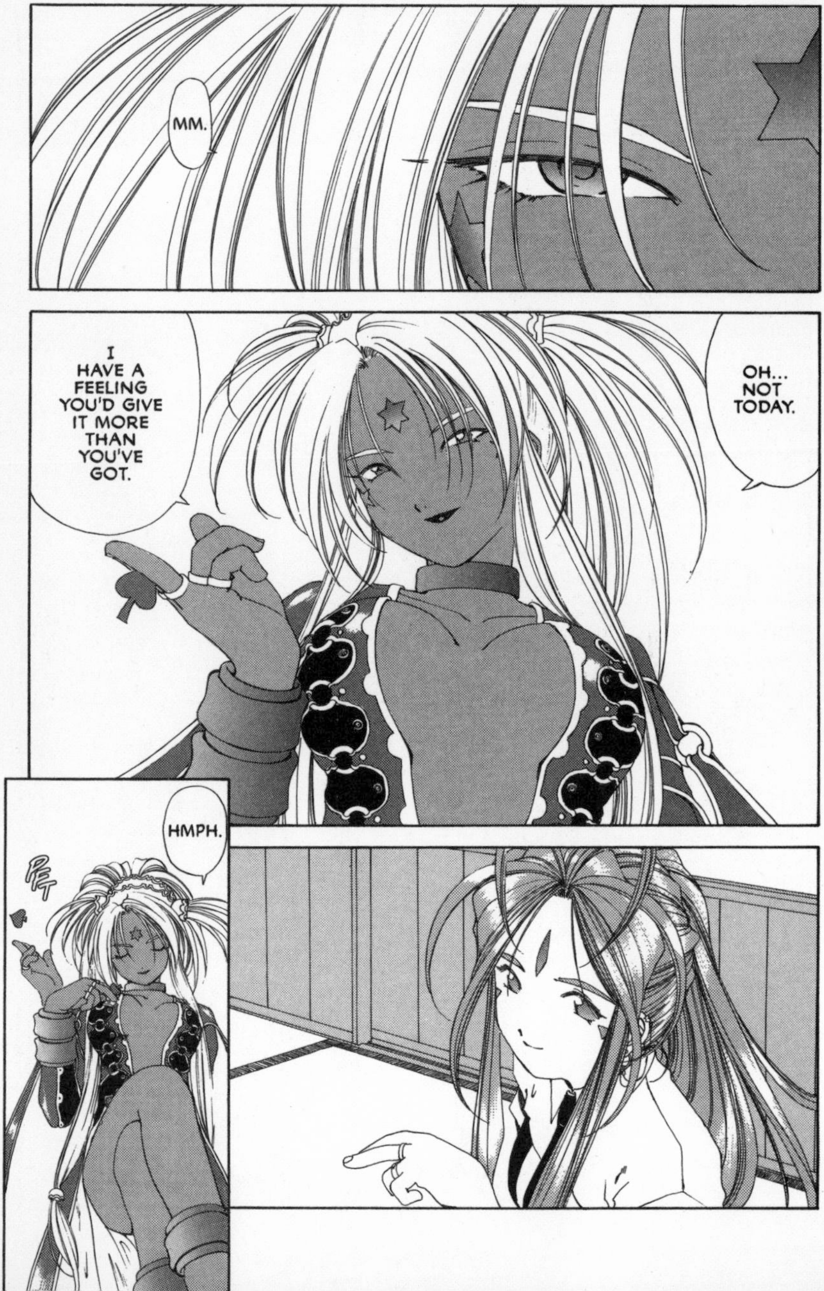
MM.
OH... NOT TODAY.
I HAVE A FEELING YOU'D GIVE IT MORE THAN YOU'VE GOT.
HMPH.
PFFT

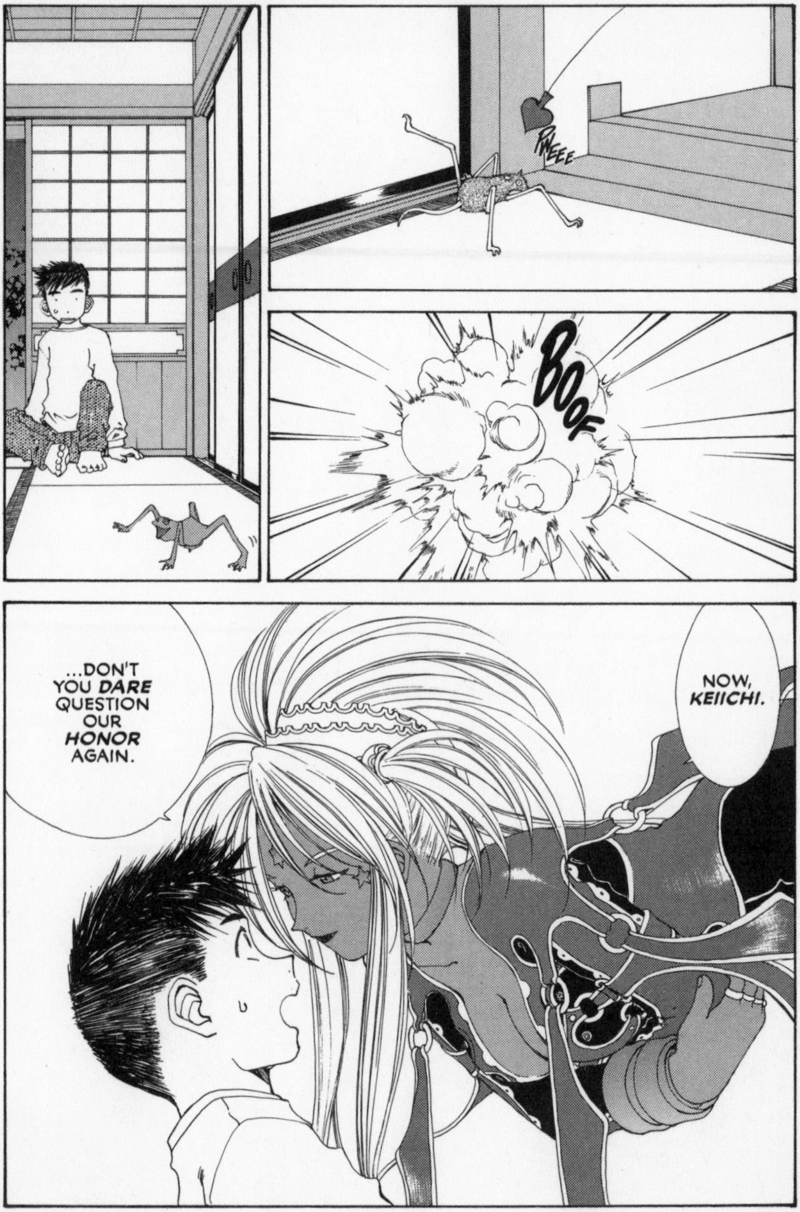
PWEEE
BOOF
NOW, KEIICHI.
...DON'T YOU DARE QUESTION OUR HONOR AGAIN.

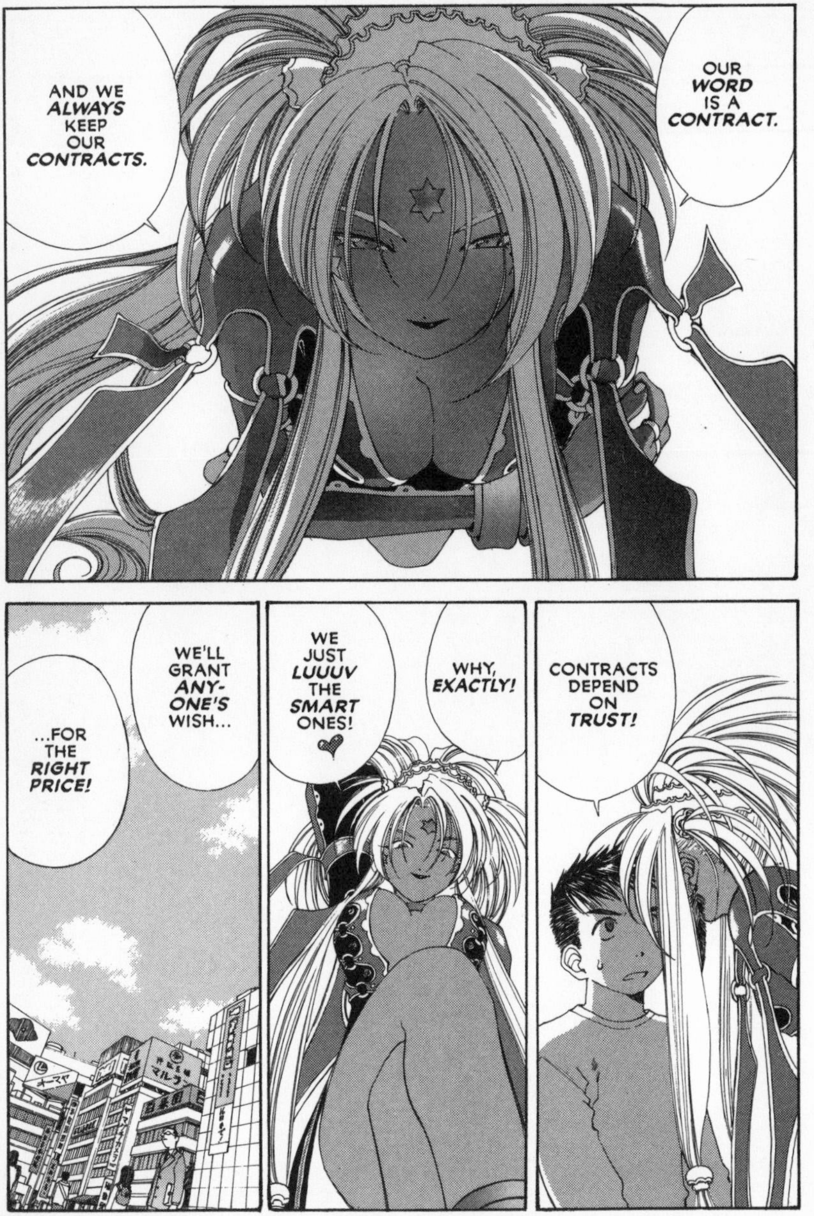
OUR WORD IS A CONTRACT.
AND WE ALWAYS KEEP OUR CONTRACTS.
CONTRACTS DEPEND ON TRUST!
WHY, EXACTLY!
WE JUST LUUUV THE SMART ONES! ♥
WE'LL GRANT ANY-ONE'S WISH...
...FOR THE RIGHT PRICE!

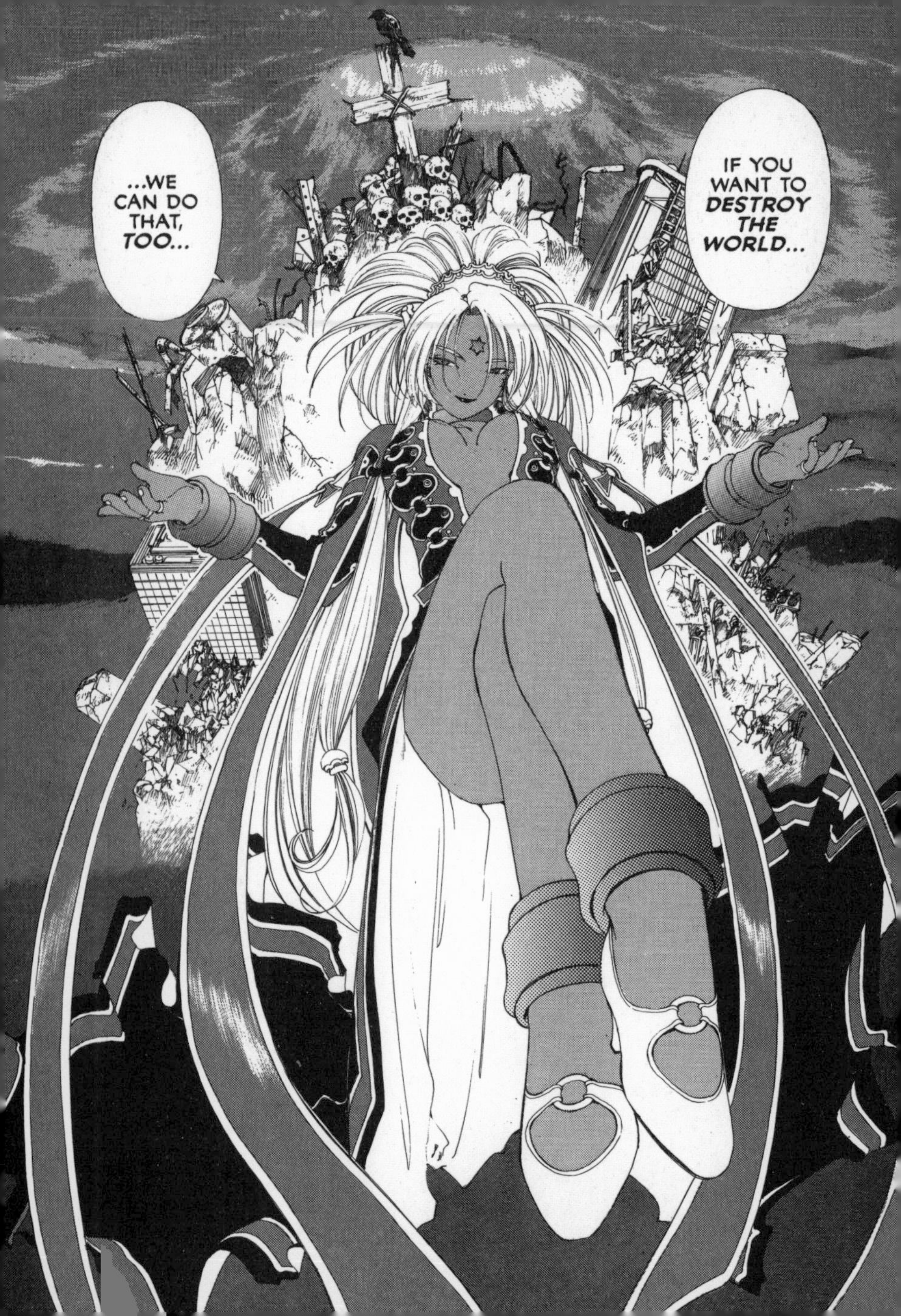
IF YOU WANT TO *DESTROY THE WORLD*...
...WE CAN DO THAT, *TOO*...

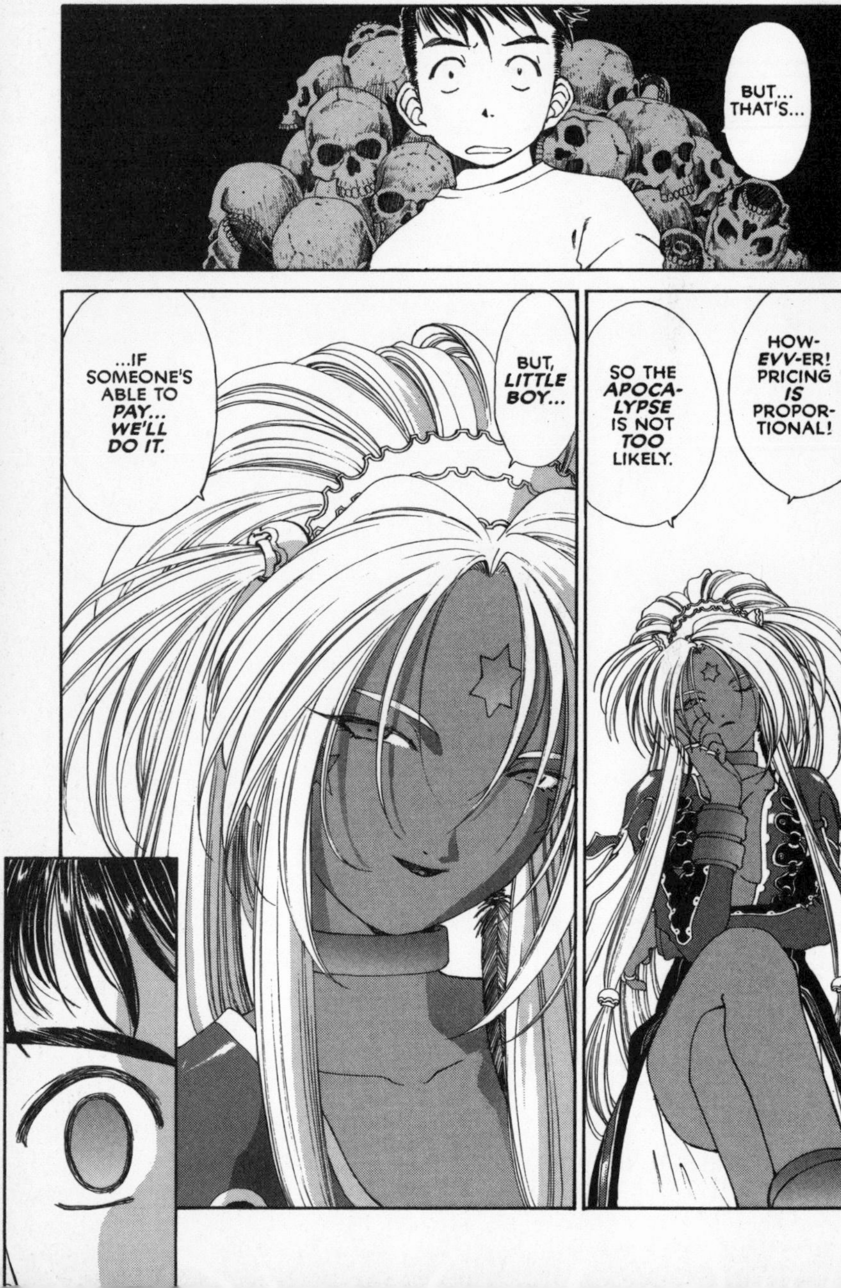
BUT... THAT'S...
HOW-EVV-ER! PRICING IS PROPORTIONAL!
SO THE APOCALYPSE IS NOT TOO LIKELY.
BUT, LITTLE BOY...
...IF SOMEONE'S ABLE TO PAY... WE'LL DO IT.

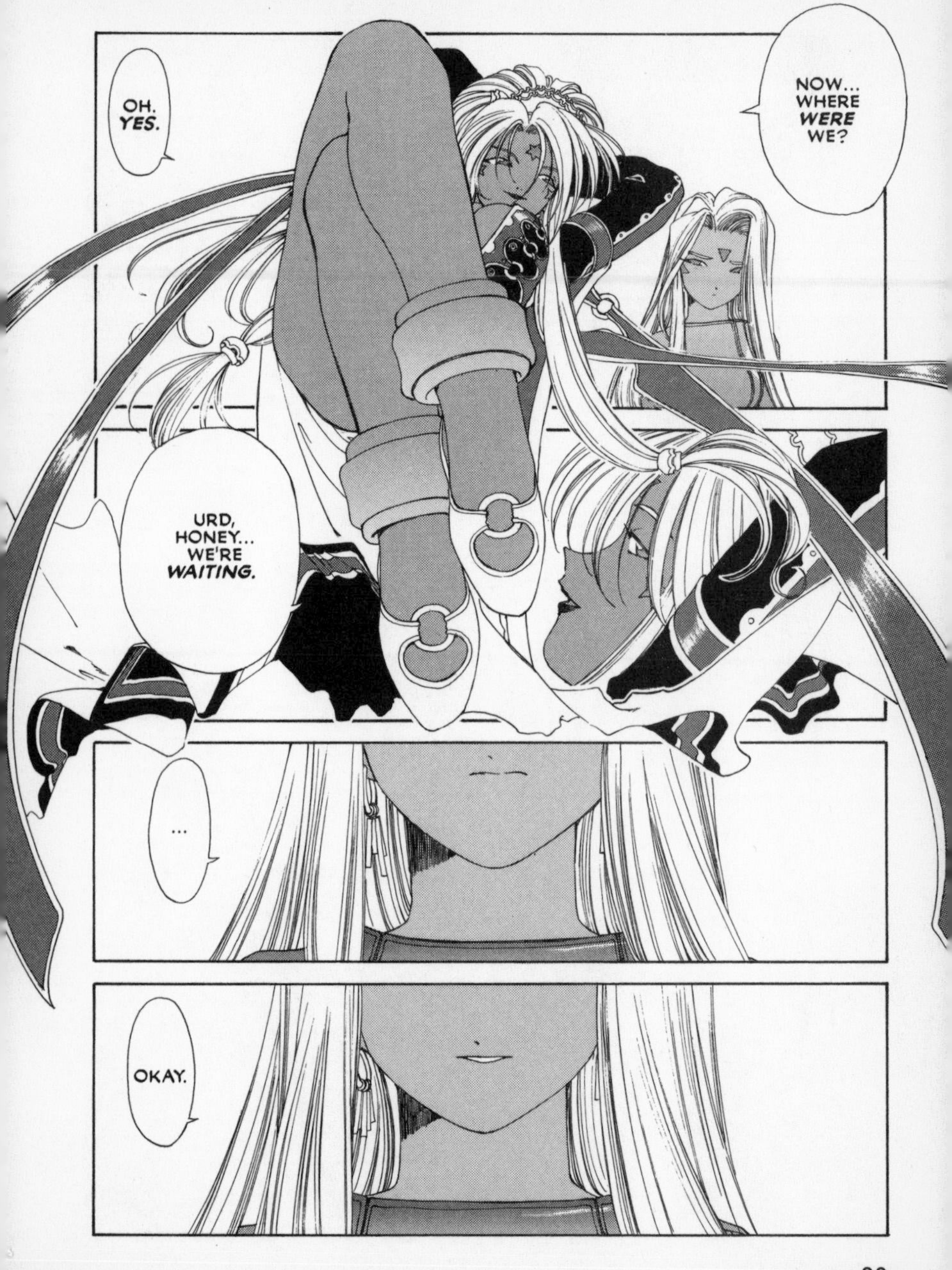
NOW... WHERE *WERE* WE?
OH. *YES.*
URD, HONEY... WE'RE *WAITING.*
...
OKAY.

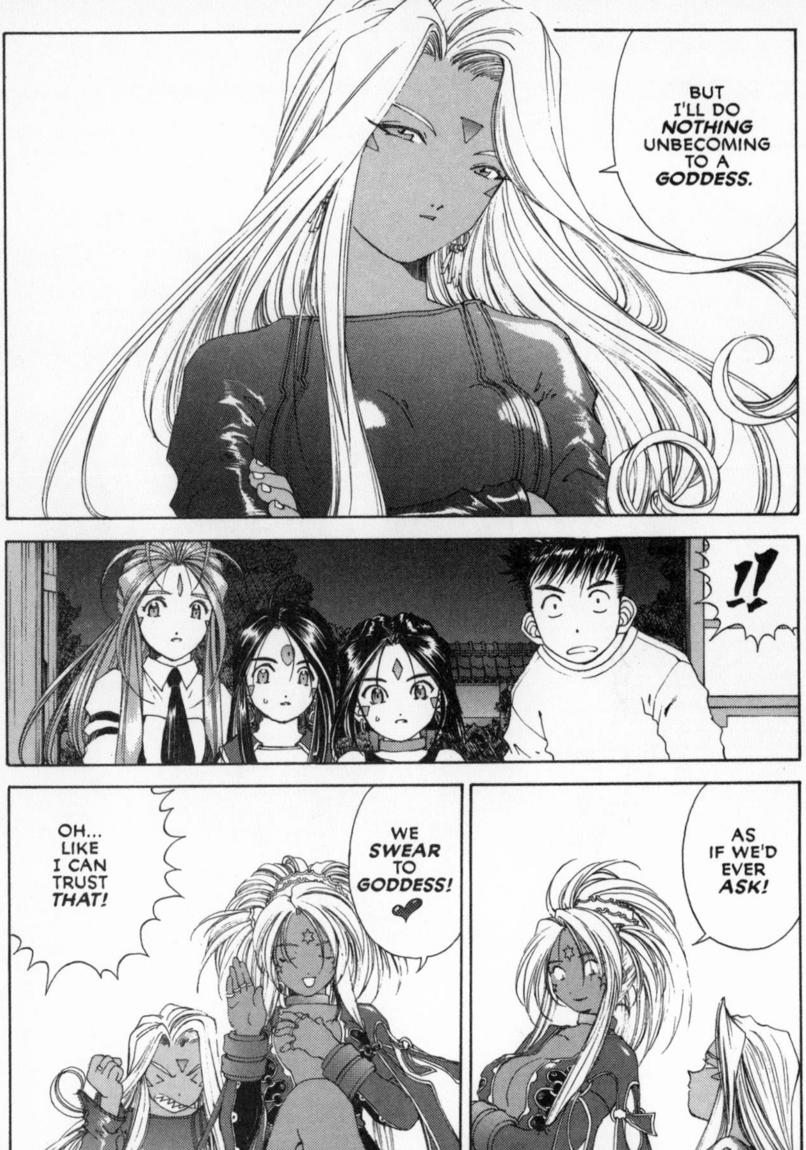
BUT I'LL DO NOTHING UNBECOMING TO A GODDESS.
!!
AS IF WE'D EVER ASK!
WE SWEAR TO GODDESS!
OH... LIKE I CAN TRUST THAT!

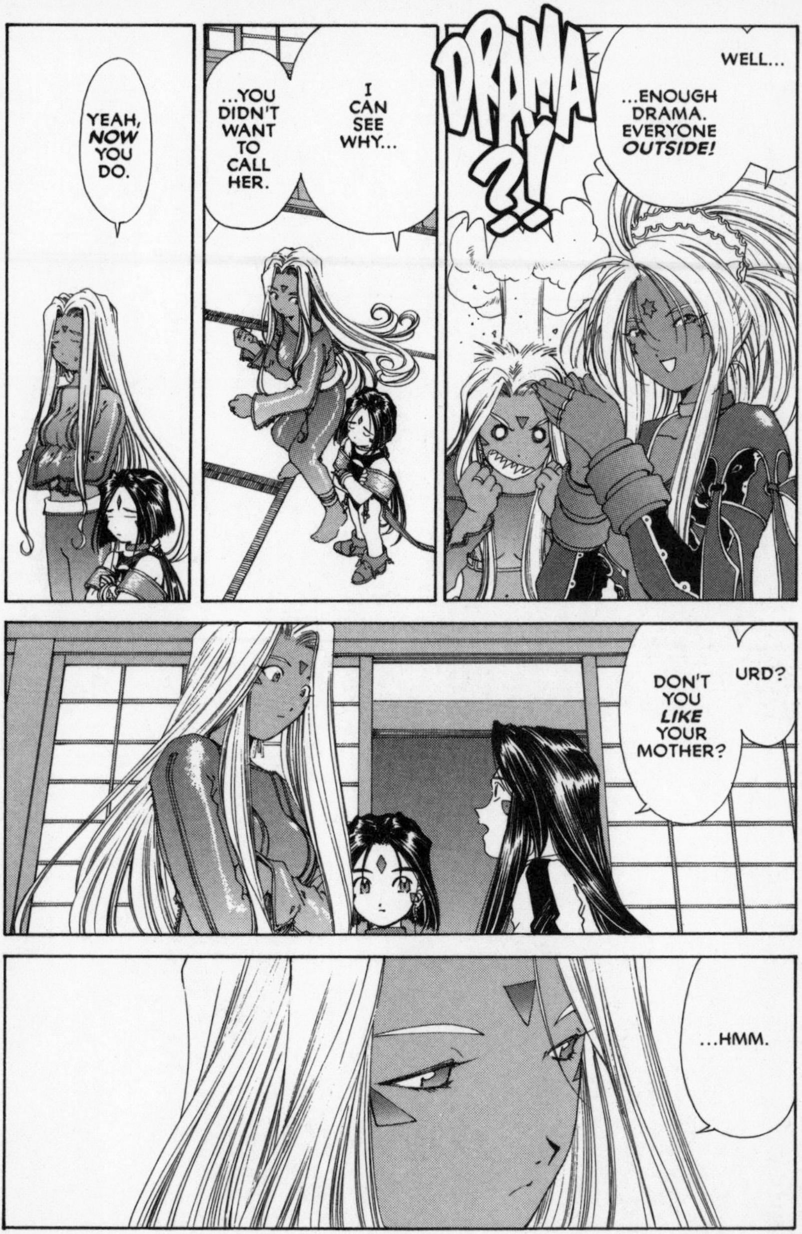
WELL...
...ENOUGH DRAMA. EVERYONE OUTSIDE!
DRAMA?!
I CAN SEE WHY...
...YOU DIDN'T WANT TO CALL HER.
YEAH, NOW YOU DO.
URD?
DON'T YOU LIKE YOUR MOTHER?
...HMM.

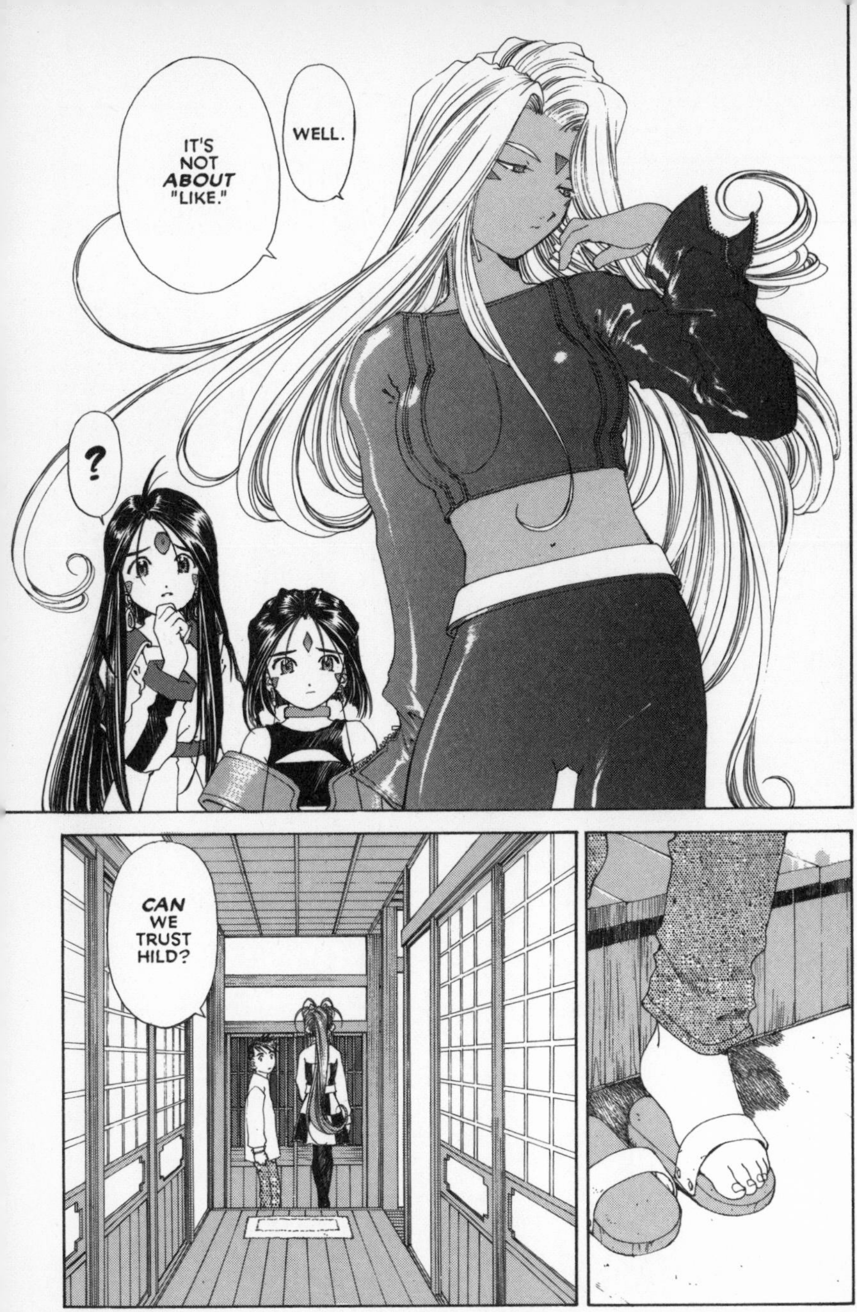
WELL.
IT'S NOT ***ABOUT*** "LIKE."
?
CAN WE TRUST HILD?

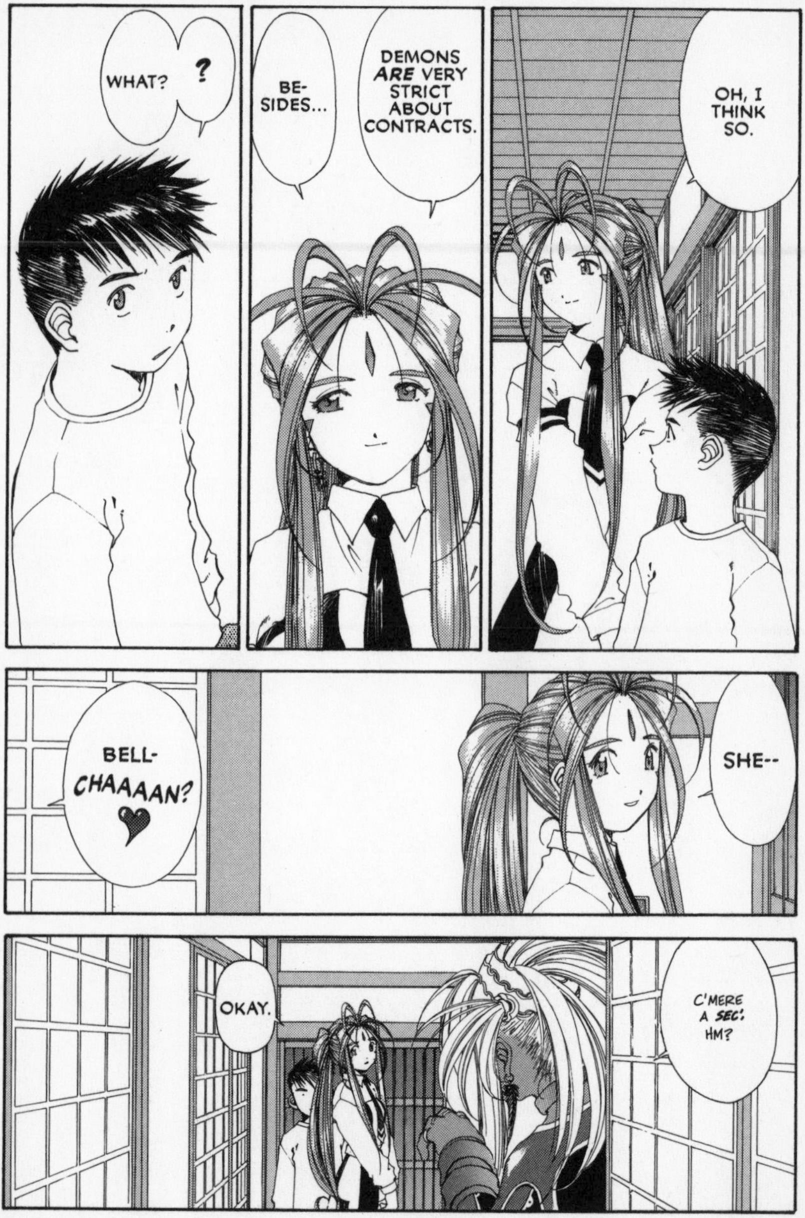
OH, I THINK SO.
DEMONS *ARE* VERY STRICT ABOUT CONTRACTS.
BE-SIDES...
?
WHAT?
SHE--
BELL-CHAAAAN? ♥
C'MERE A SEC; HM?
OKAY.

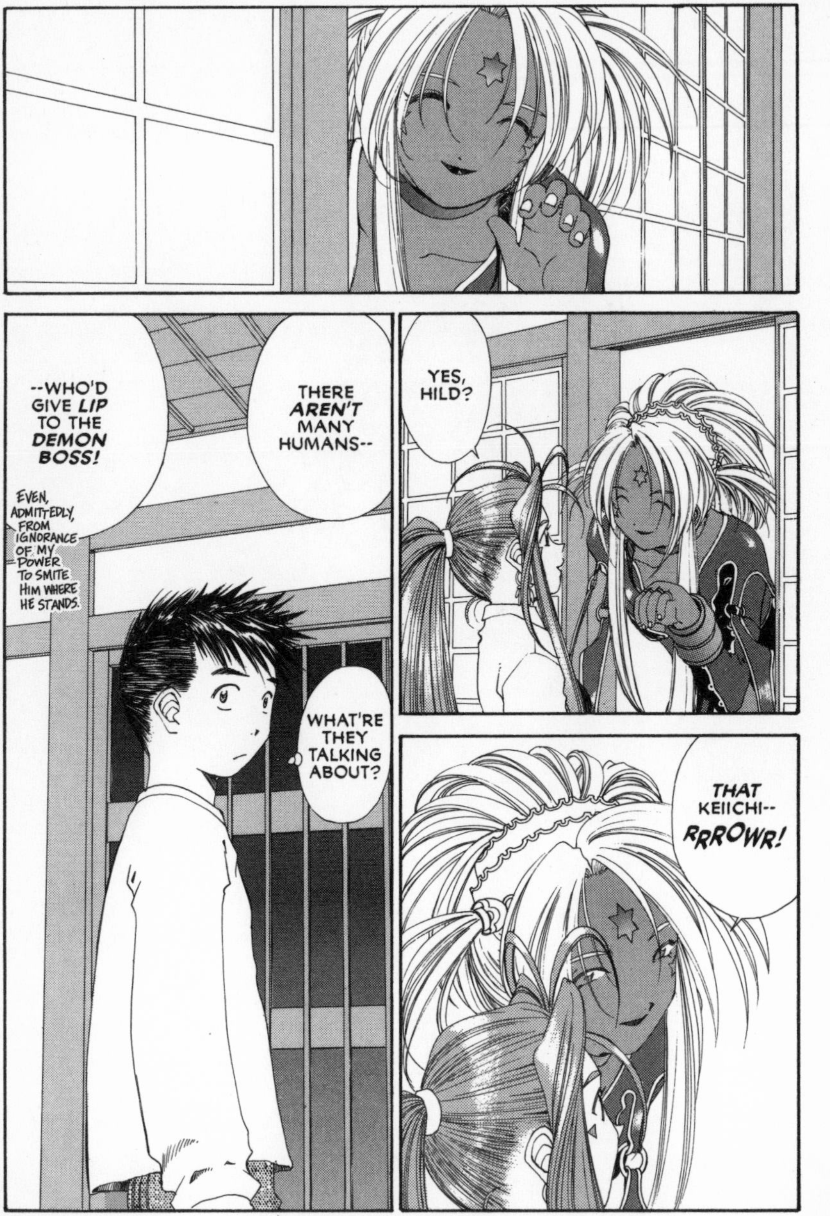
YES, HILD?
THAT KEIICHI-- RRROWR!
THERE AREN'T MANY HUMANS--
--WHO'D GIVE LIP TO THE DEMON BOSS!
EVEN, ADMITTEDLY, FROM IGNORANCE OF MY POWER TO SMITE HIM WHERE HE STANDS.
WHAT'RE THEY TALKING ABOUT?

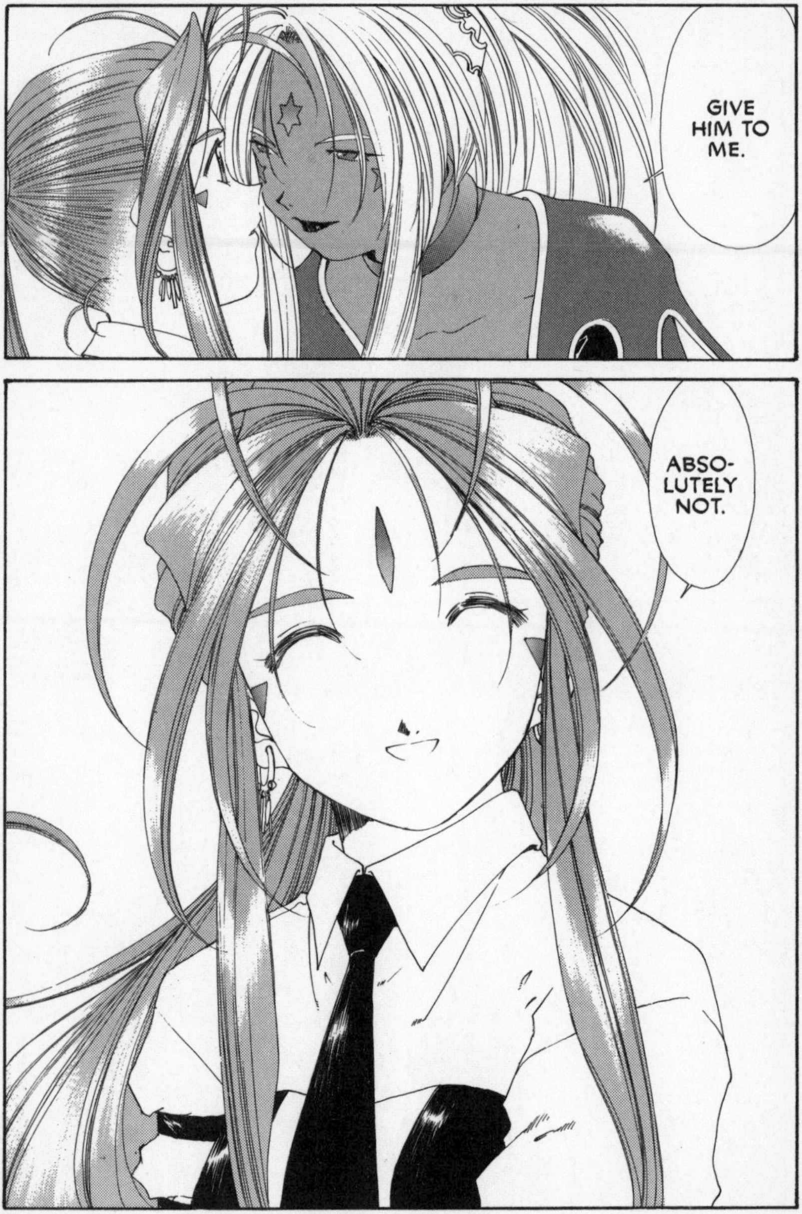
GIVE HIM TO ME.
ABSOLUTELY NOT.

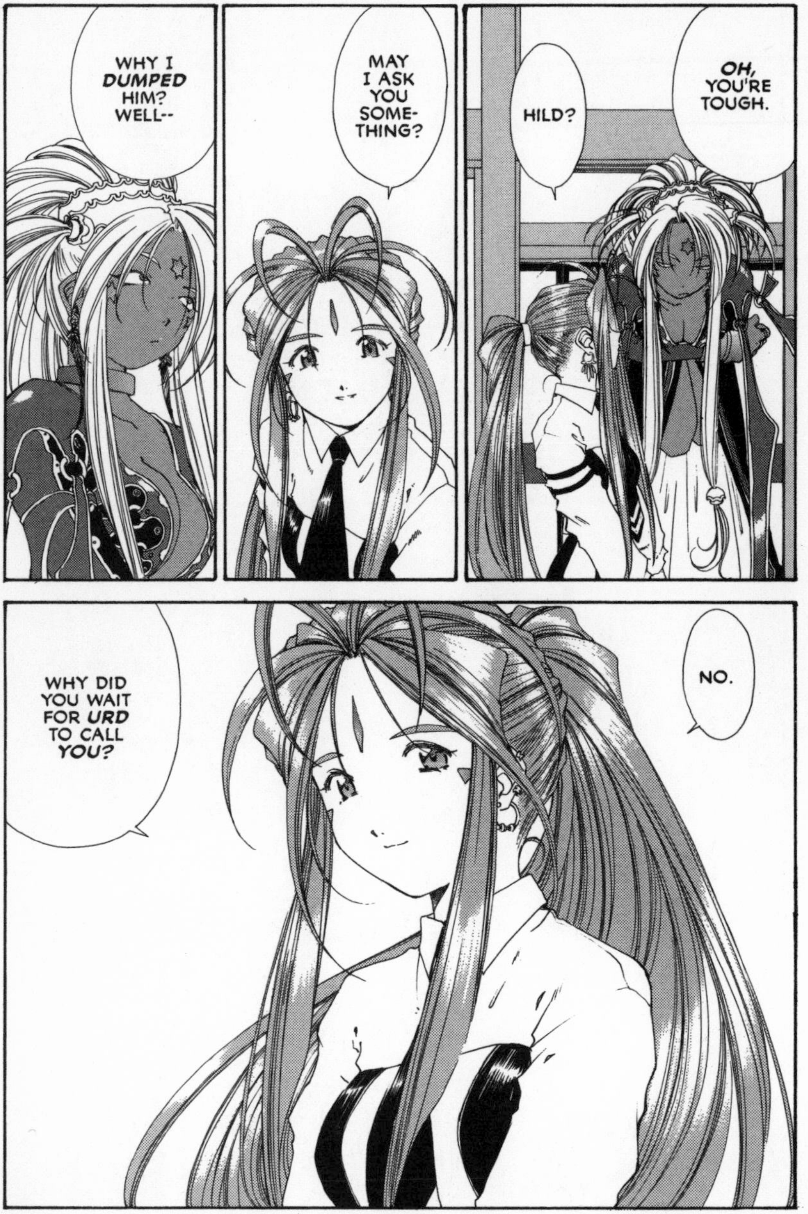
OH, YOU'RE TOUGH.
HILD?
MAY I ASK YOU SOMETHING?
WHY I *DUMPED* HIM? WELL--
NO.
WHY DID YOU WAIT FOR *URD* TO CALL *YOU?*

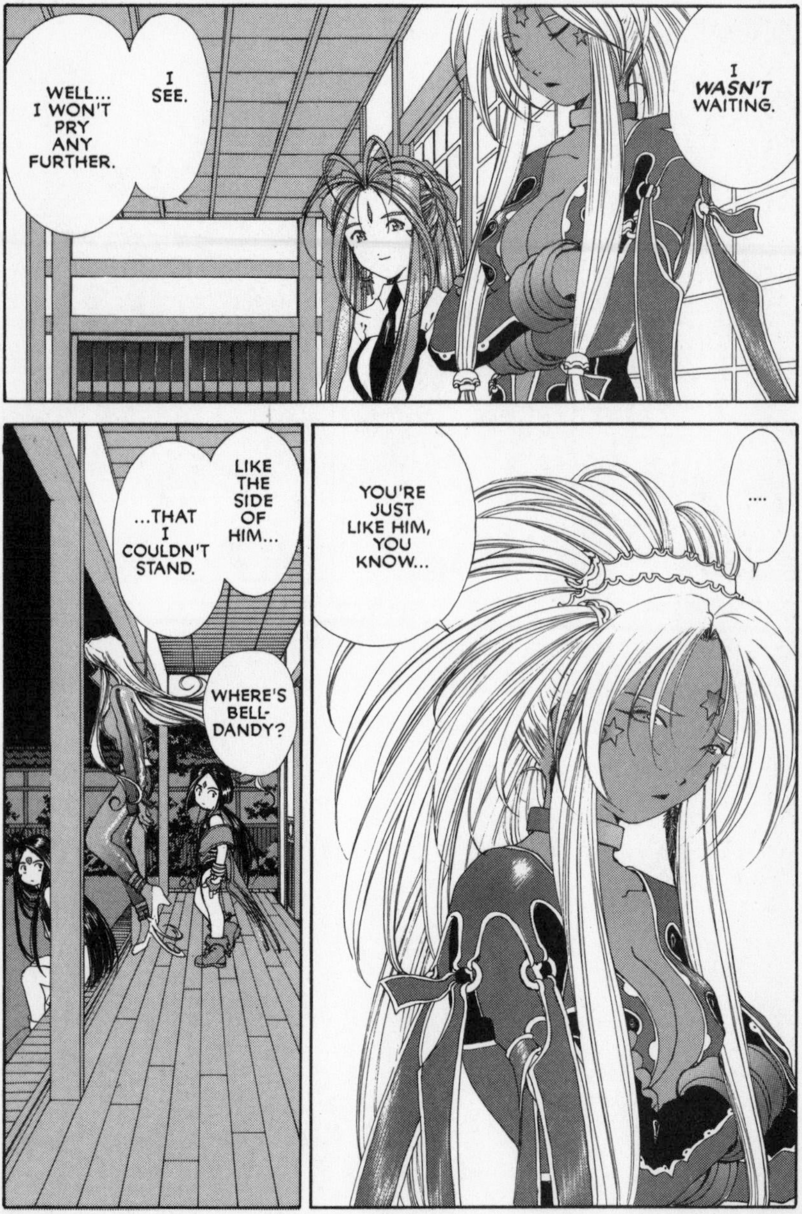
I *WASN'T* WAITING.
I SEE.
WELL... I WON'T PRY ANY FURTHER.
....
YOU'RE JUST LIKE HIM, YOU KNOW...
LIKE THE SIDE OF HIM...
...THAT I COULDN'T STAND.
WHERE'S BELL-DANDY?

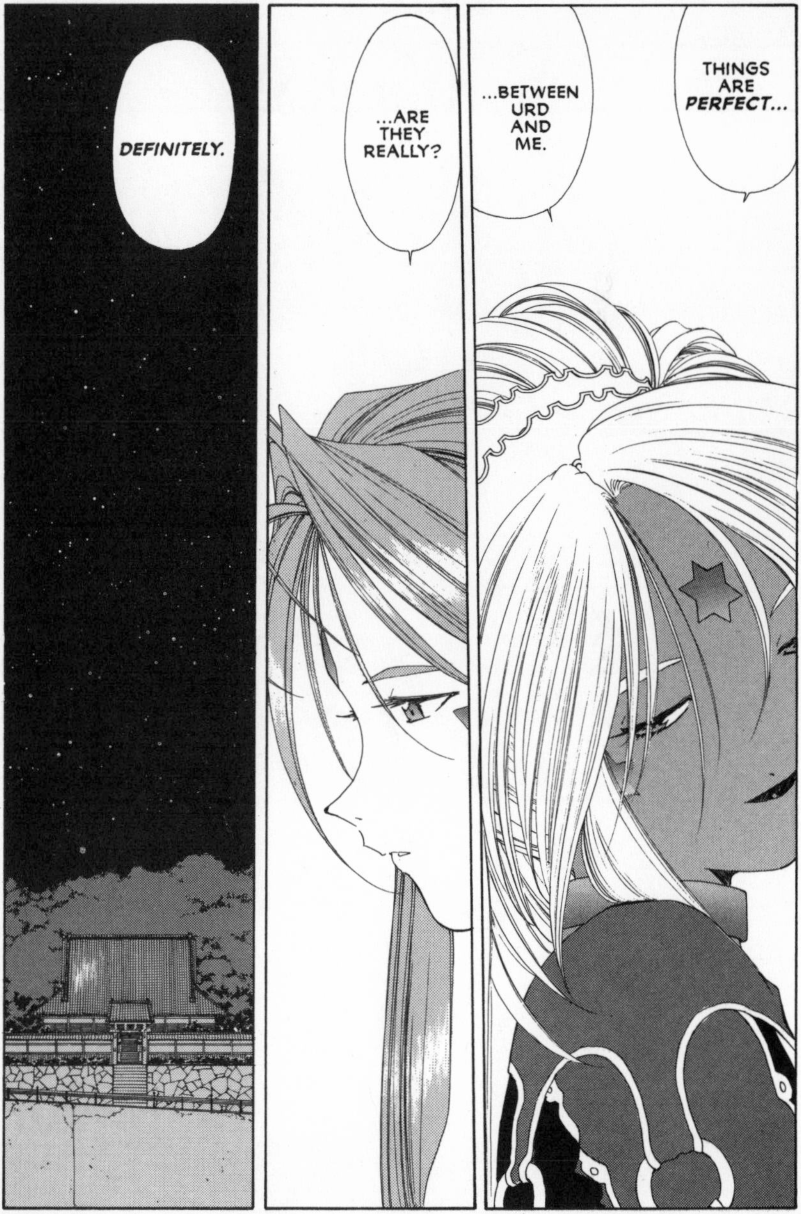
THINGS ARE *PERFECT*...
...BETWEEN URD AND ME.
...ARE THEY REALLY?
DEFINITELY.

Oh My Goddess!
HILD

CHAPTER 137

Sister Act

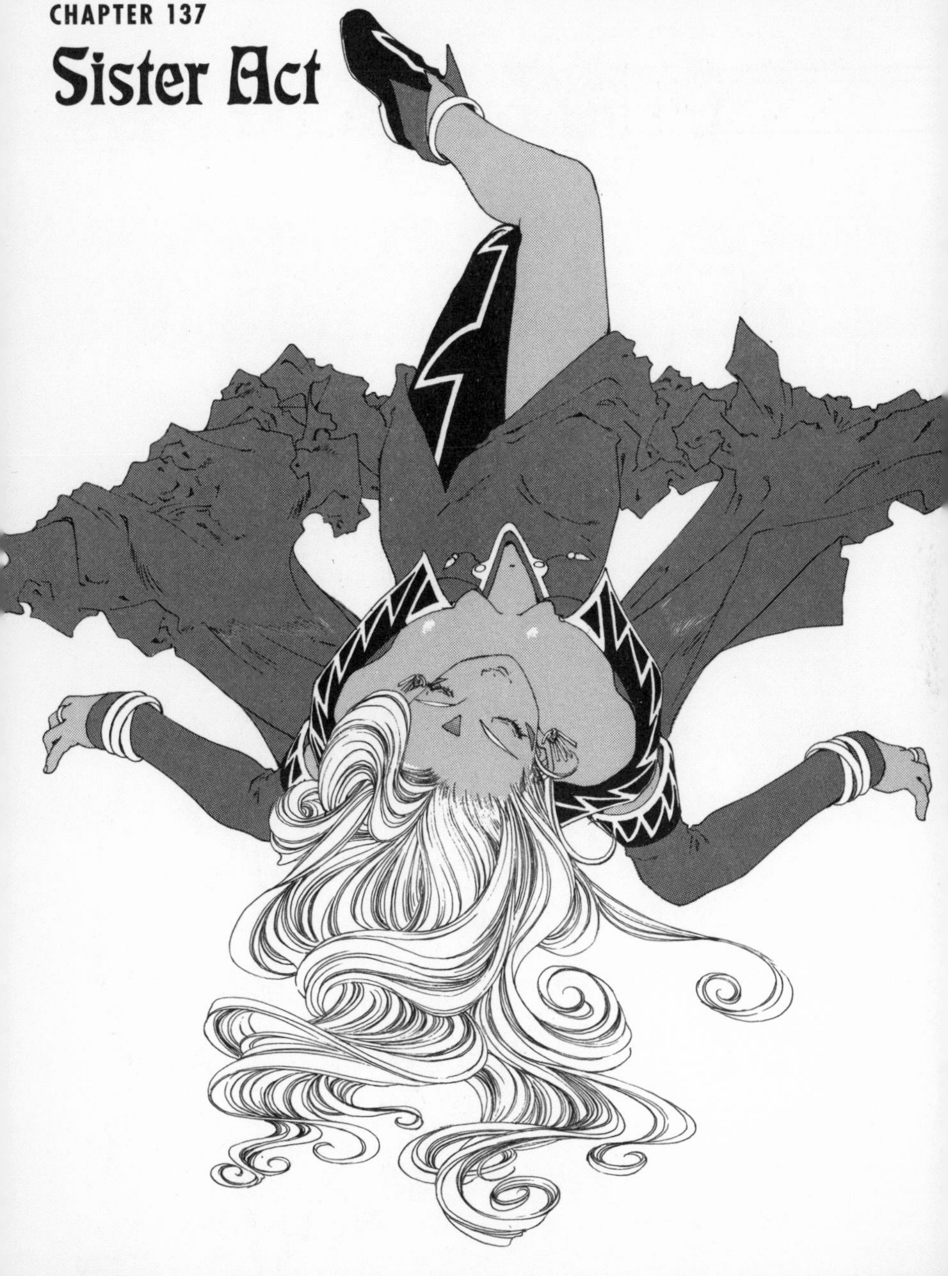

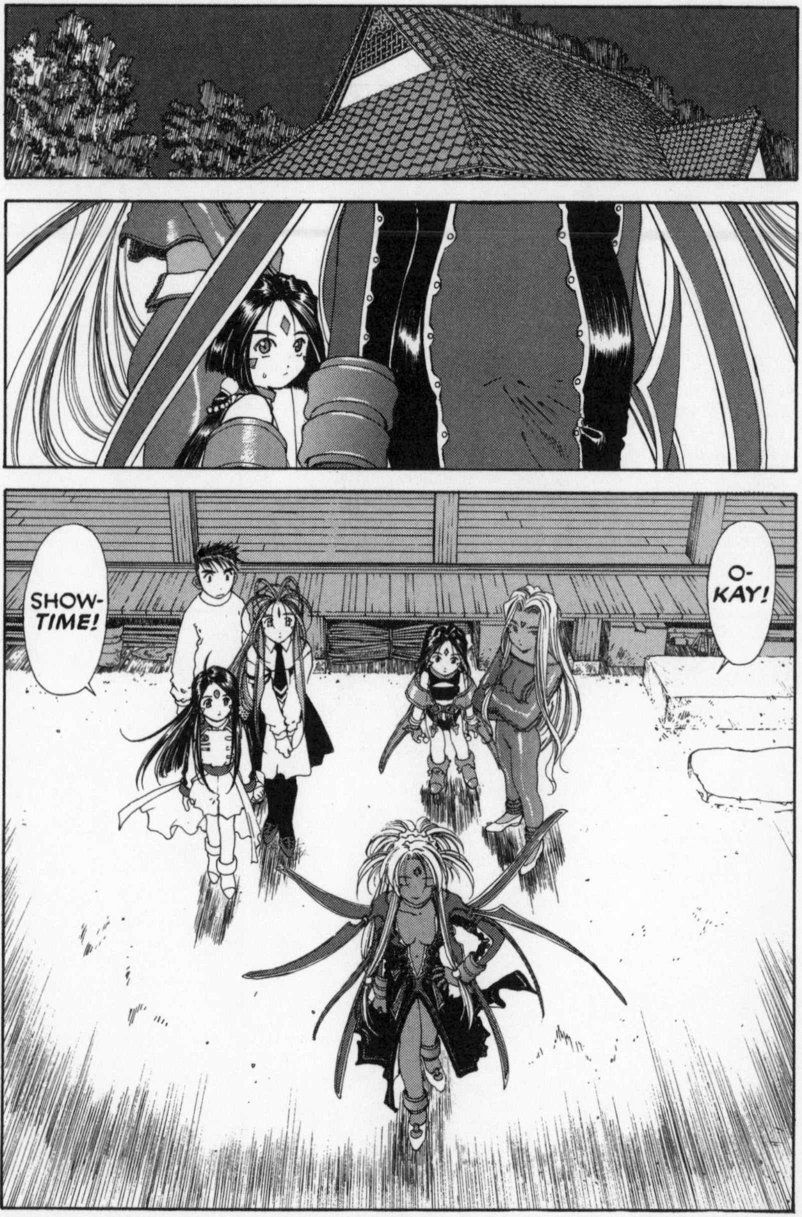
O-KAY!
SHOW-TIME!

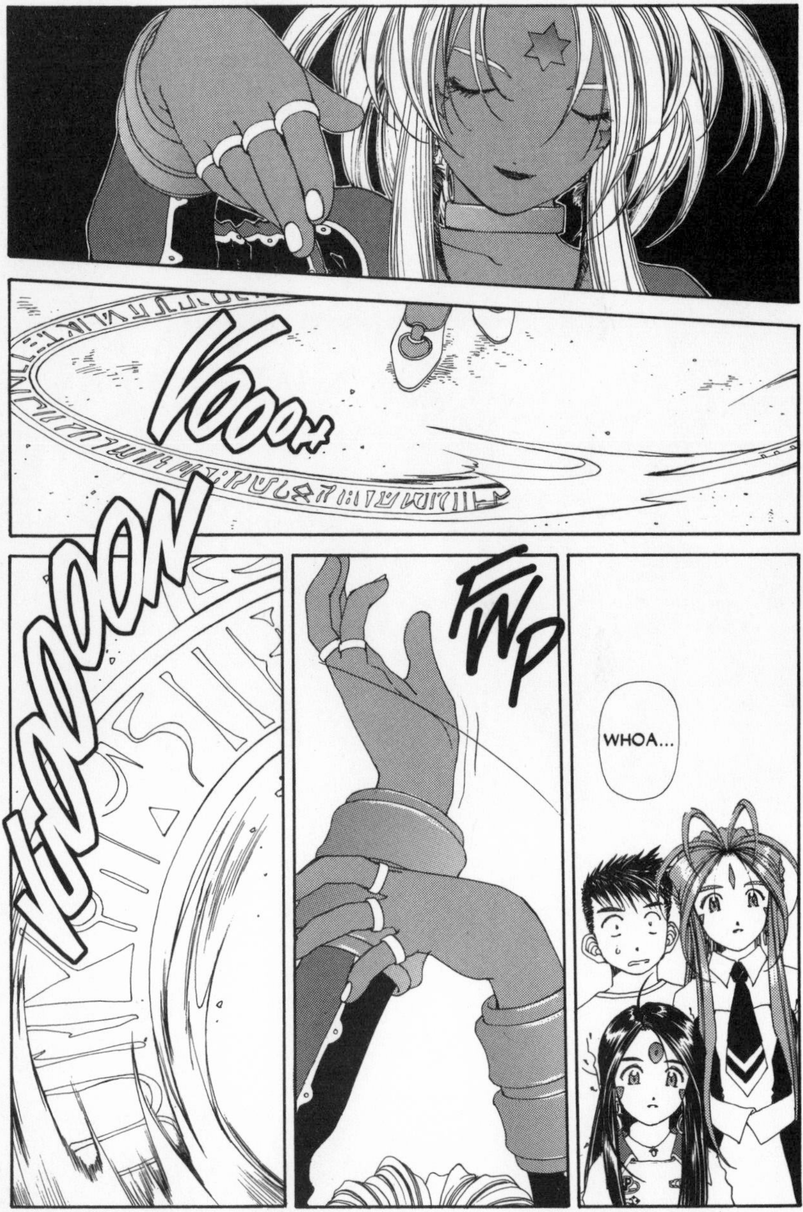
VOOO
WHOA...
FWP
VOOOOON

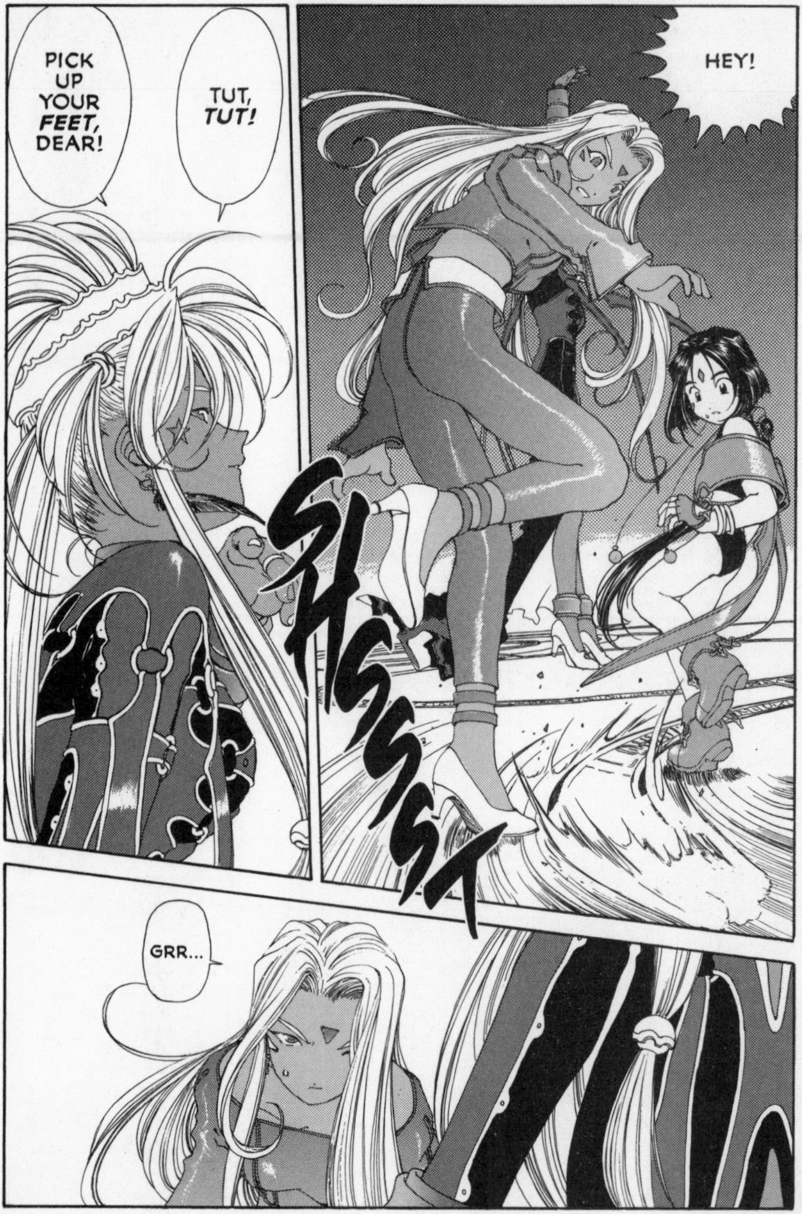
HEY!
TUT, TUT!
PICK UP YOUR FEET, DEAR!
SHSSSST
GRR...

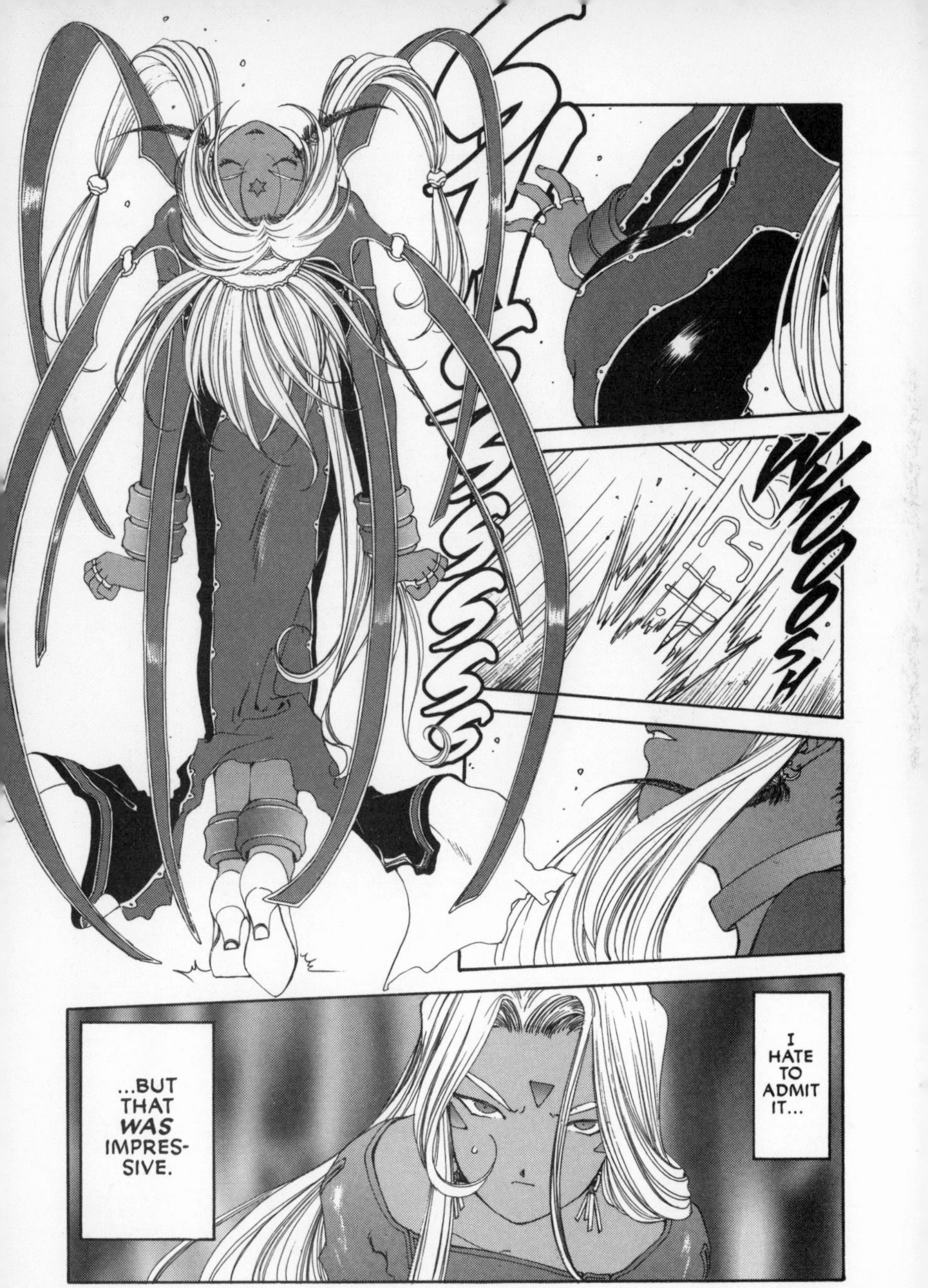
WHOOOOSH
I HATE TO ADMIT IT...
...BUT THAT *WAS* IMPRESSIVE.

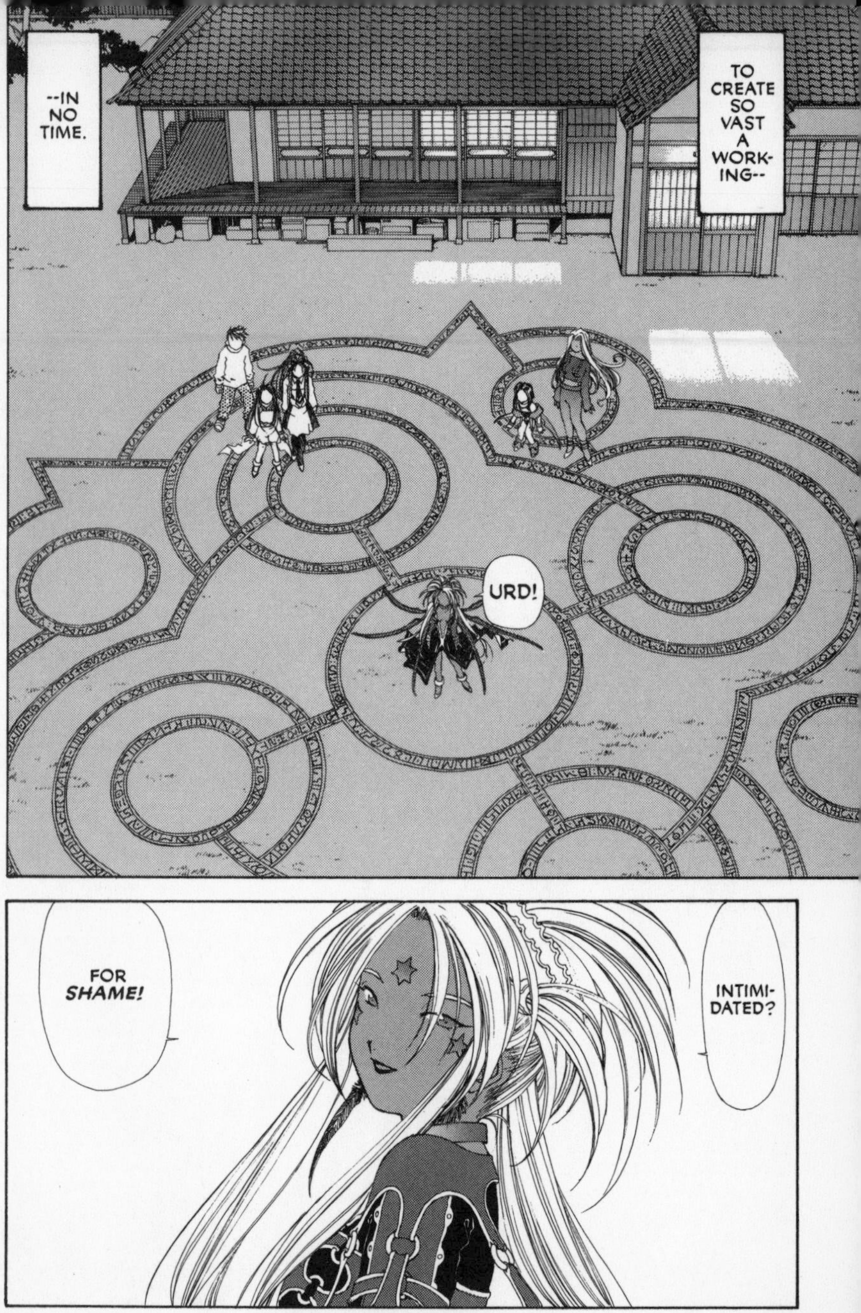
TO CREATE SO VAST A WORKING--
--IN NO TIME.
URD!
INTIMIDATED?
FOR *SHAME!*

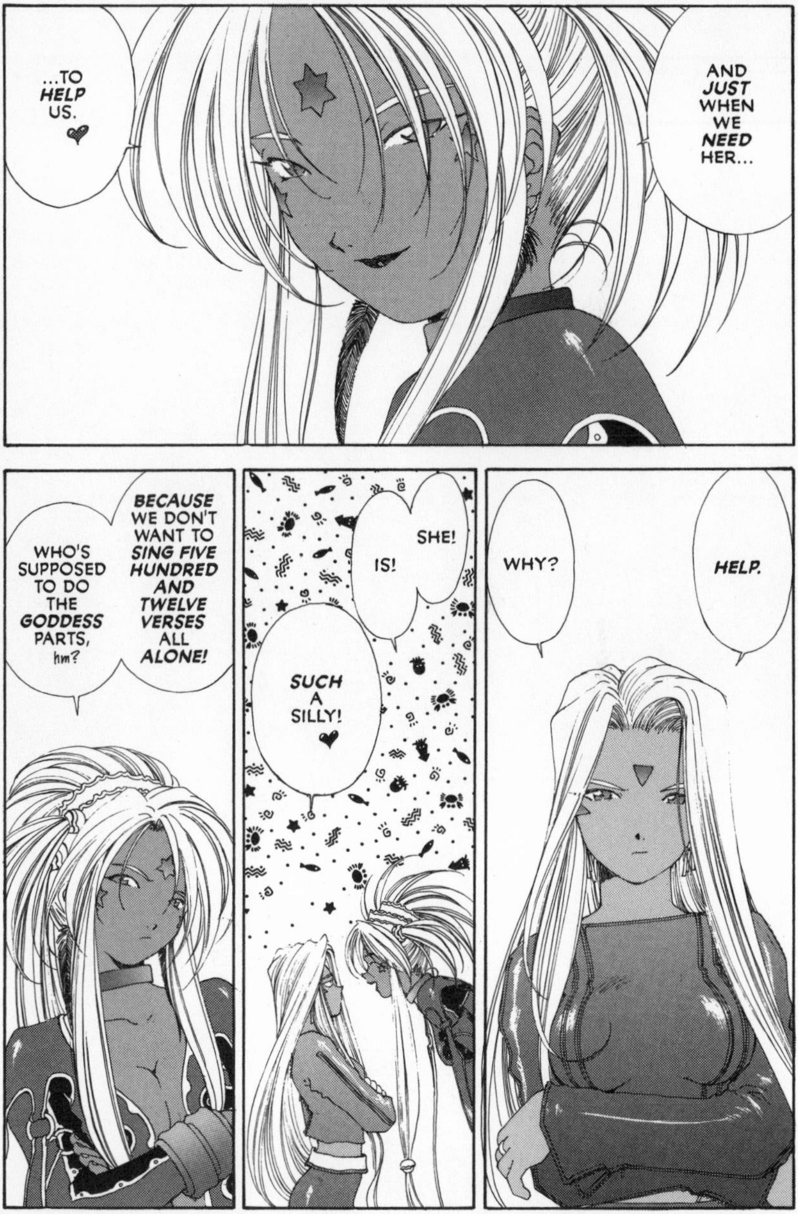
AND JUST WHEN WE NEED HER...
...TO HELP US. ♥
HELP.
WHY?
SHE!
IS!
SUCH A SILLY! ♥
BECAUSE WE DON'T WANT TO SING FIVE HUNDRED AND TWELVE VERSES ALL ALONE!
WHO'S SUPPOSED TO DO THE GODDESS PARTS, hm?

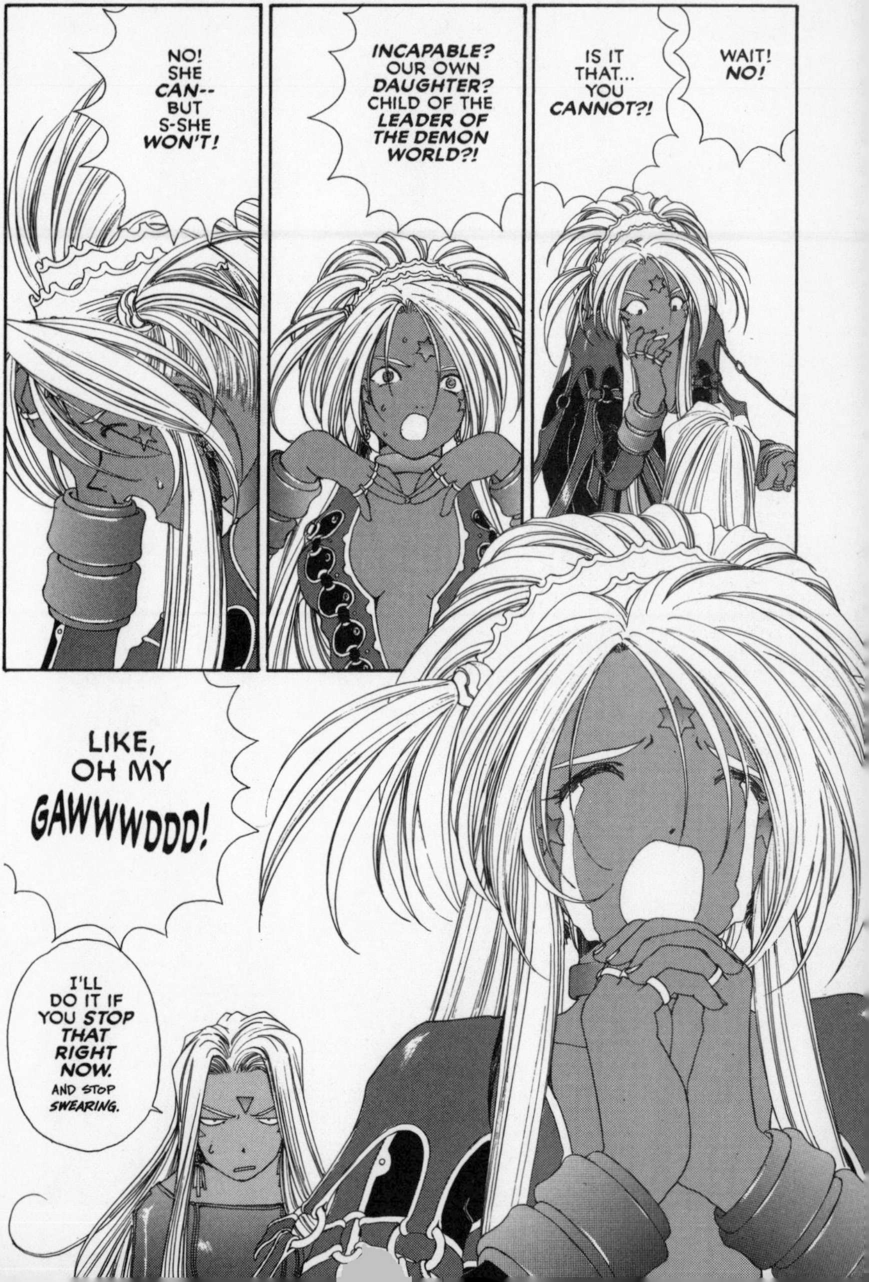
WAIT! NO!
IS IT THAT... YOU CANNOT?!
INCAPABLE? OUR OWN DAUGHTER? CHILD OF THE LEADER OF THE DEMON WORLD?!
NO! SHE CAN-- BUT S-SHE WON'T!
LIKE, OH MY GAWWWDDD!
I'LL DO IT IF YOU STOP THAT RIGHT NOW. AND STOP SWEARING.

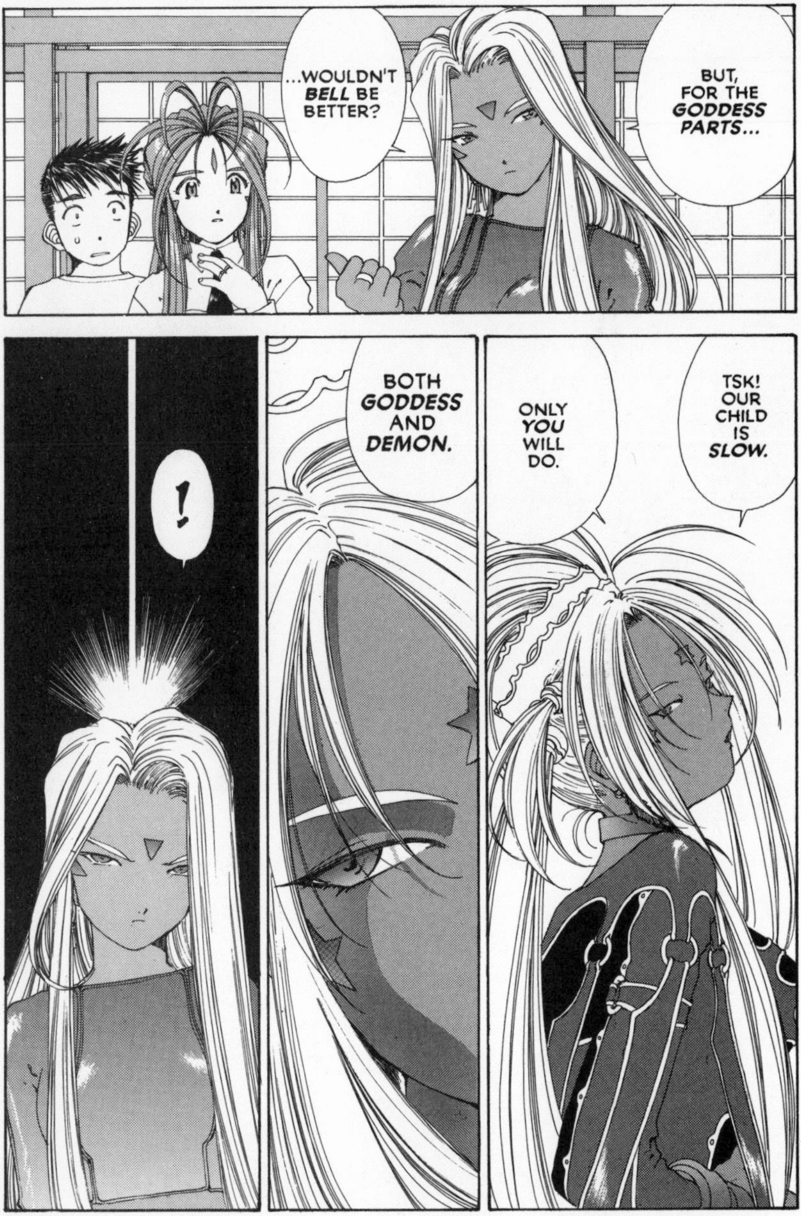
BUT, FOR THE GODDESS PARTS...
...WOULDN'T BELL BE BETTER?
TSK! OUR CHILD IS SLOW.
ONLY YOU WILL DO.
BOTH GODDESS AND DEMON.
!

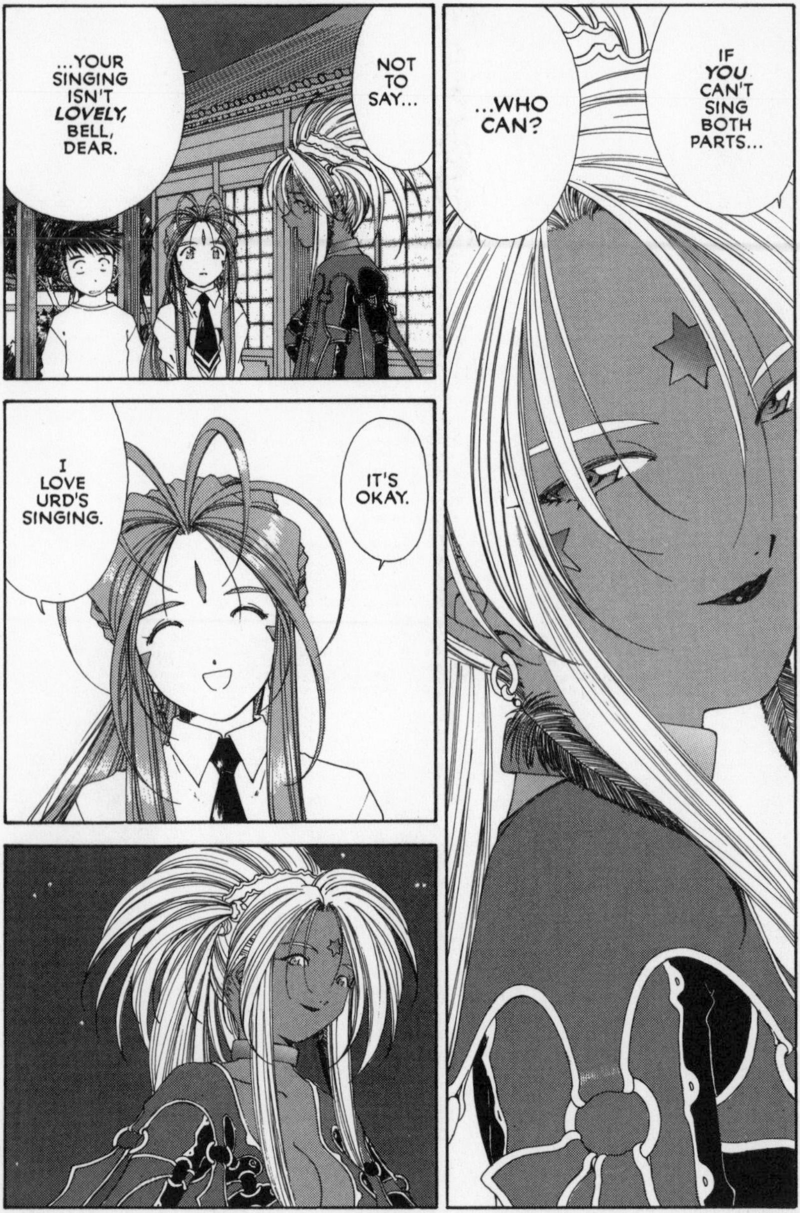
IF *YOU* CAN'T SING BOTH PARTS...
...WHO CAN?
NOT TO SAY...
...YOUR SINGING ISN'T *LOVELY,* BELL, DEAR.
IT'S OKAY.
I LOVE URD'S SINGING.

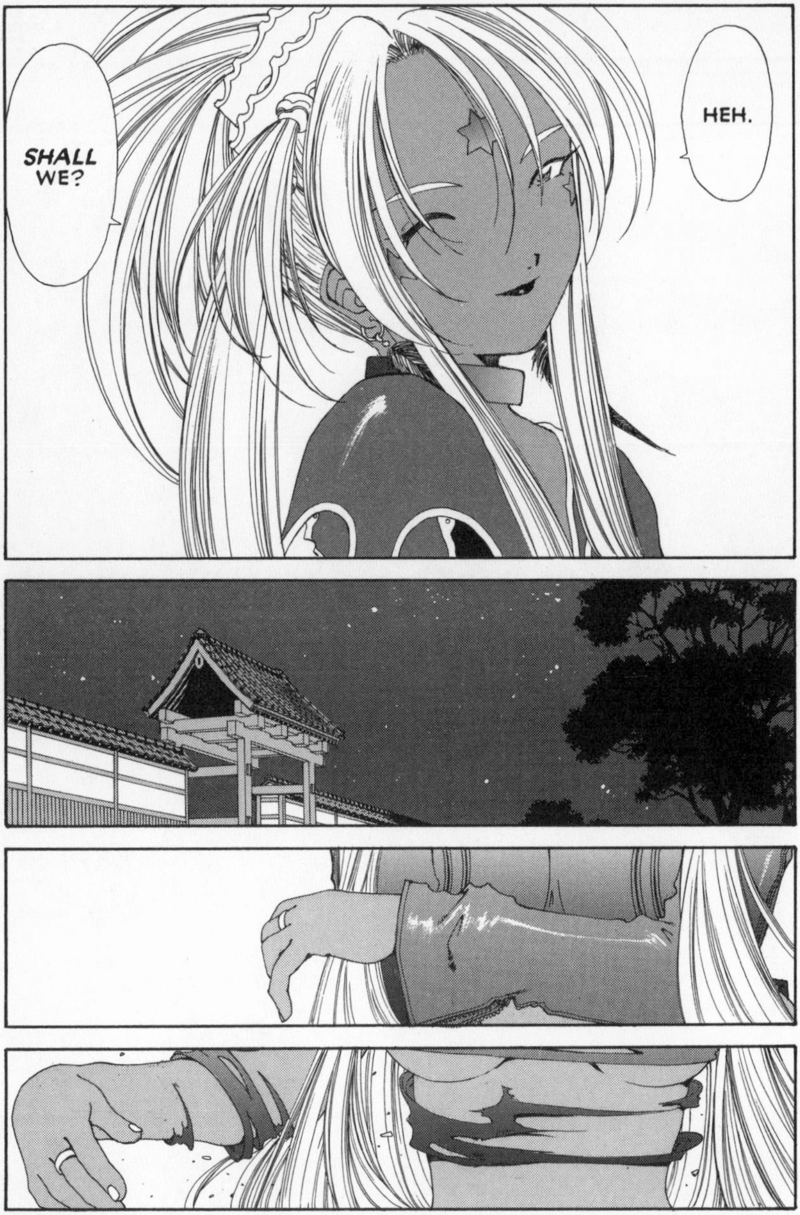
HEH.
SHALL WE?

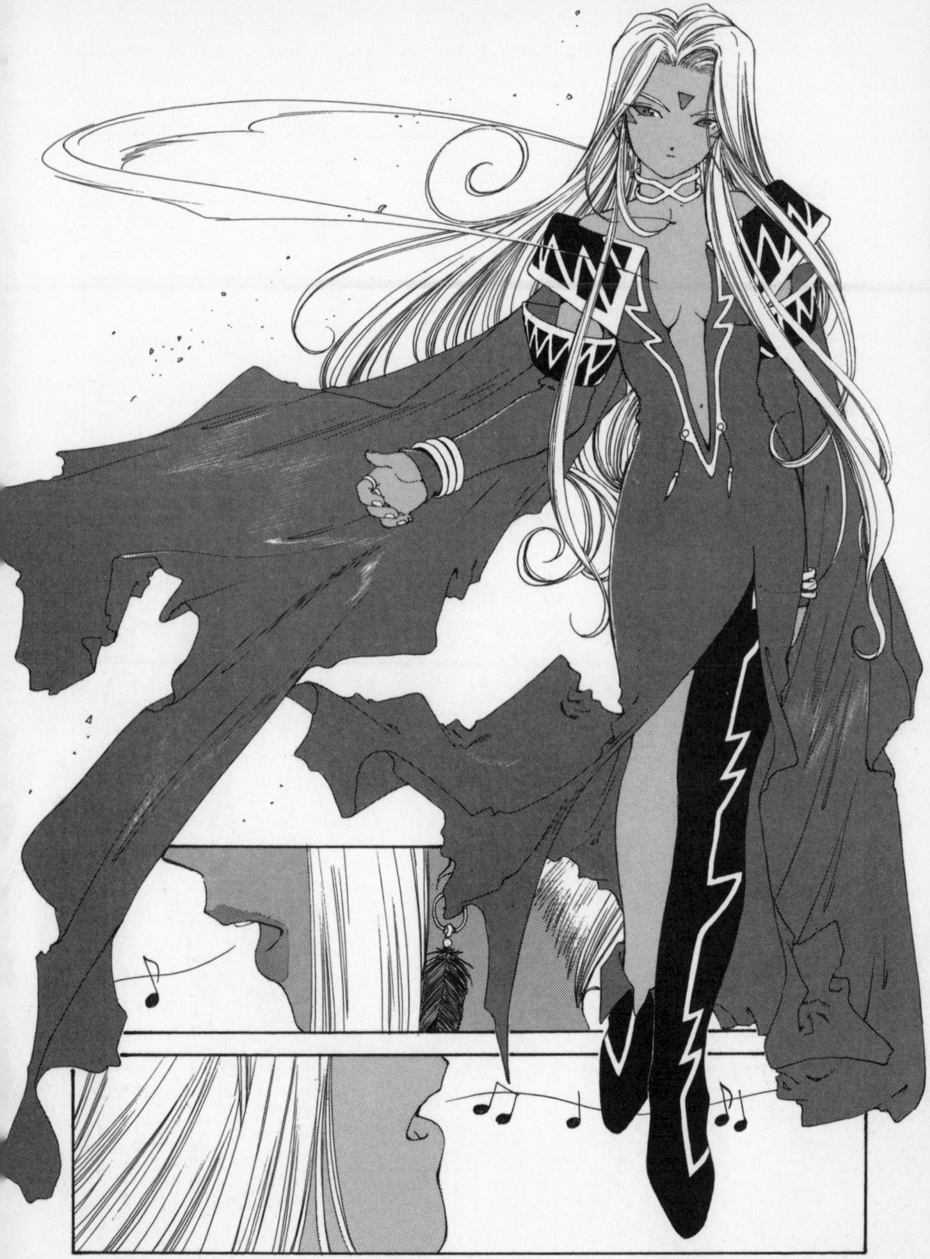

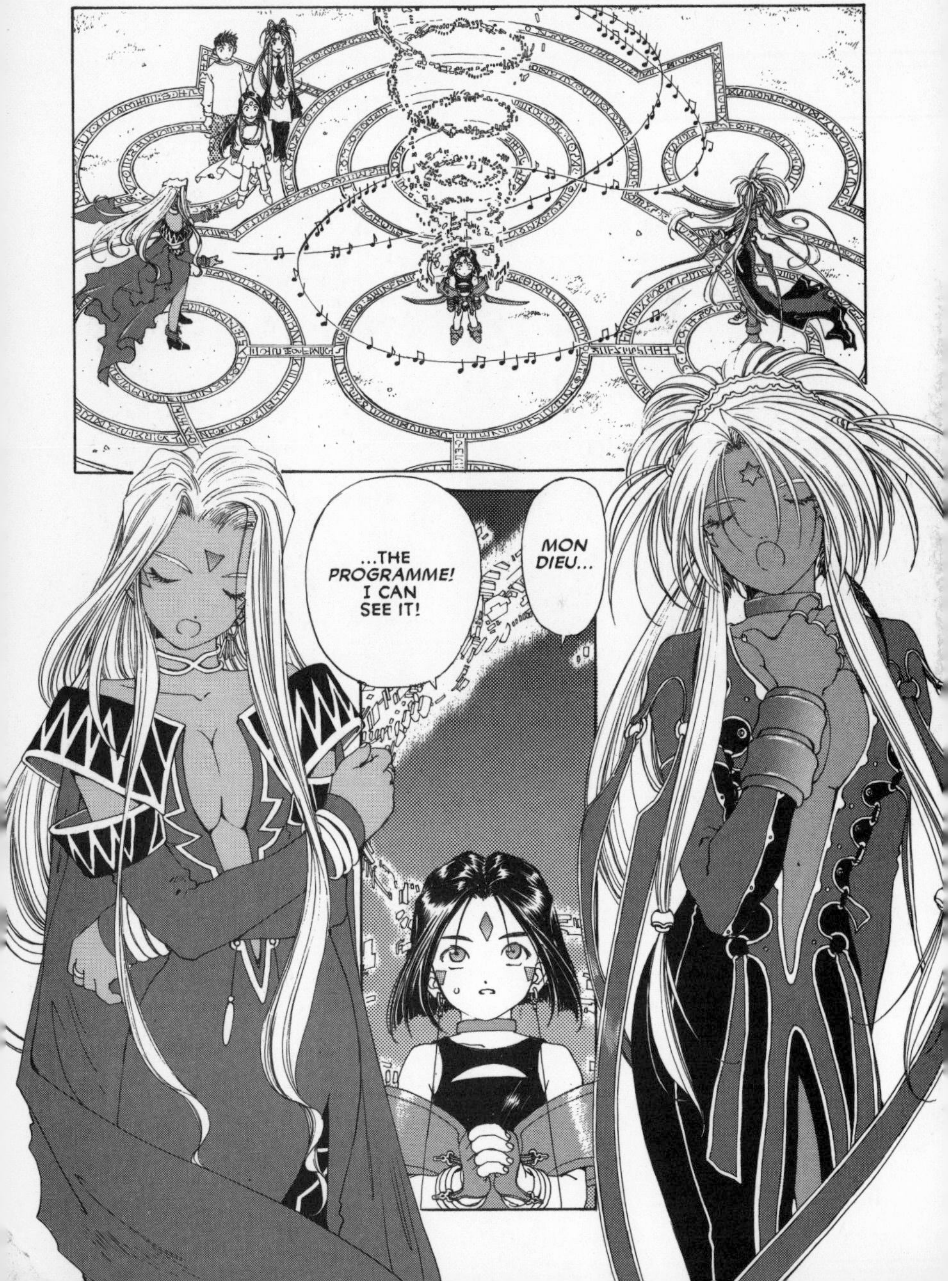
MON DIEU...
...THE PROGRAMME! I CAN SEE IT!

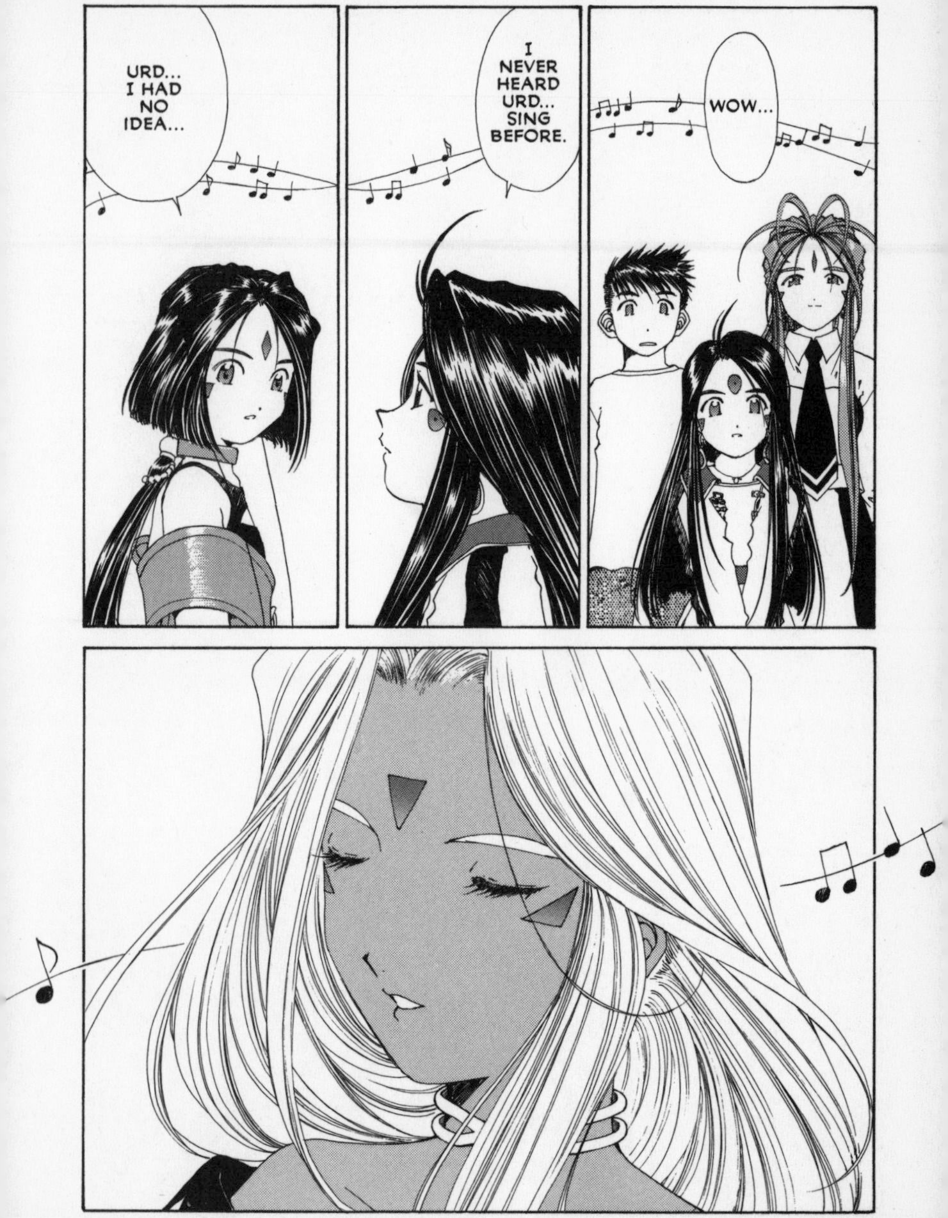
WOW...
I NEVER HEARD URD... SING BEFORE.
URD... I HAD NO IDEA...

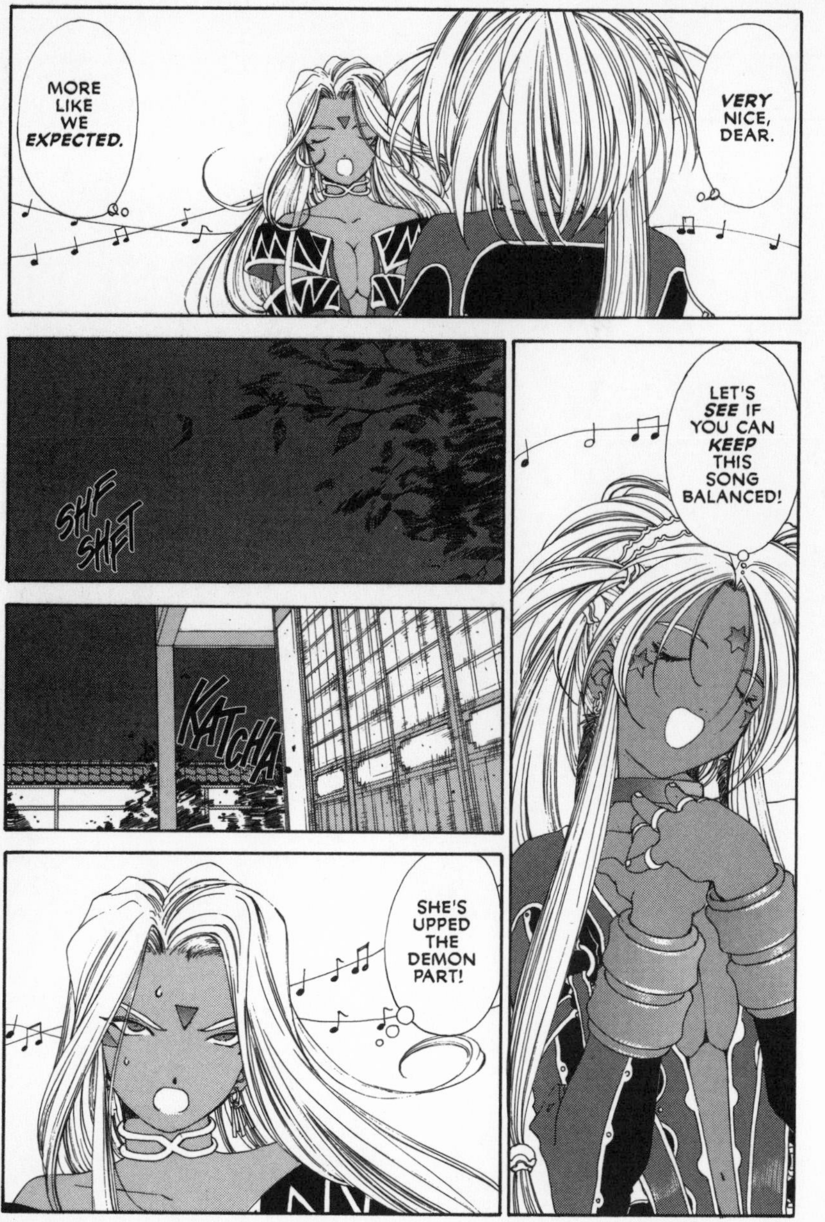
VERY NICE, DEAR.
MORE LIKE WE EXPECTED.
LET'S SEE IF YOU CAN KEEP THIS SONG BALANCED!
SHF SHFT
KATCHA
SHE'S UPPED THE DEMON PART!

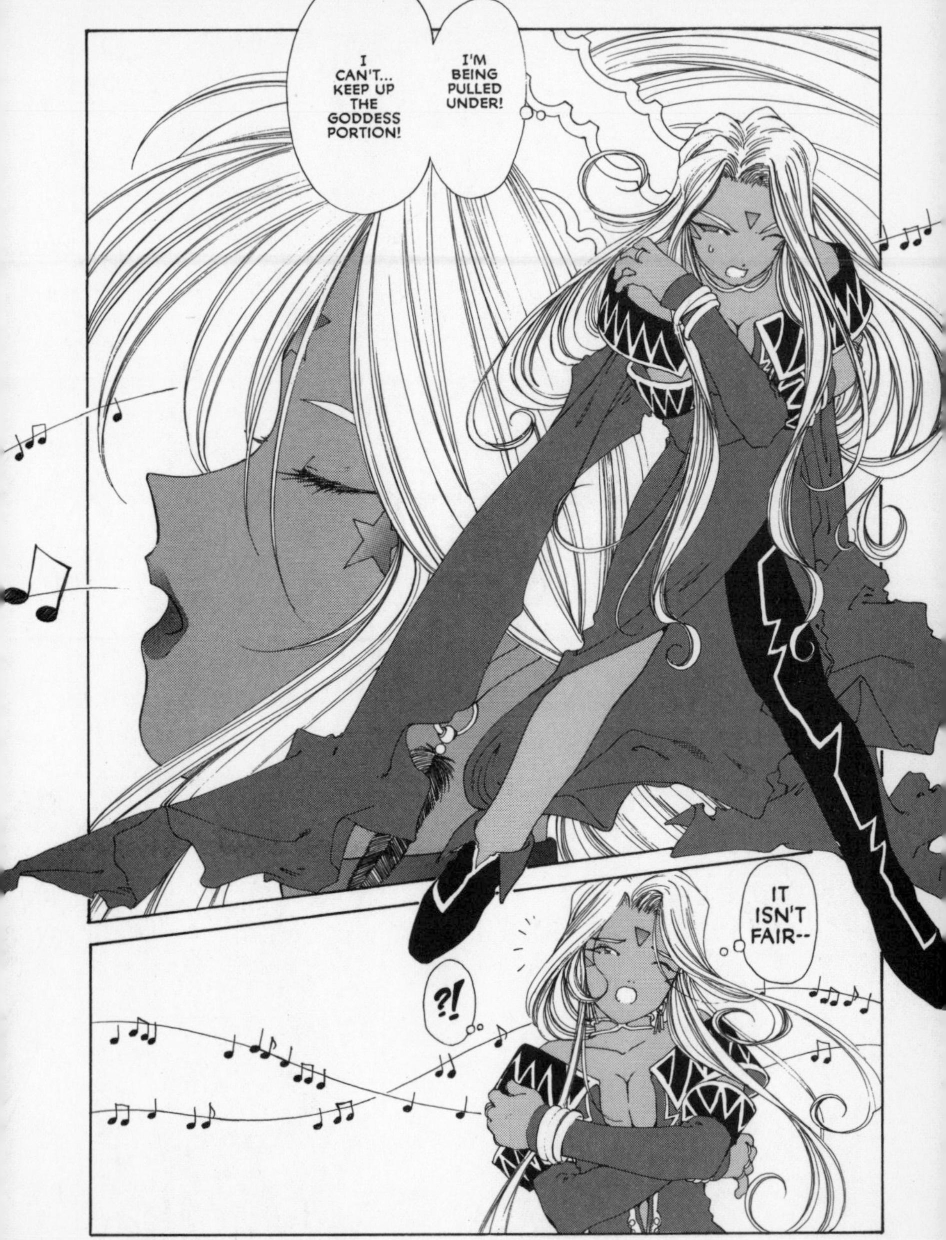
I'M BEING PULLED UNDER!
I CAN'T... KEEP UP THE GODDESS PORTION!
IT ISN'T FAIR--
?!

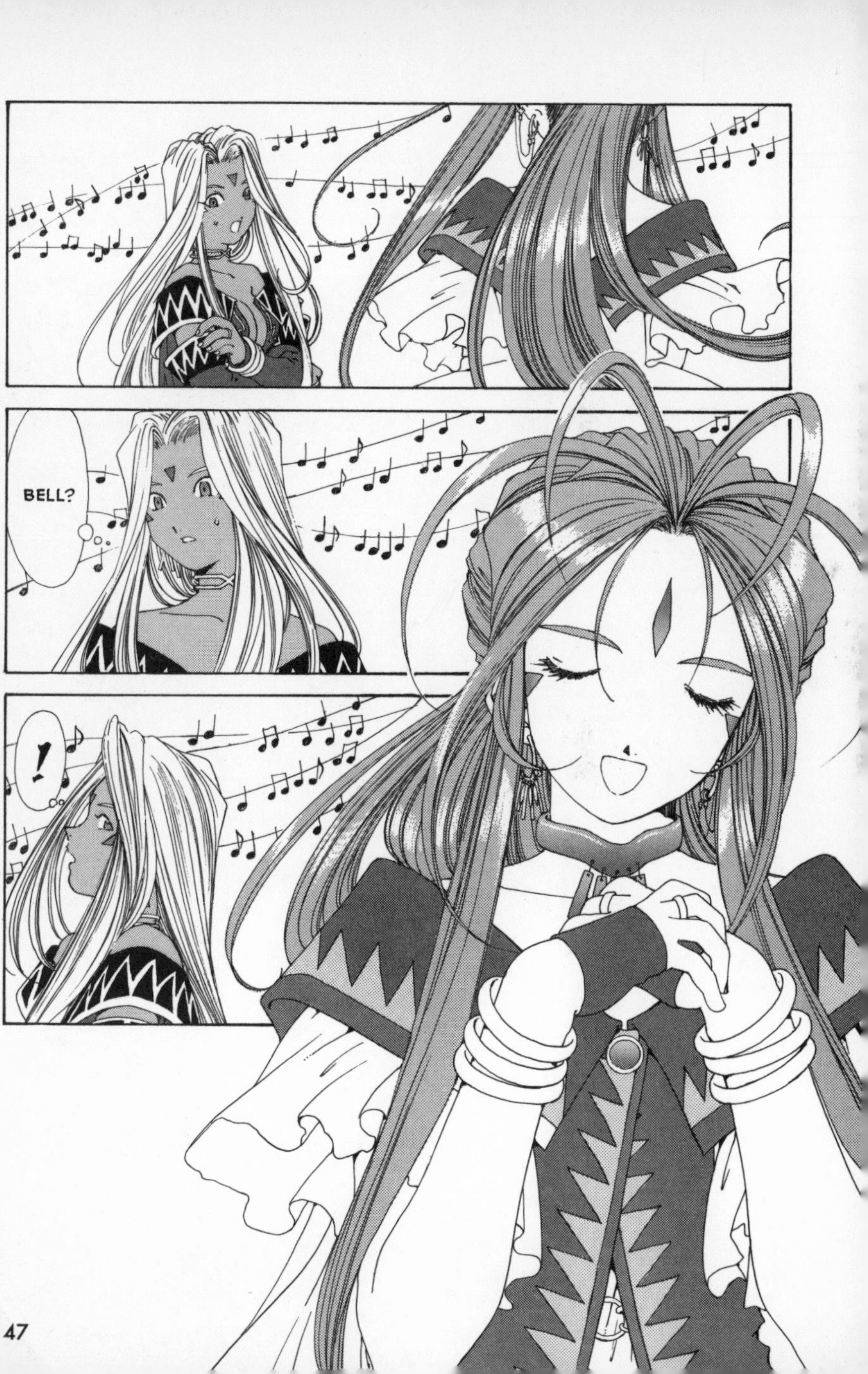
BELL?
!

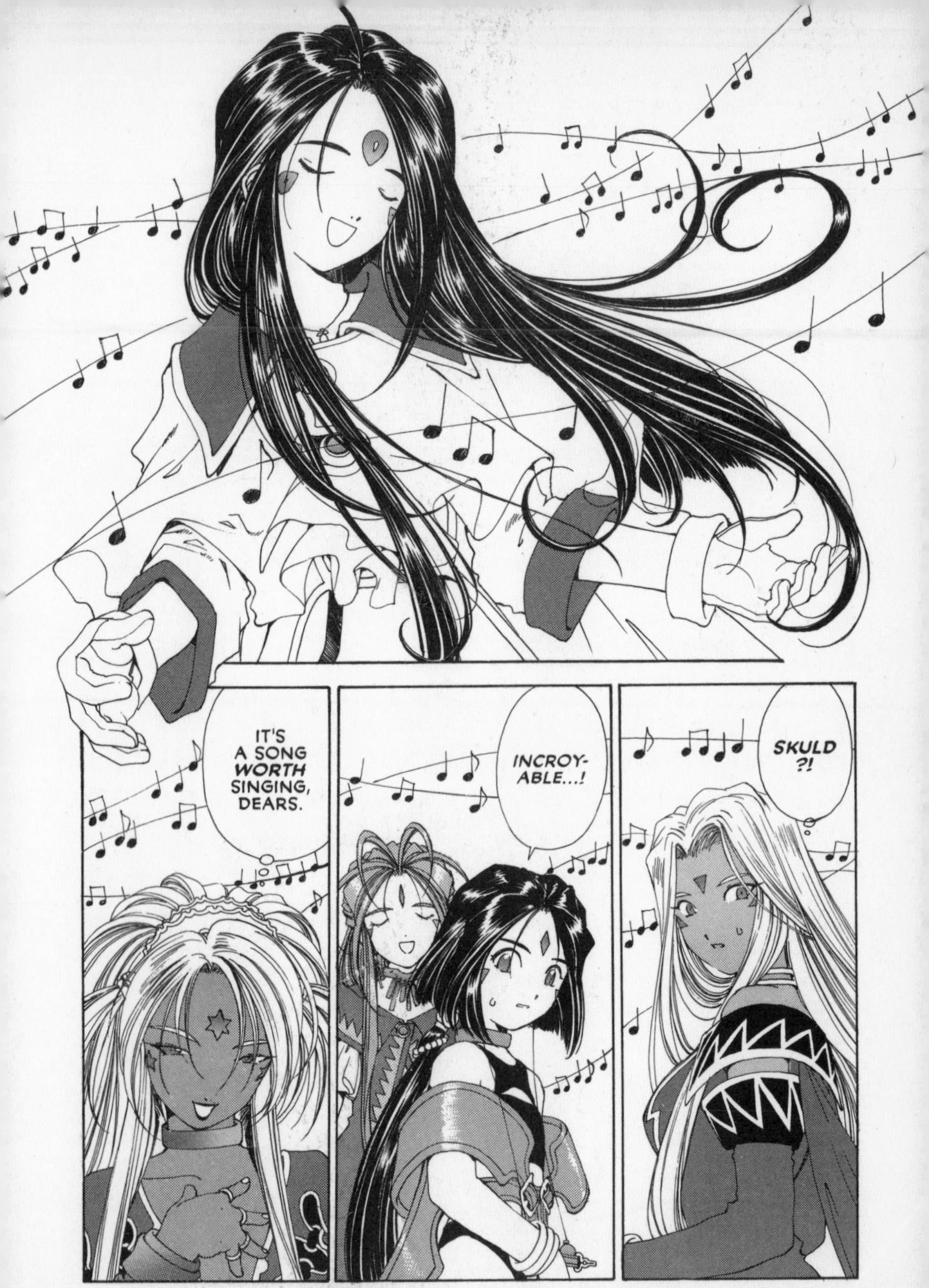
SKULD ?!
INCROY-ABLE...!
IT'S A SONG WORTH SINGING, DEARS.

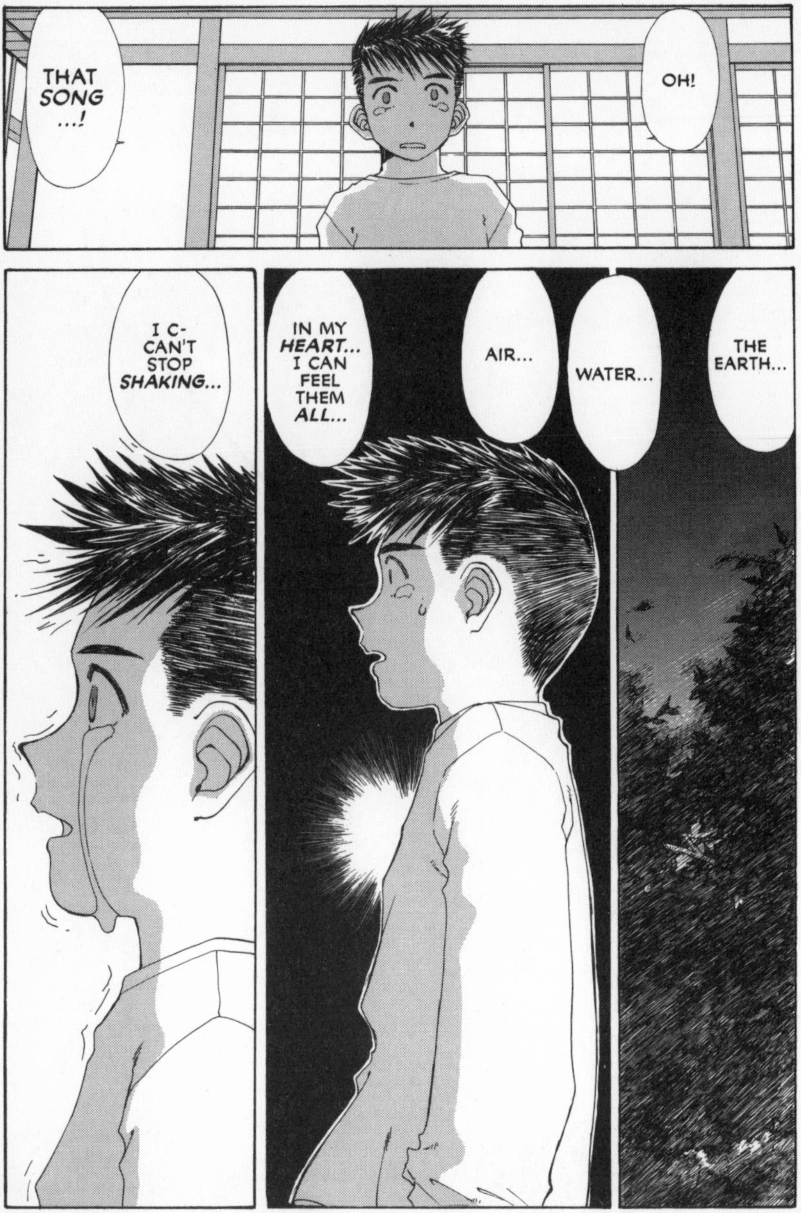
OH!
THAT *SONG* ...!
THE EARTH...
WATER...
AIR...
IN MY *HEART*... I CAN FEEL THEM *ALL*...
I C- CAN'T STOP *SHAKING*...

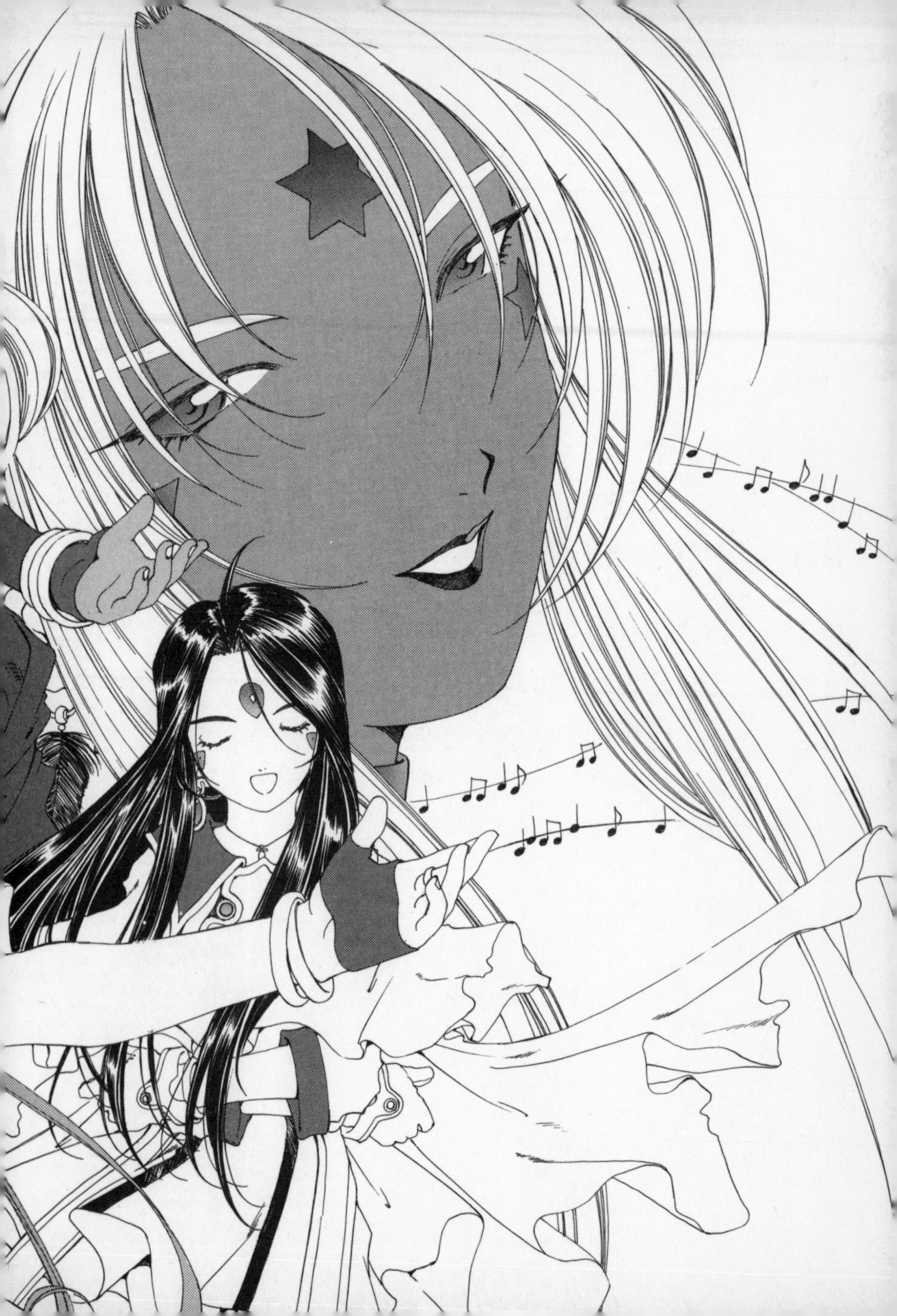

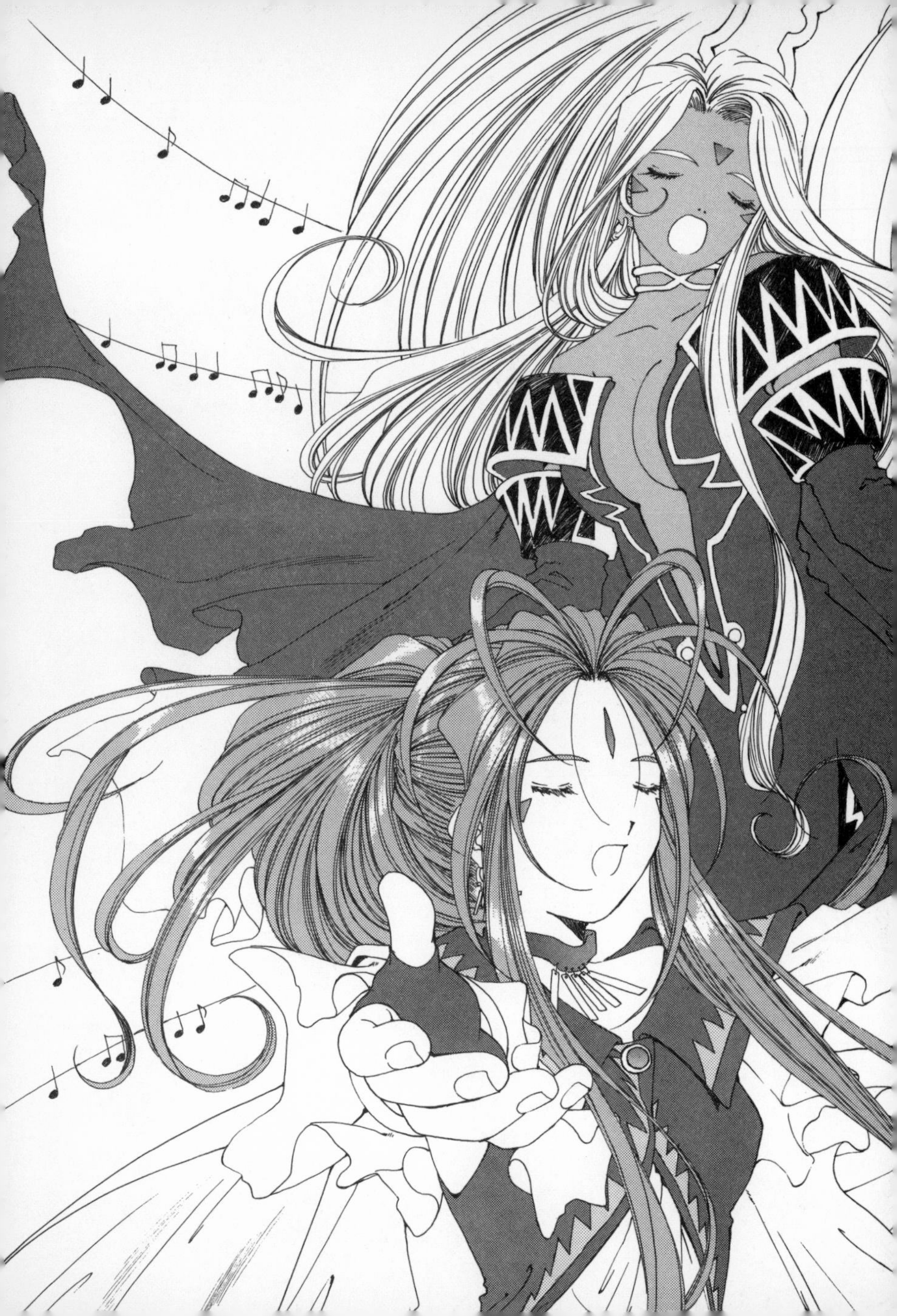

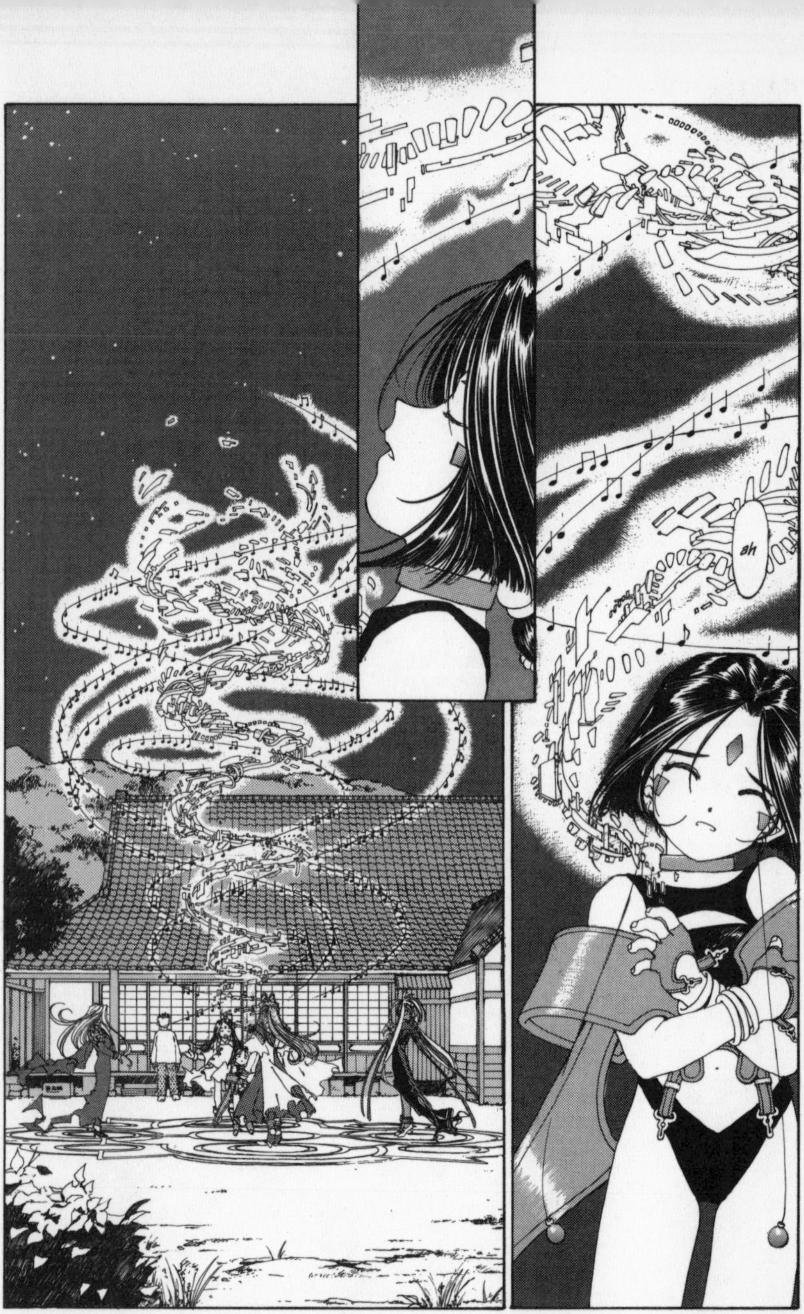
ah

CHAPTER 138

Maybe . . . ?

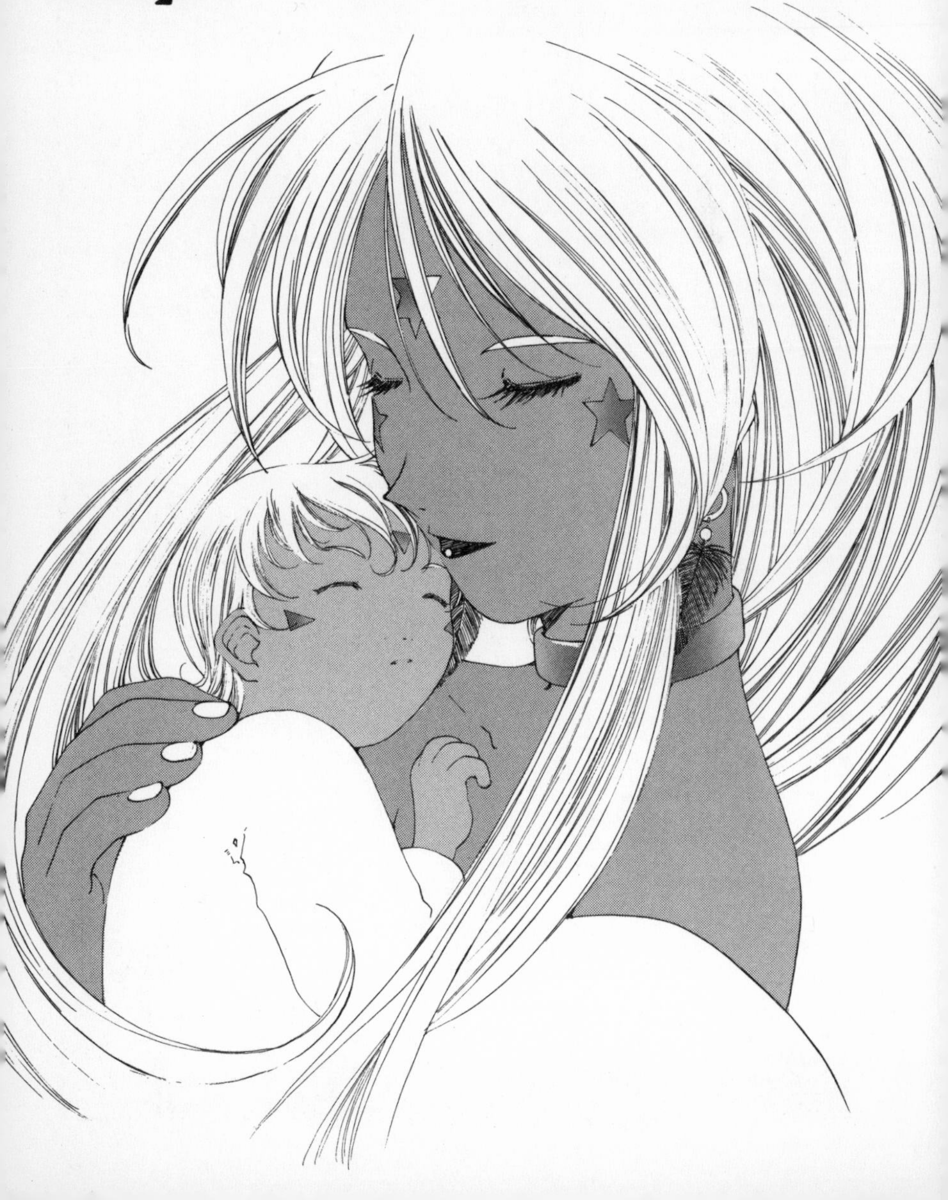

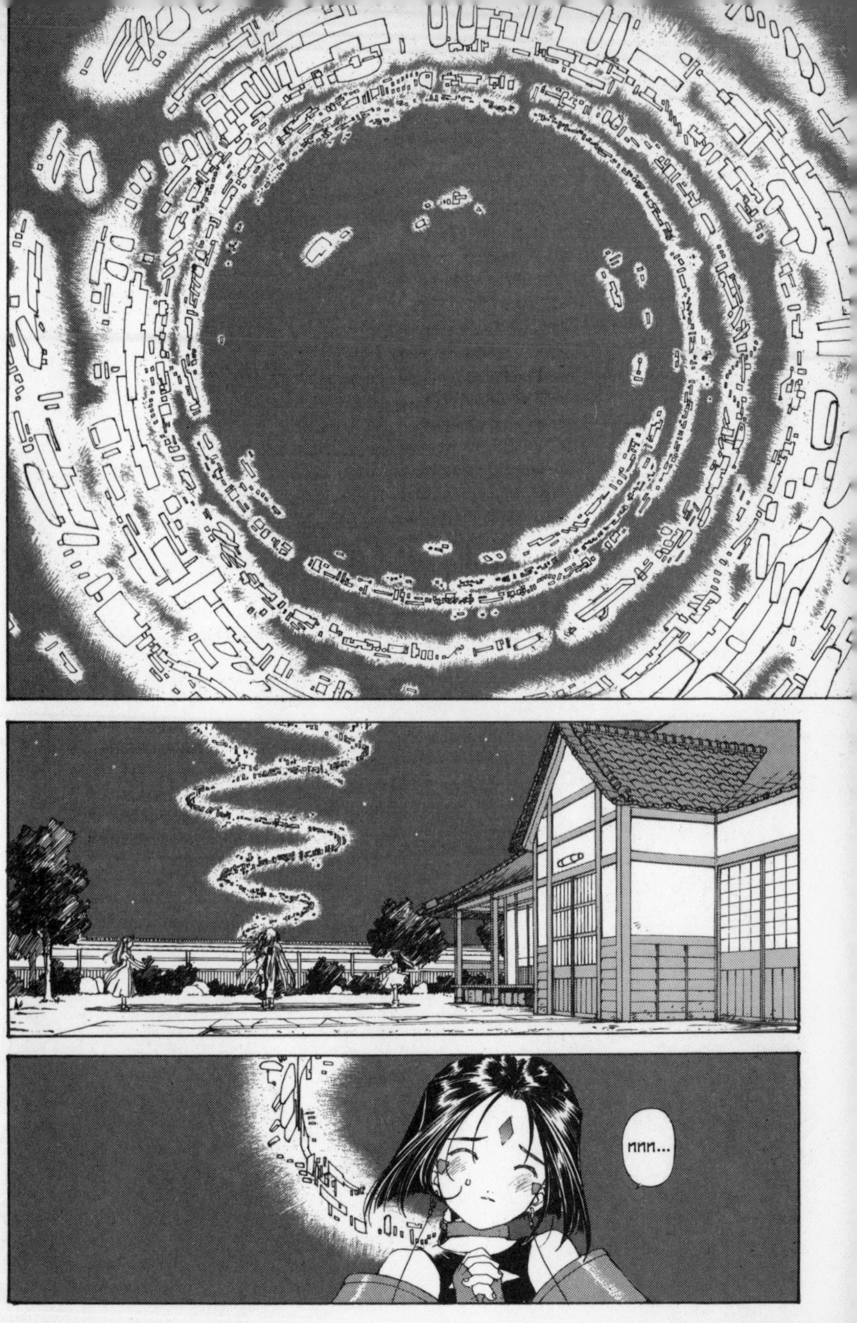
MMM...

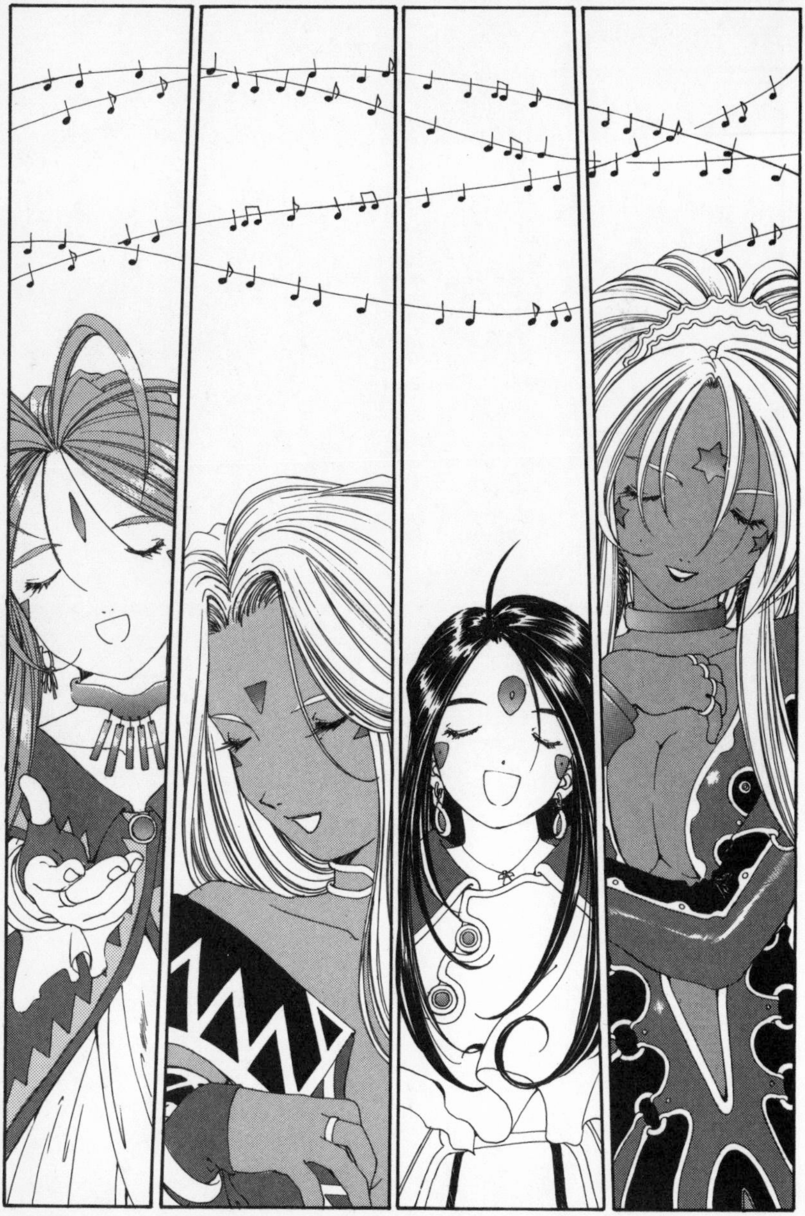

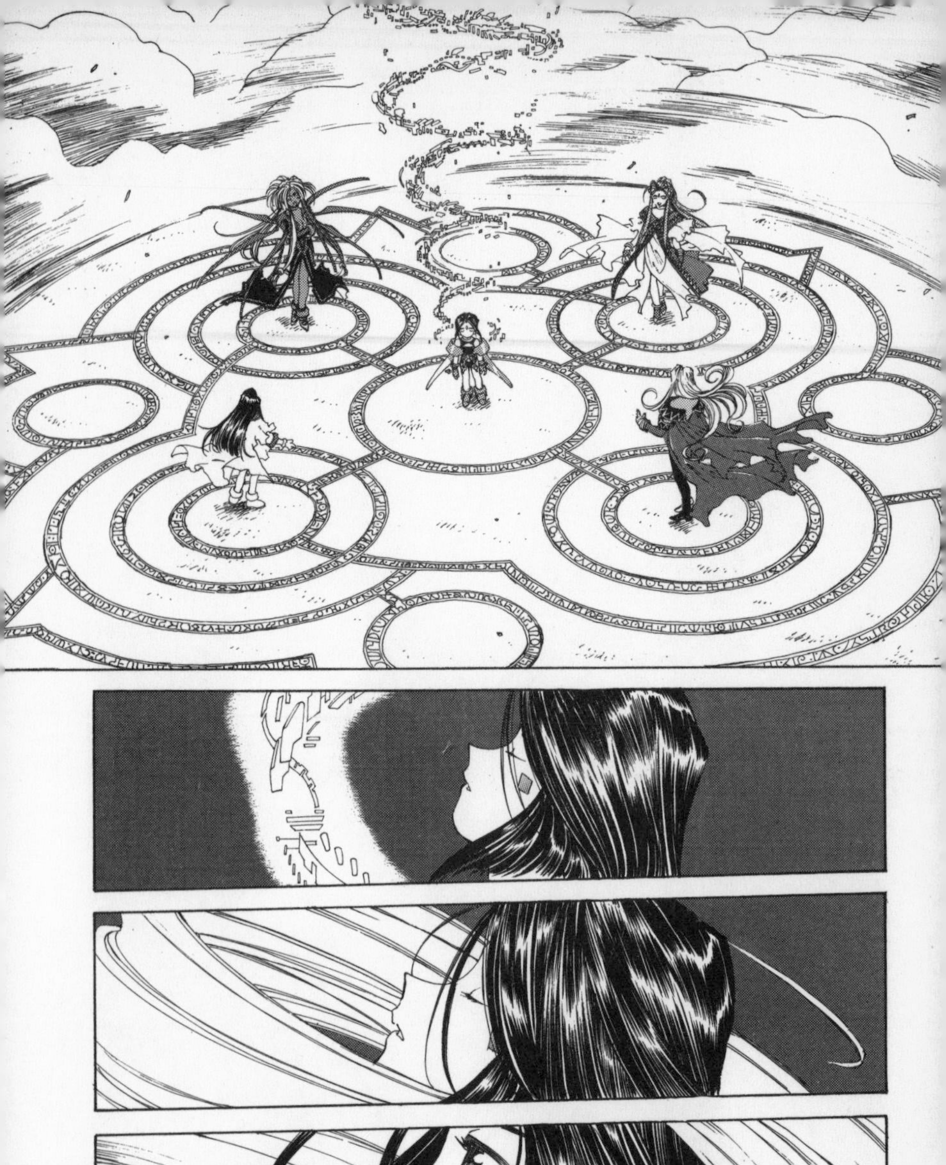

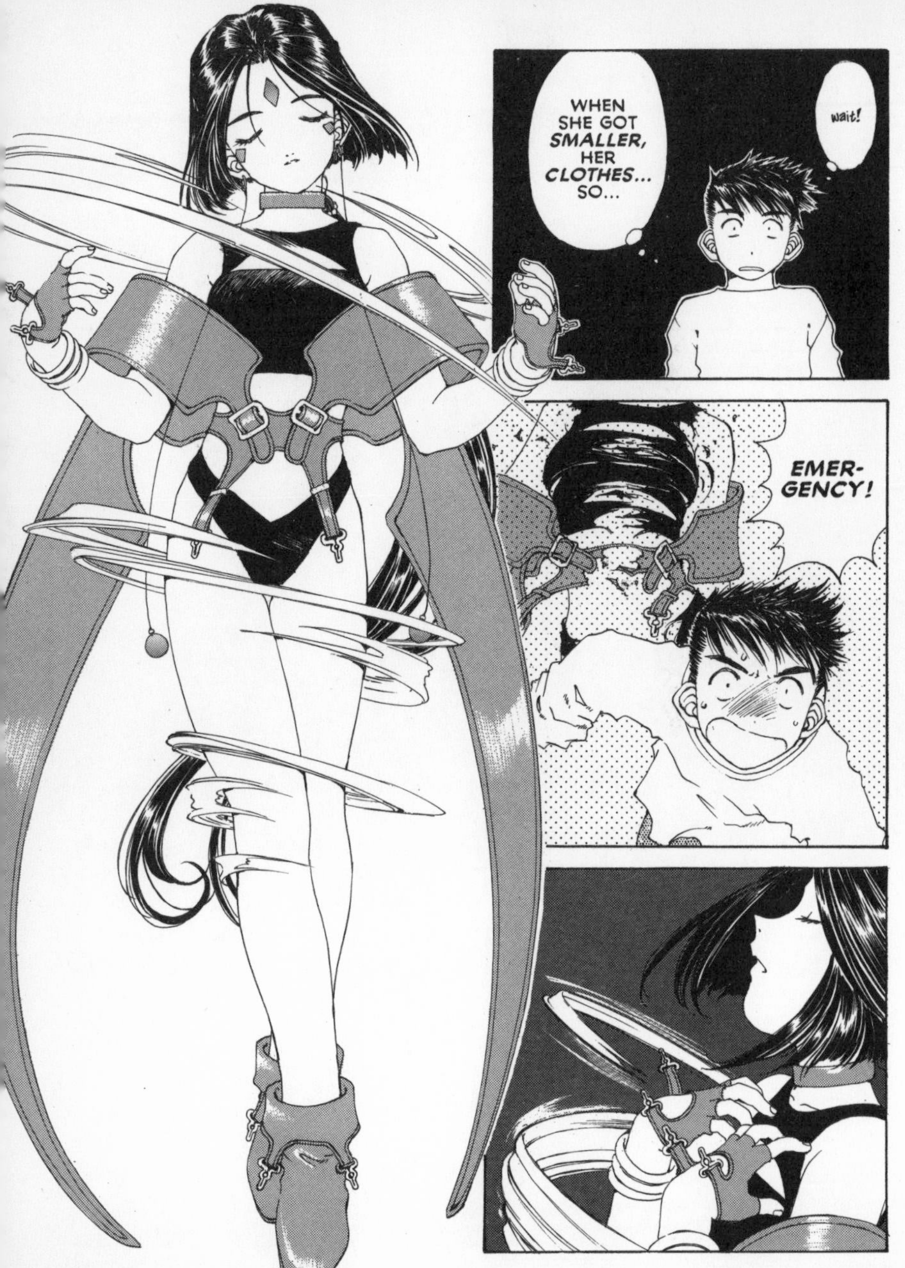
wait!
WHEN SHE GOT SMALLER, HER CLOTHES... SO...
EMER-GENCY!

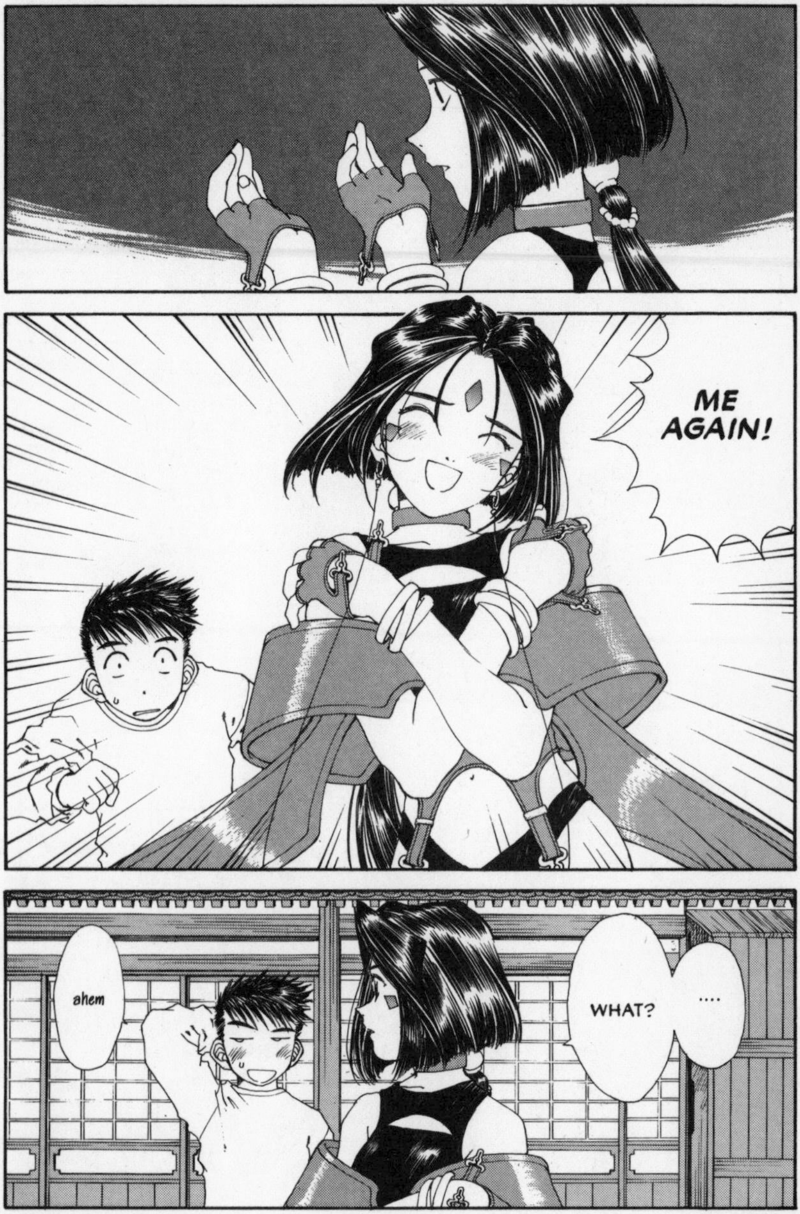
ME AGAIN!
....
WHAT?
ahem

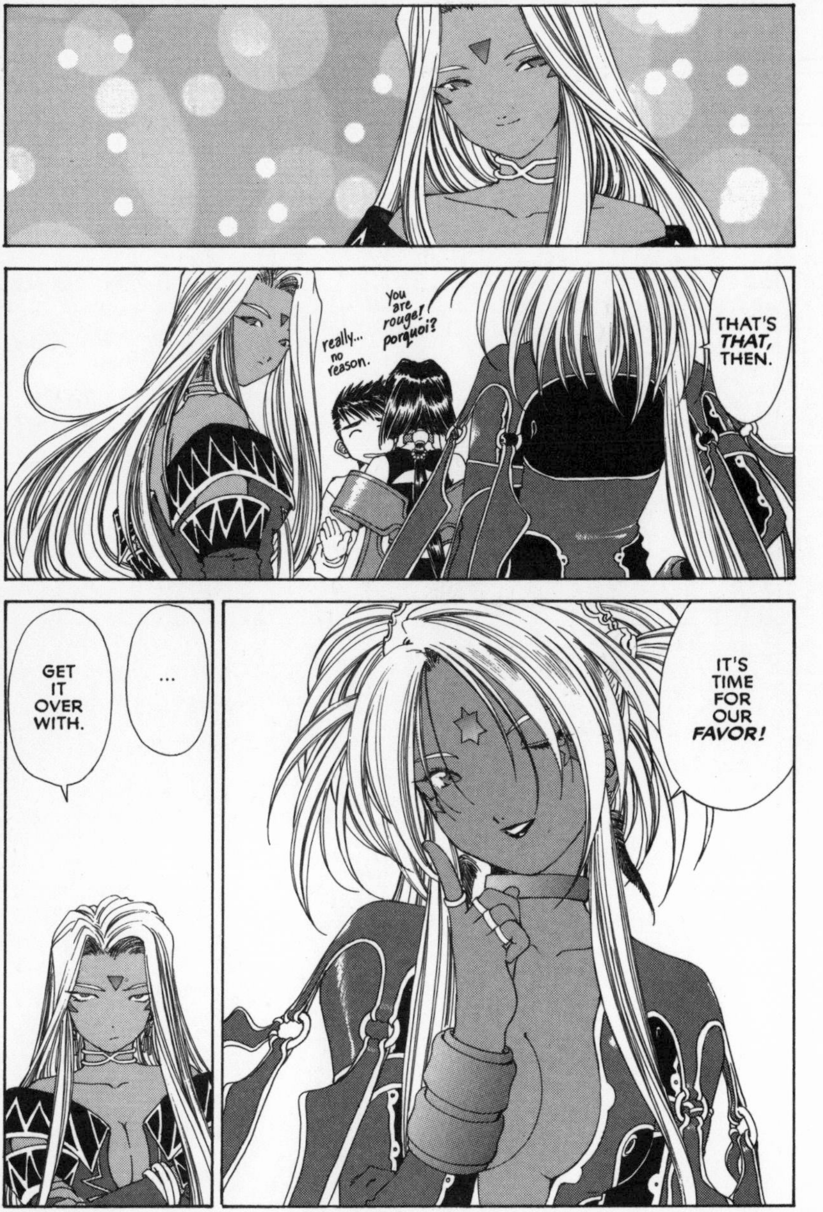
THAT'S *THAT*, THEN.
You are rouge! porquoi?
really... no reason.
IT'S TIME FOR OUR *FAVOR!*
...
GET IT OVER WITH.

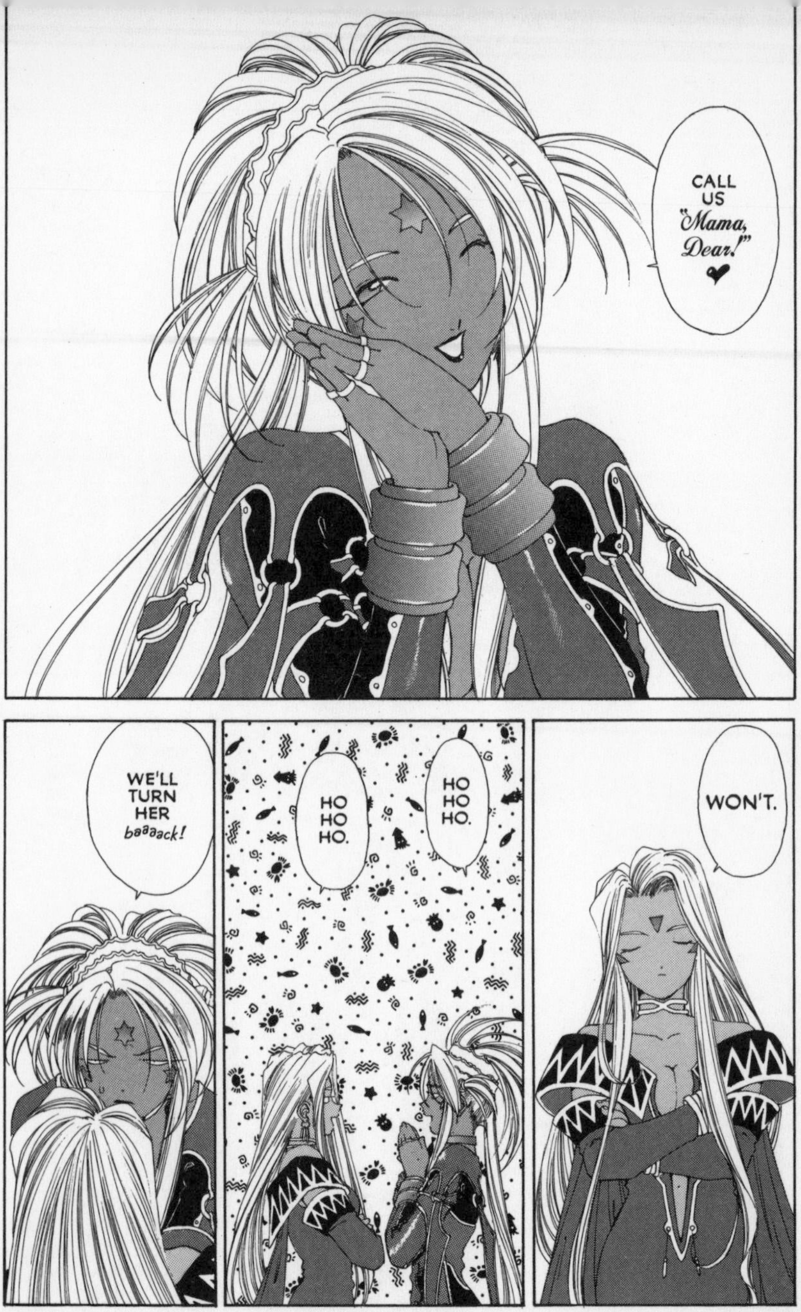
CALL US "Mama, Dear!" ❤
WON'T.
HO HO HO.
HO HO HO.
WE'LL TURN HER baaaack!

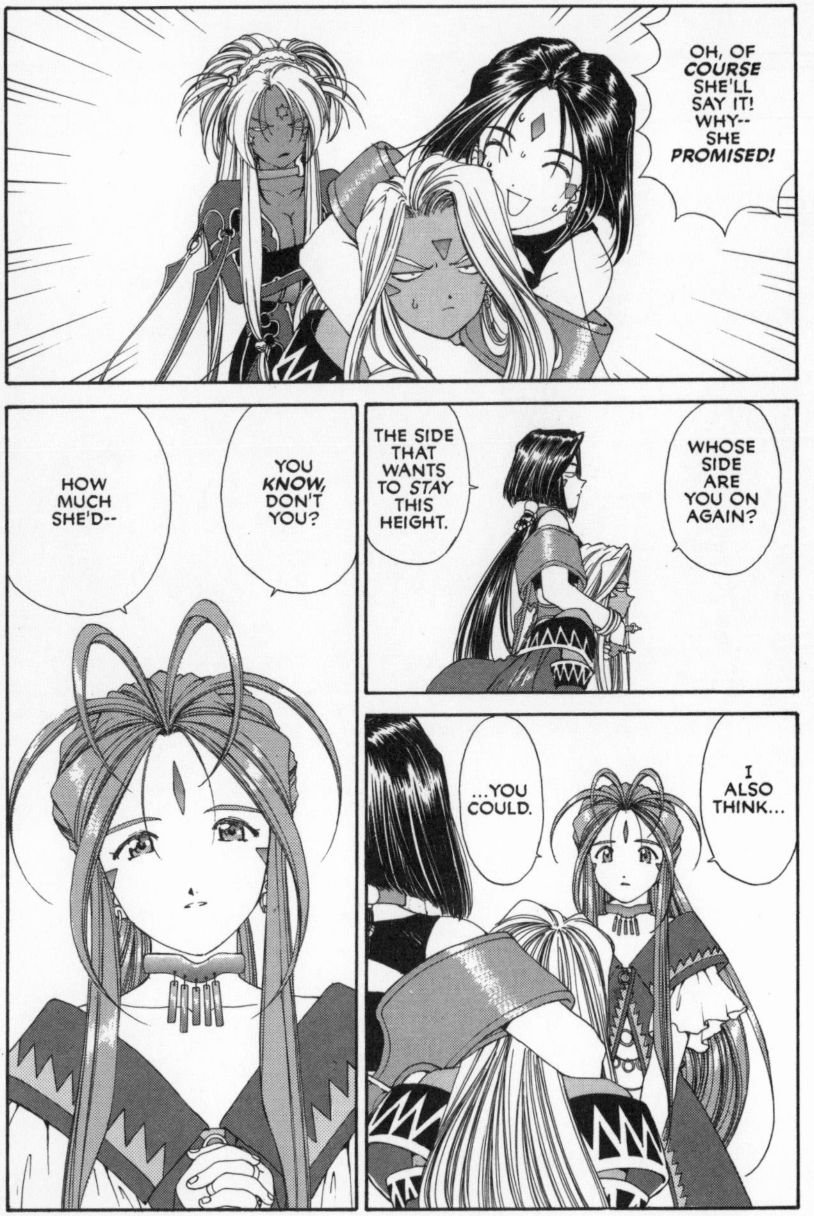
OH, OF COURSE SHE'LL SAY IT! WHY-- SHE PROMISED!
WHOSE SIDE ARE YOU ON AGAIN?
THE SIDE THAT WANTS TO STAY THIS HEIGHT.
I ALSO THINK...
...YOU COULD.
YOU KNOW, DON'T YOU?
HOW MUCH SHE'D--

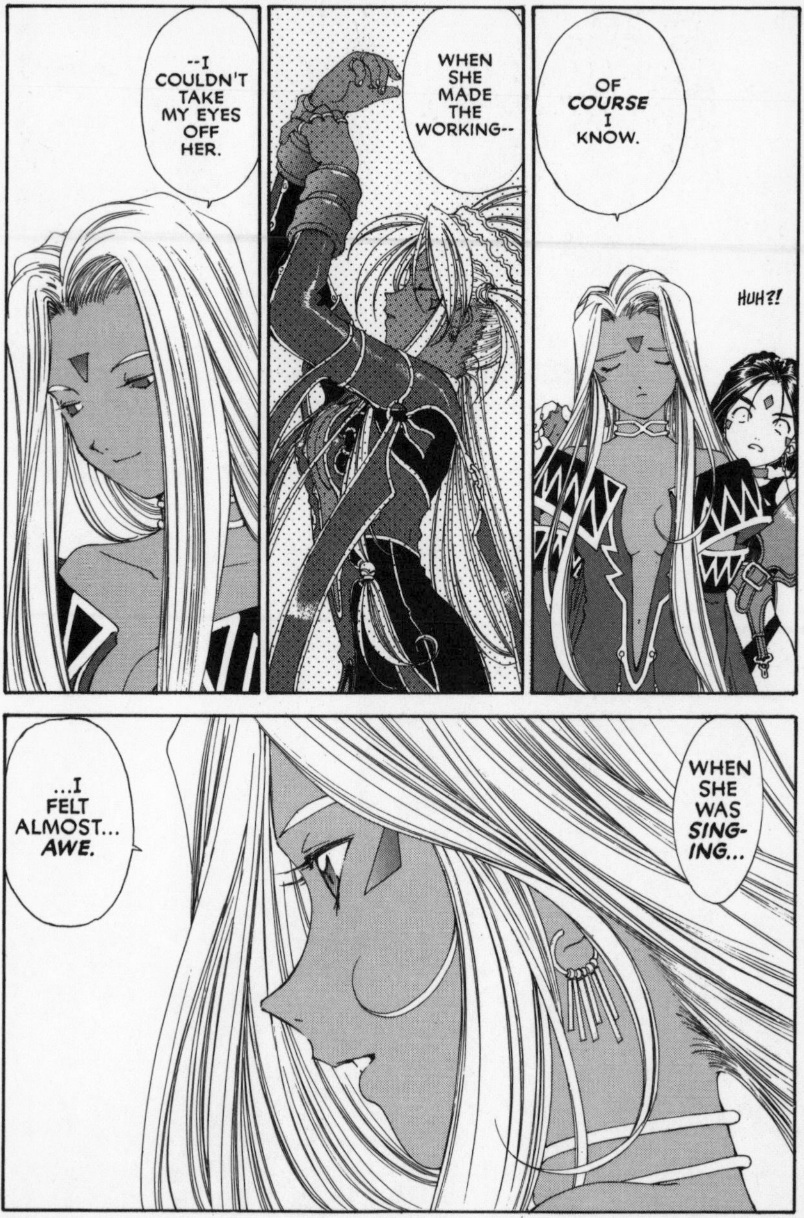
OF COURSE I KNOW.
HUH?!
WHEN SHE MADE THE WORKING--
--I COULDN'T TAKE MY EYES OFF HER.
WHEN SHE WAS SING-ING...
...I FELT ALMOST... AWE.

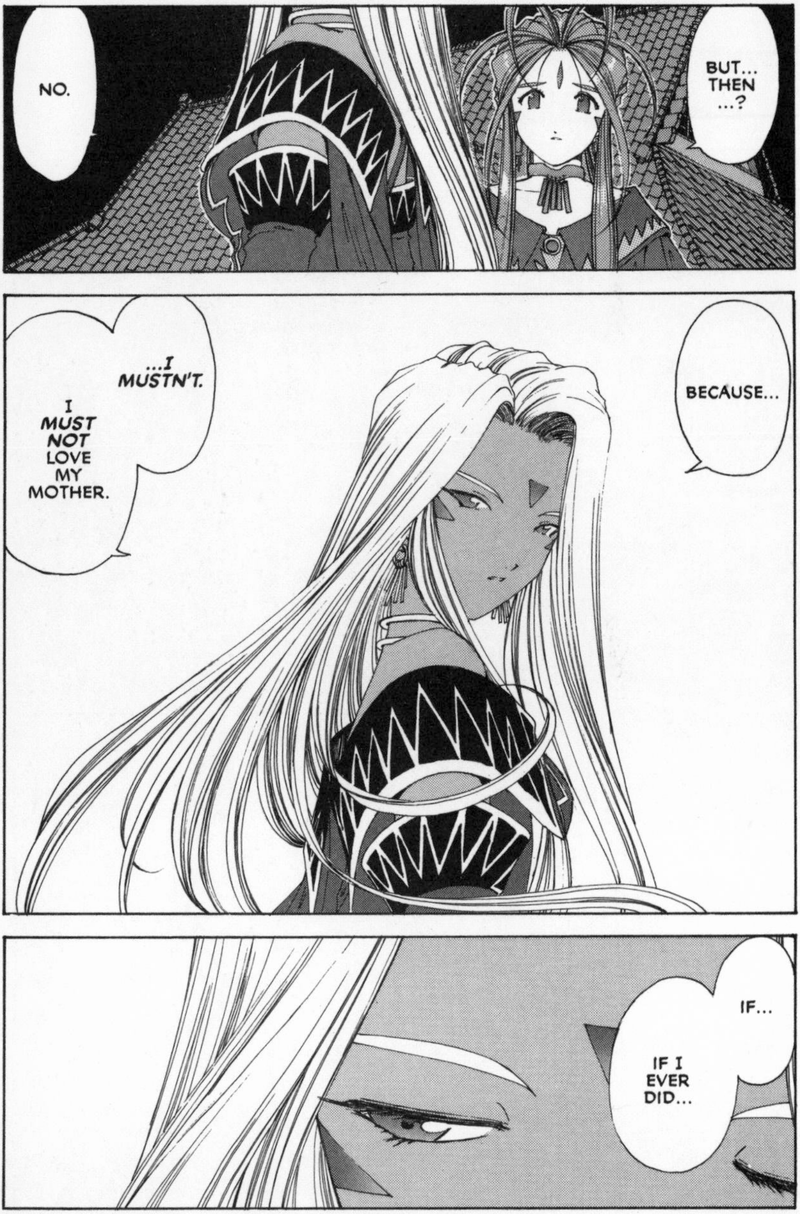
BUT... THEN ...?
NO.
BECAUSE...
...I MUSTN'T.
I MUST NOT LOVE MY MOTHER.
IF...
IF I EVER DID...

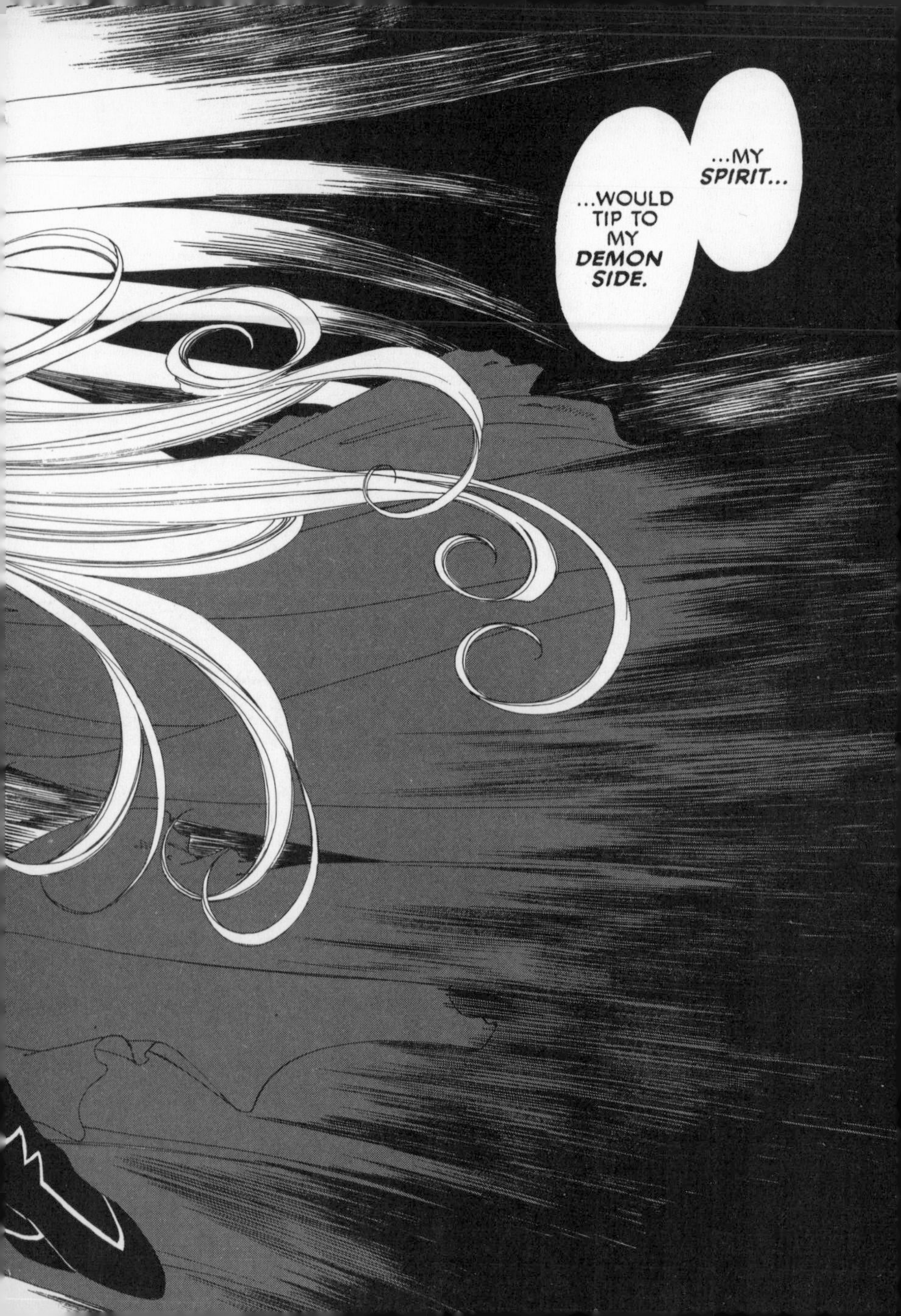
...MY SPIRIT...
...WOULD TIP TO MY DEMON SIDE.

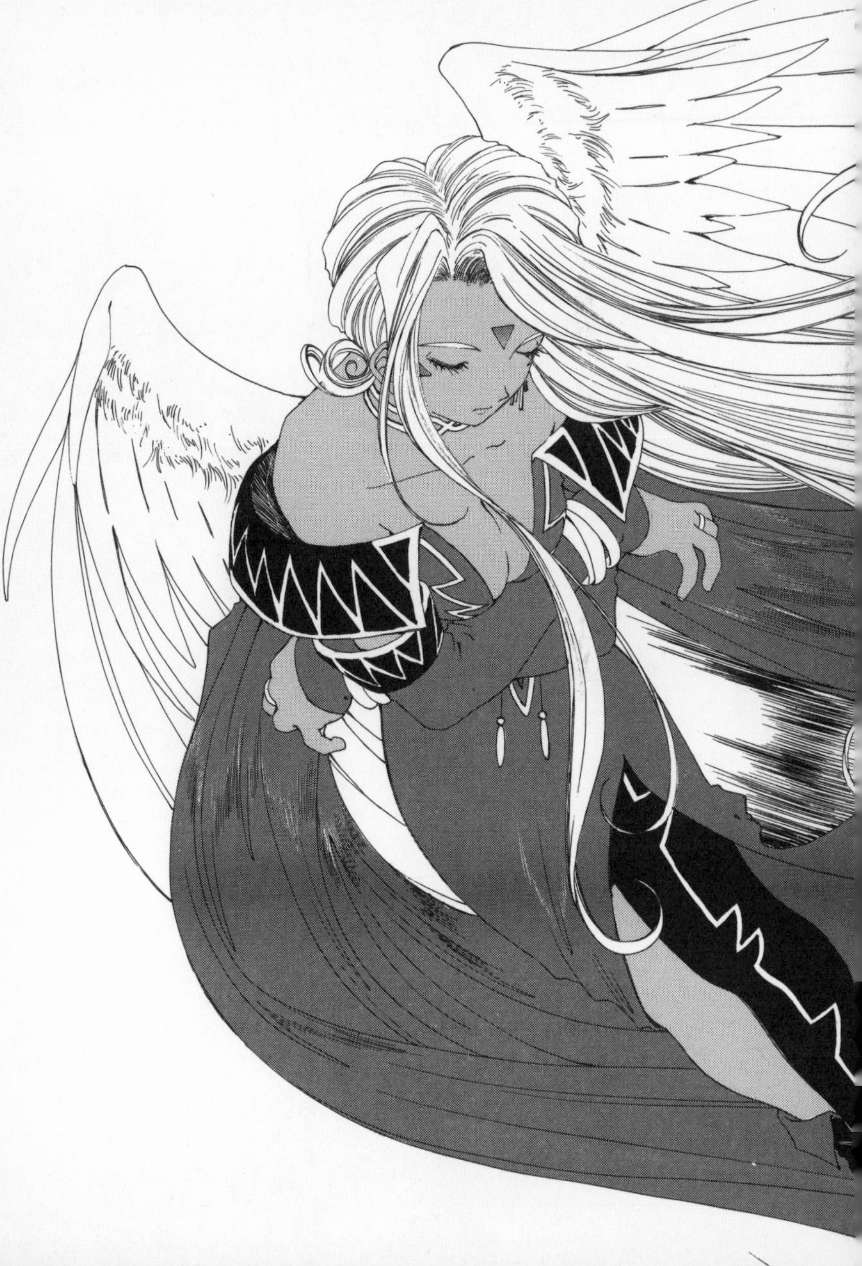

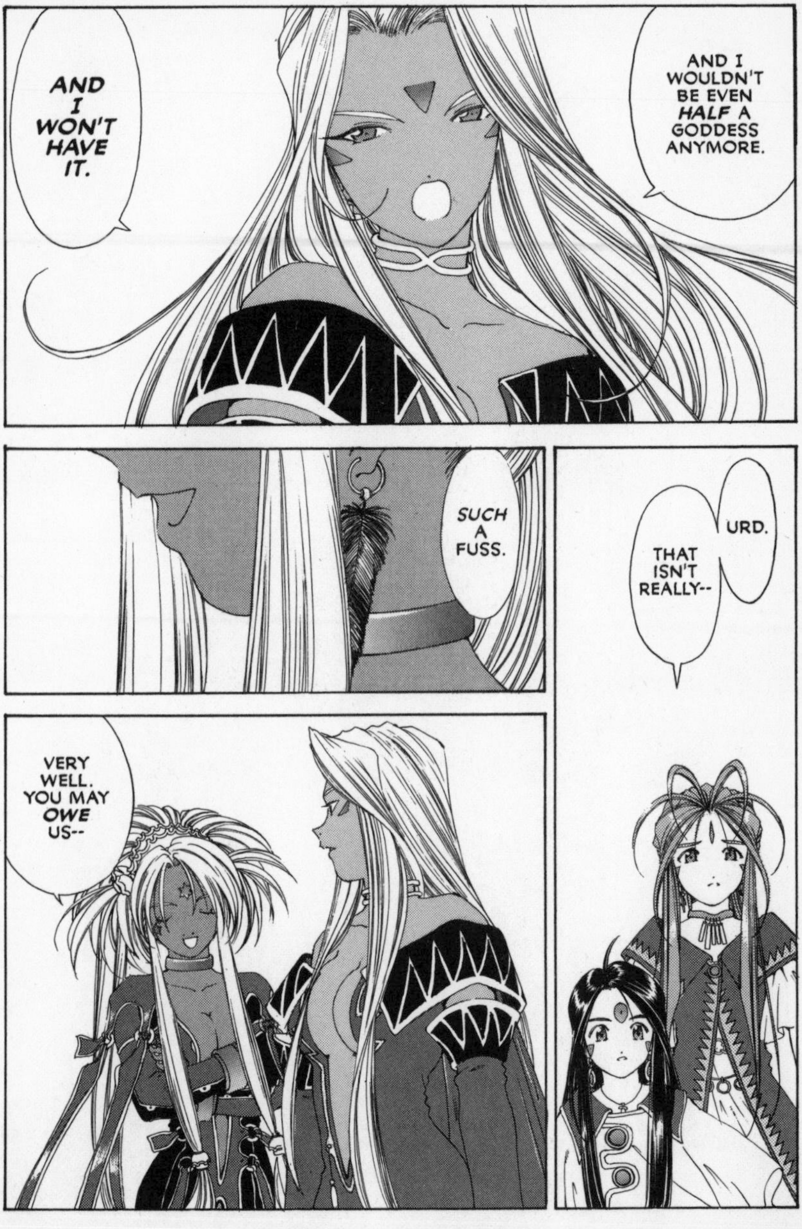
AND I WOULDN'T BE EVEN *HALF* A GODDESS ANYMORE.
AND I WON'T HAVE IT.
URD.
THAT ISN'T REALLY--
SUCH A FUSS.
VERY WELL. YOU MAY *OWE* US--

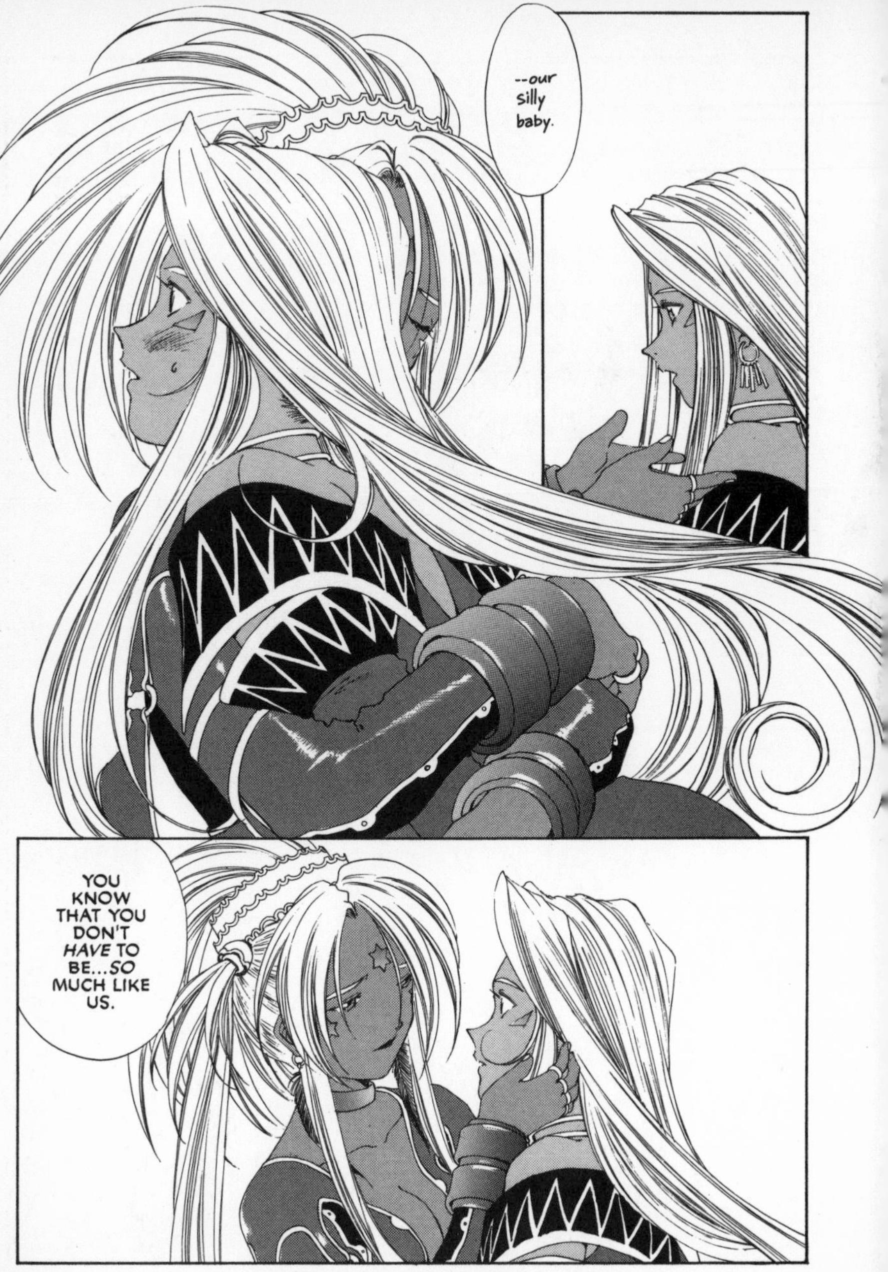
--our silly baby.
YOU KNOW THAT YOU DON'T *HAVE* TO BE...*SO* MUCH LIKE US.

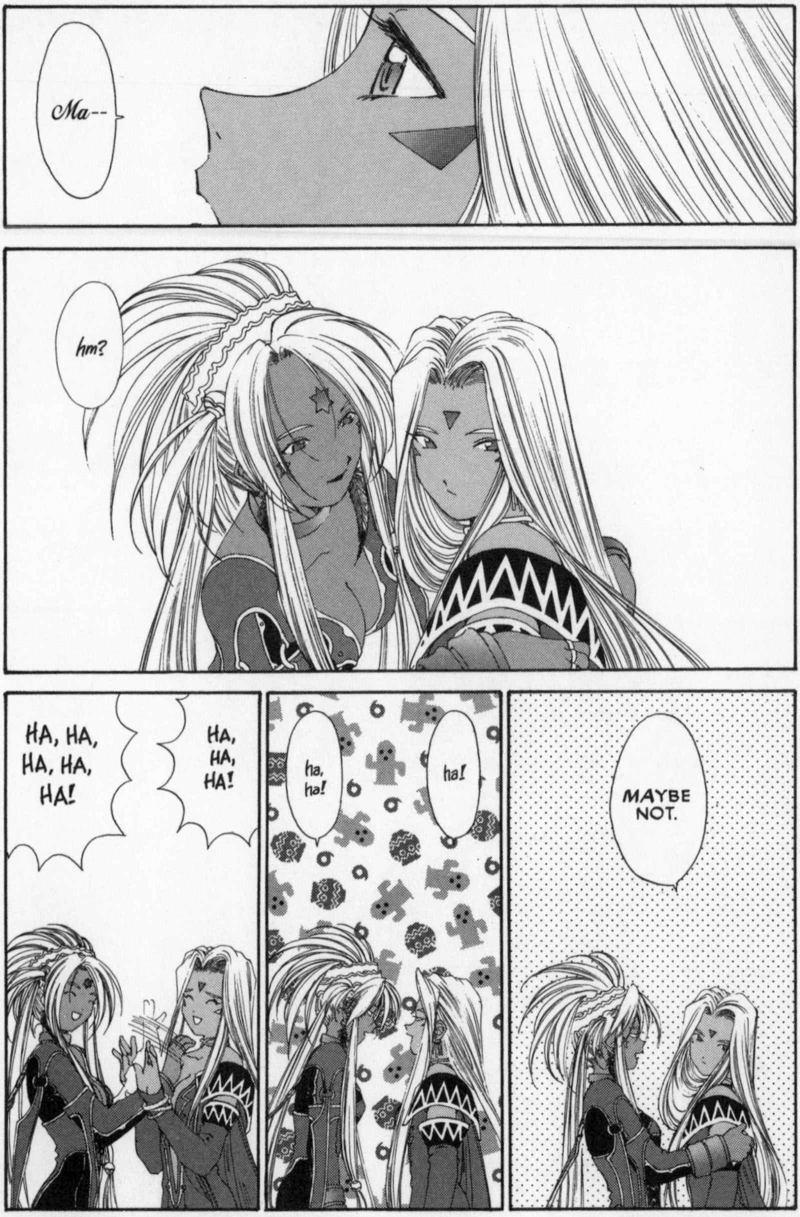
Ma--
hm?
MAYBE NOT.
ha!
ha, ha!
HA, HA, HA!
HA, HA, HA, HA, HA!

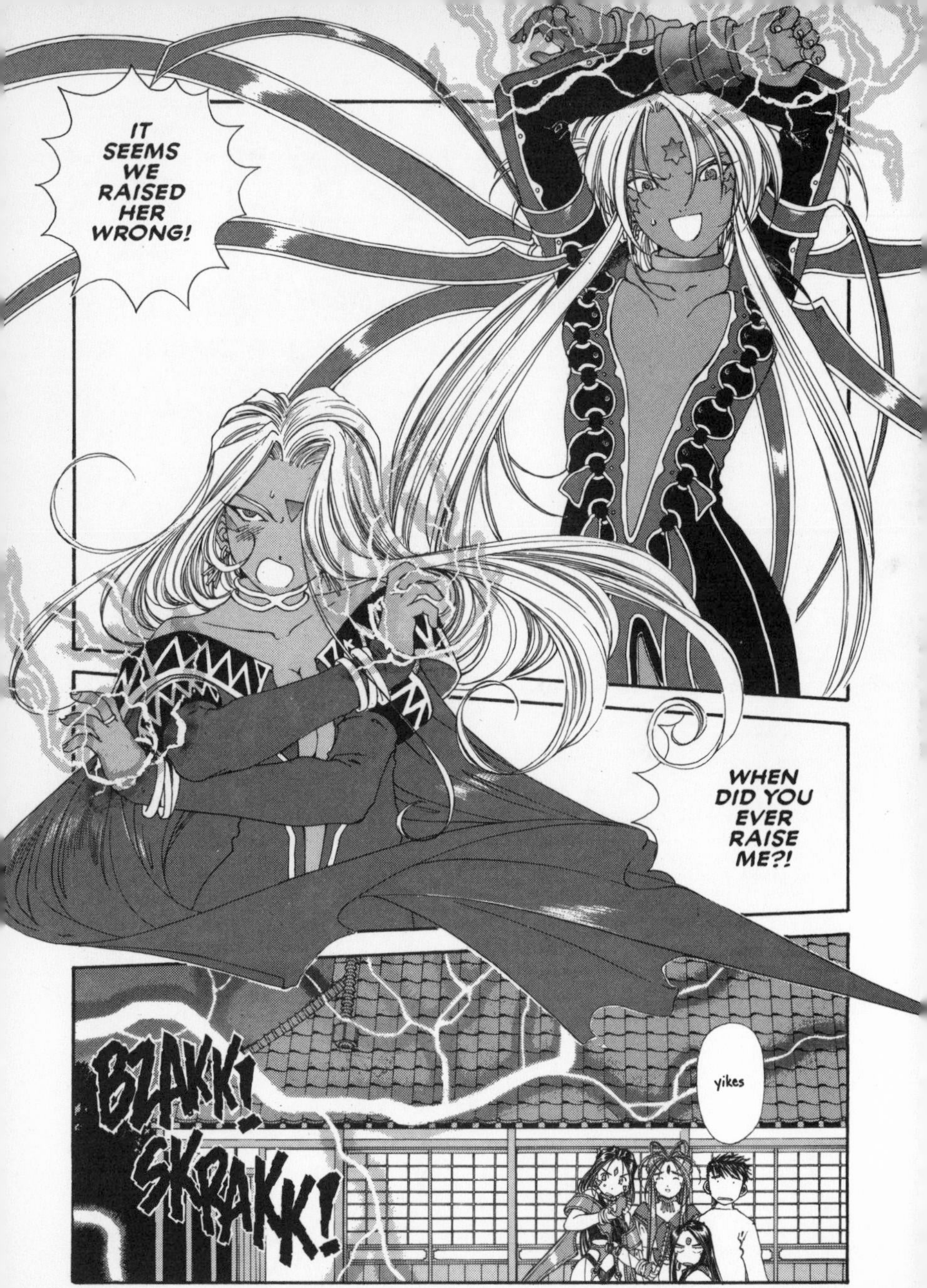
IT SEEMS WE RAISED HER WRONG!
WHEN DID YOU EVER RAISE ME?!
yikes
BZAKK! SKRAKK!

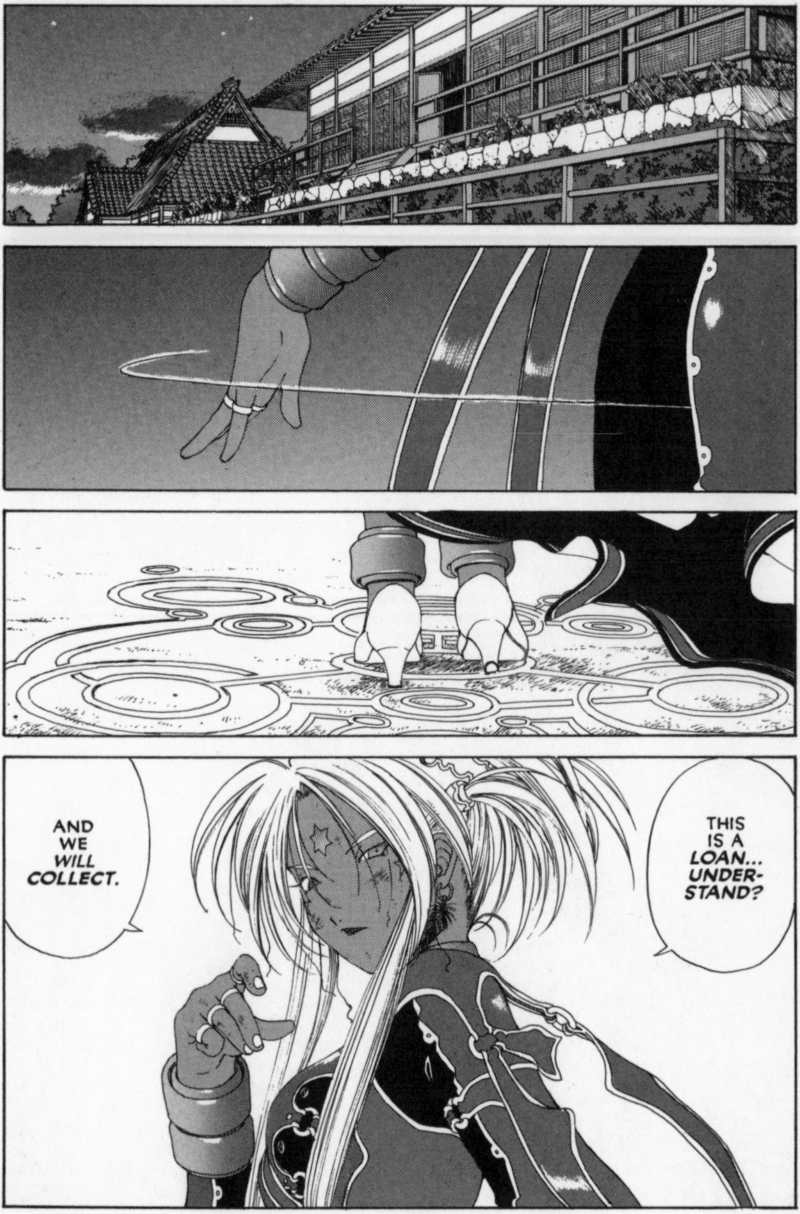
THIS IS A LOAN... UNDER-STAND?
AND WE WILL COLLECT.

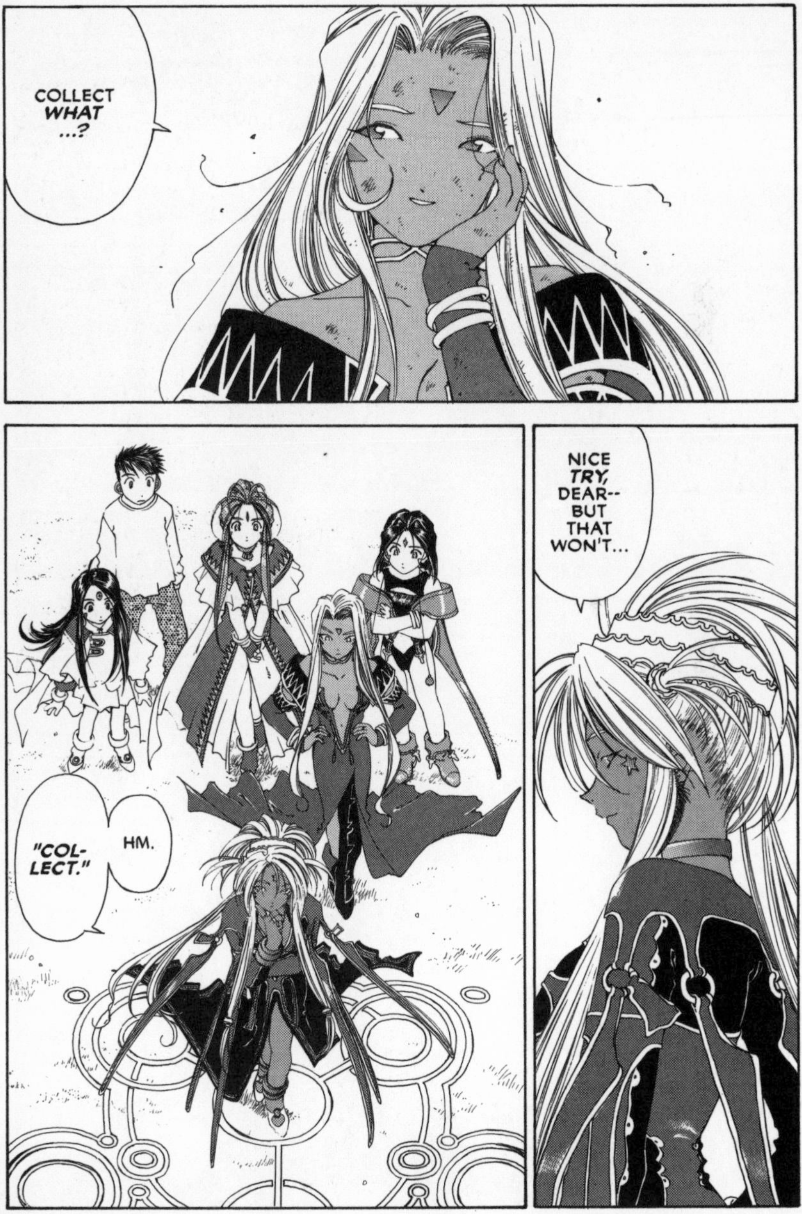
COLLECT *WHAT* ...?
NICE *TRY,* DEAR-- BUT THAT WON'T...
HM.
"COL-LECT."

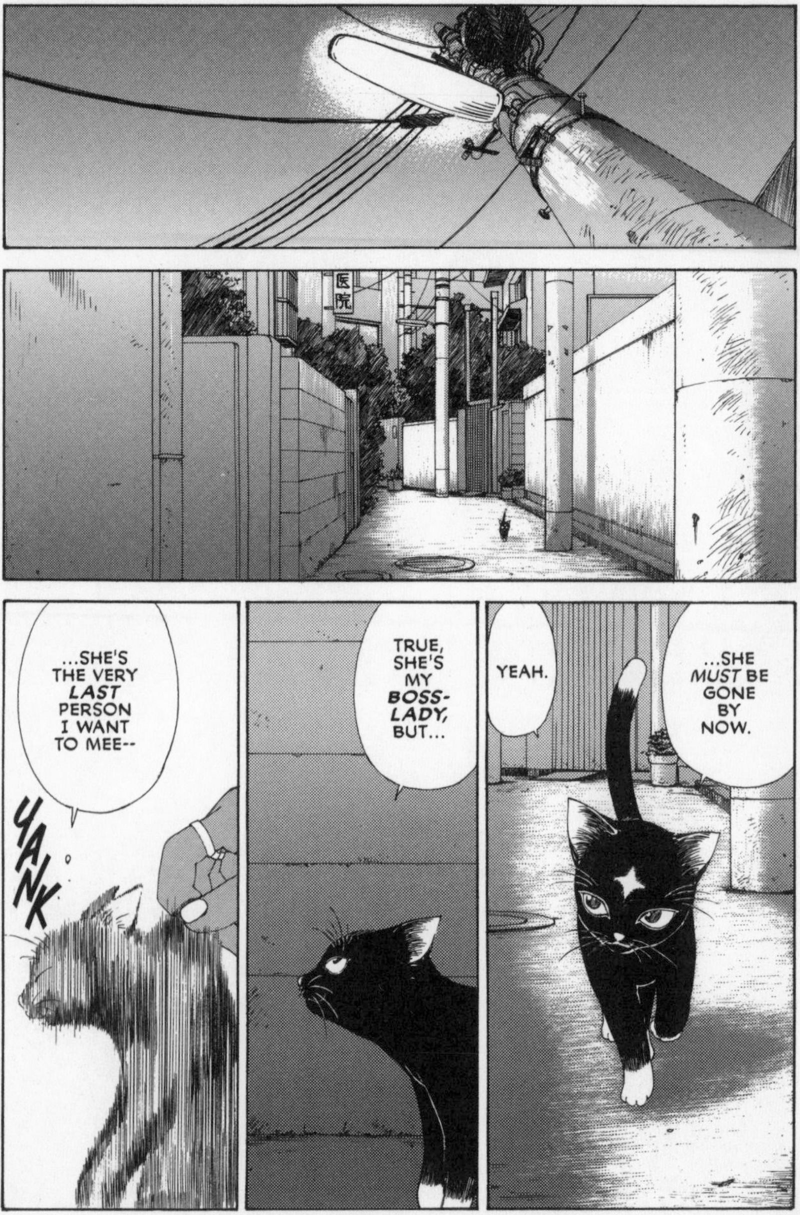
医院
...SHE *MUST* BE GONE BY NOW.
YEAH.
TRUE, SHE'S MY *BOSS-LADY,* BUT...
...SHE'S THE VERY *LAST* PERSON I WANT TO MEE--
YANK

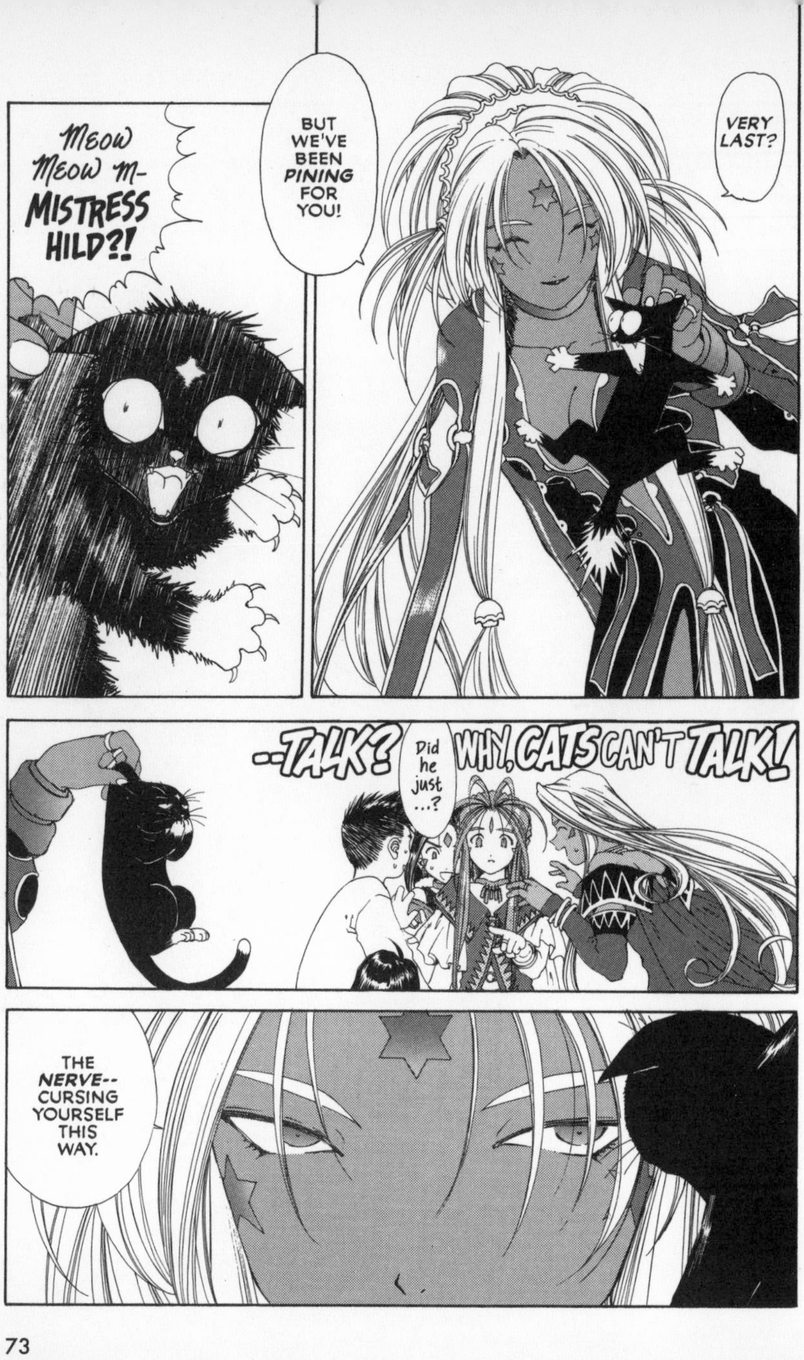
VERY LAST?
BUT WE'VE BEEN *PINING* FOR YOU!
MEOW MEOW M-MISTRESS HILD?!
Did he just ...?
--TALK? WHY, CATS CAN'T TALK!
THE *NERVE*-- CURSING YOURSELF THIS WAY.

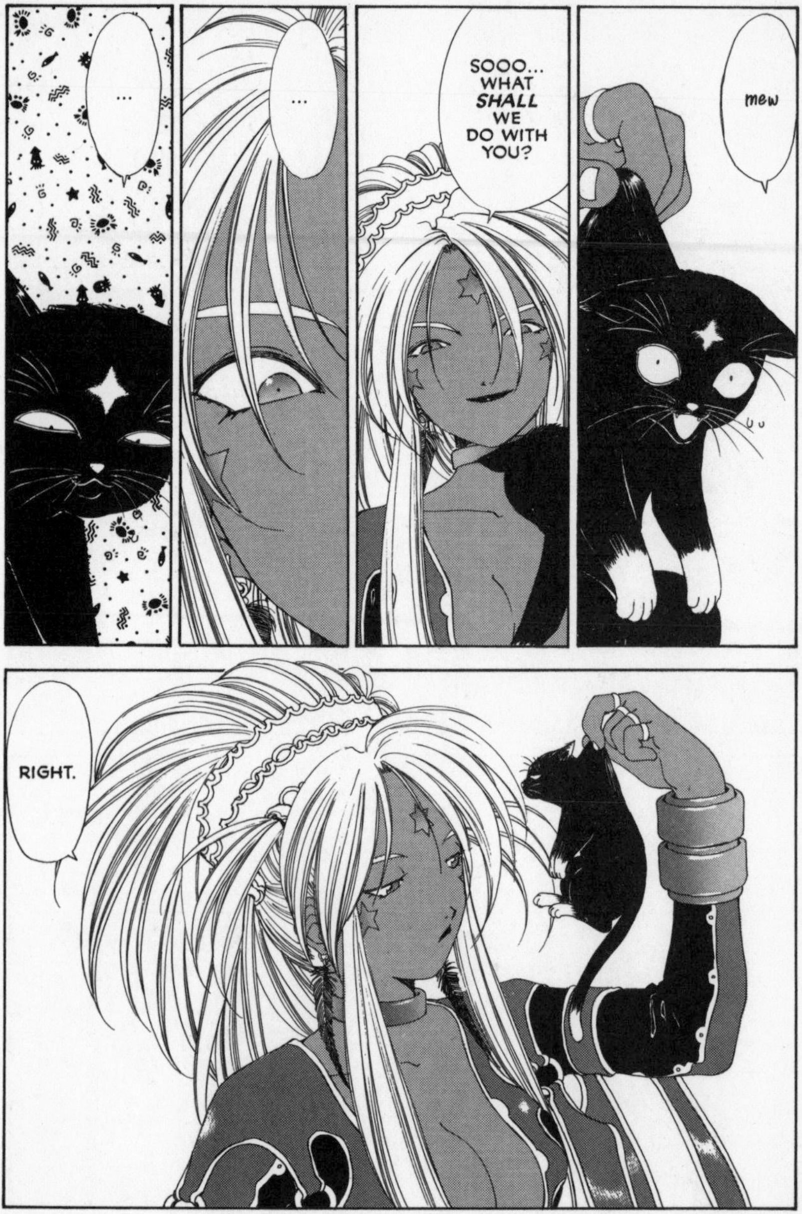
mew
SOOO... WHAT *SHALL* WE DO WITH YOU?
...
...
RIGHT.

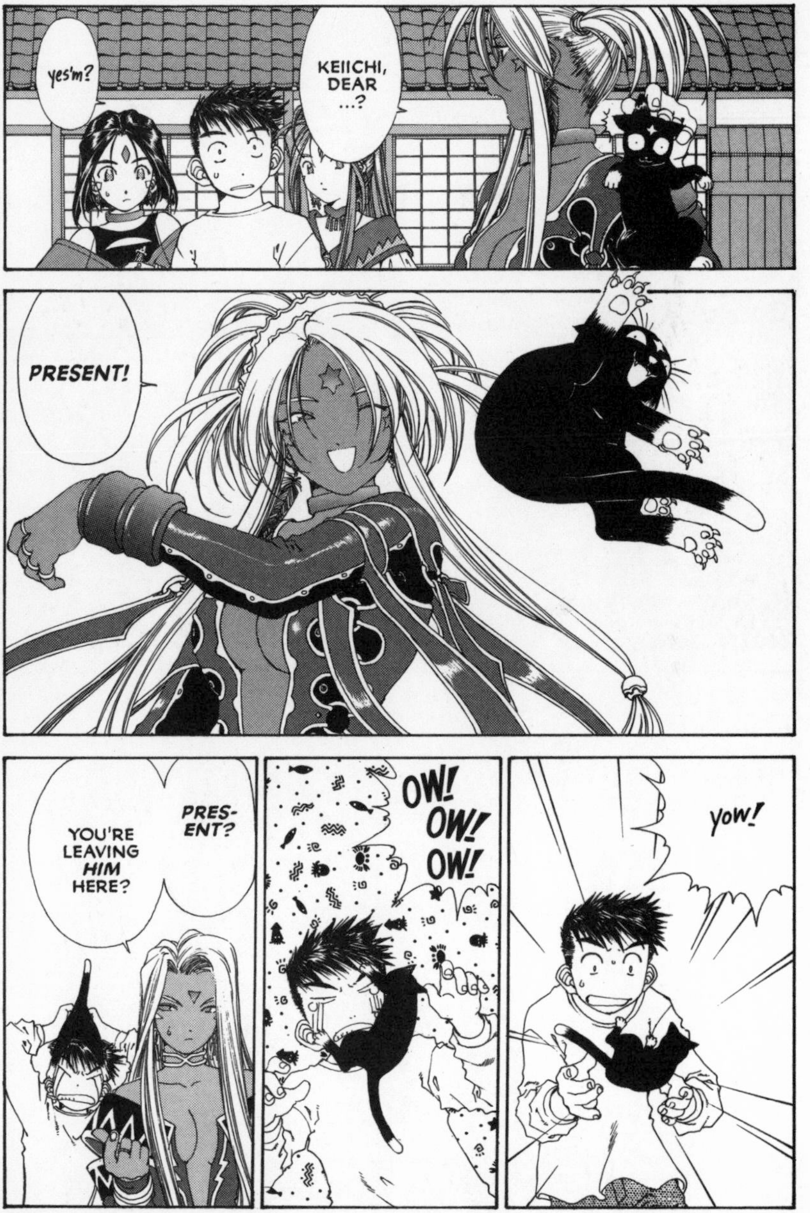
KEIICHI, DEAR ...?
yes'm?
PRESENT!
yow!
OW! OW! OW!
PRES-ENT?
YOU'RE LEAVING *HIM* HERE?

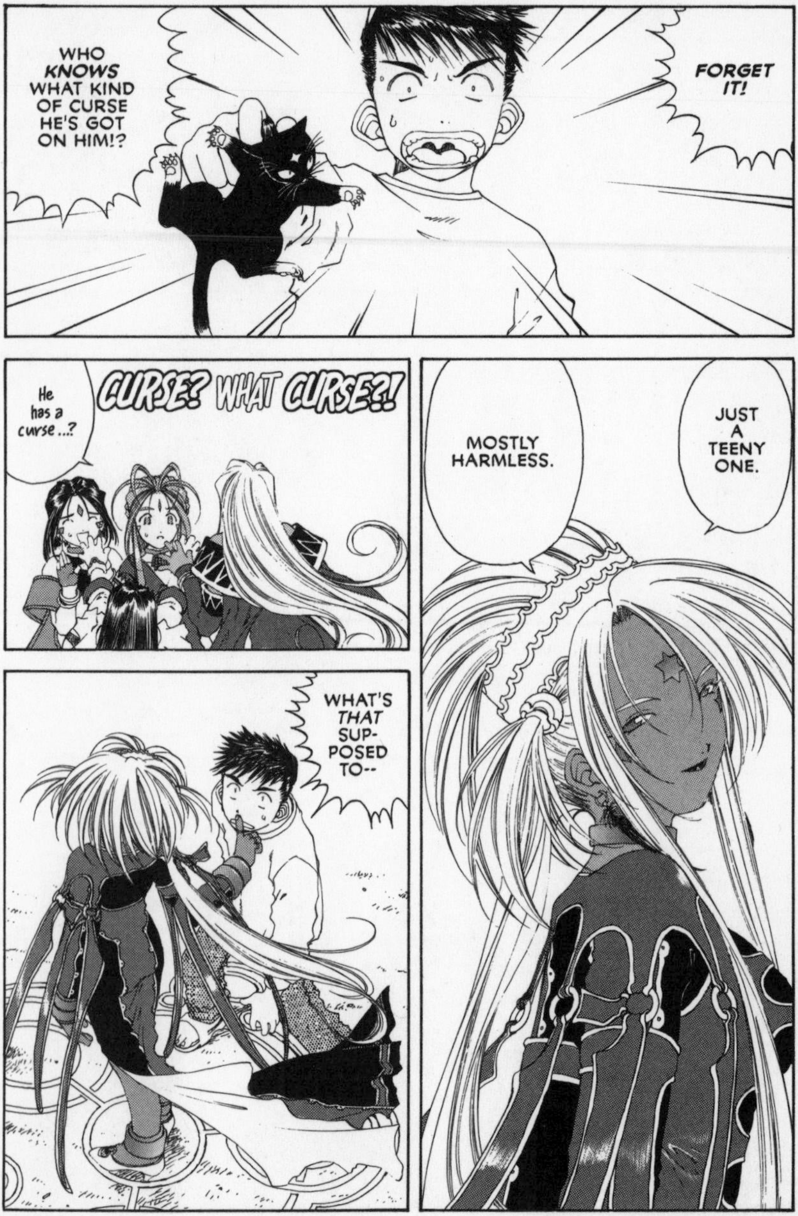
FORGET IT!
WHO KNOWS WHAT KIND OF CURSE HE'S GOT ON HIM!?
JUST A TEENY ONE.
MOSTLY HARMLESS.
CURSE? WHAT CURSE?!
He has a curse...?
WHAT'S THAT SUP-POSED TO--

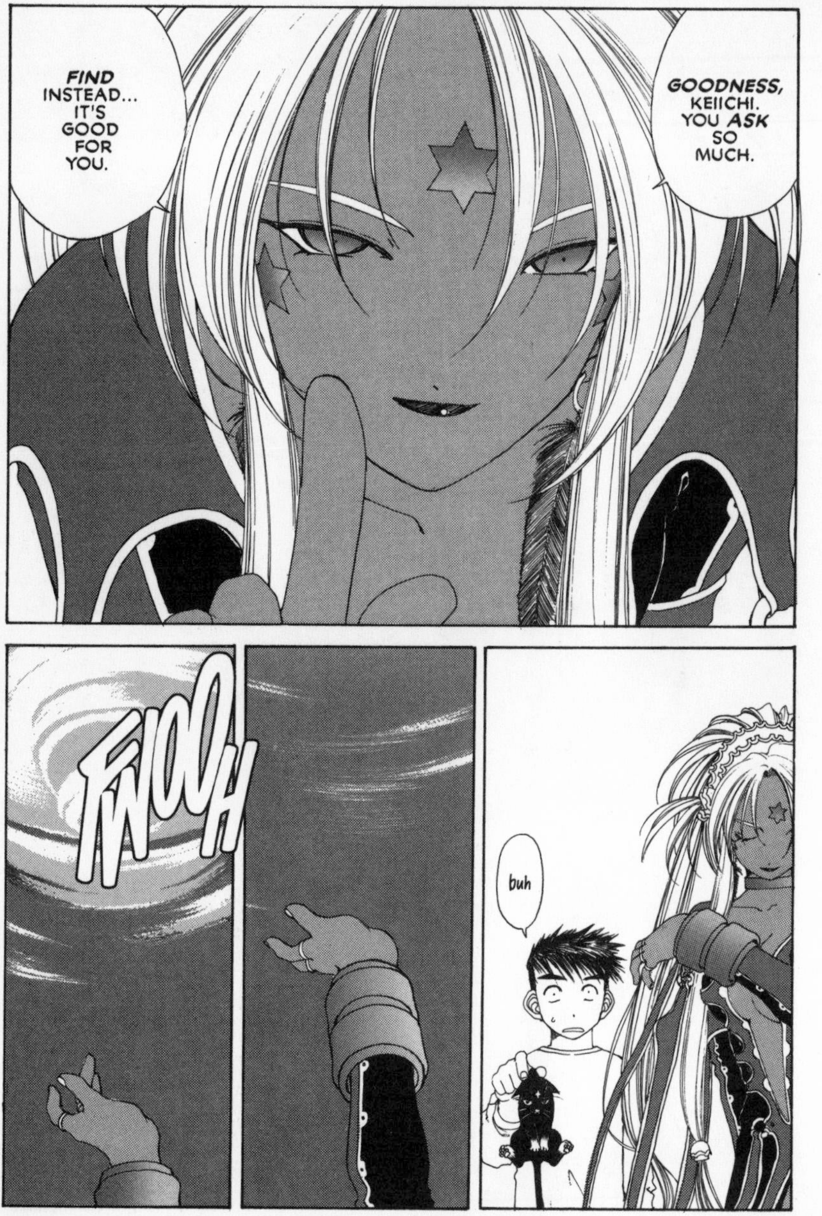
GOODNESS, KEIICHI. YOU ASK SO MUCH.
FIND INSTEAD... IT'S GOOD FOR YOU.
buh
FWOOH

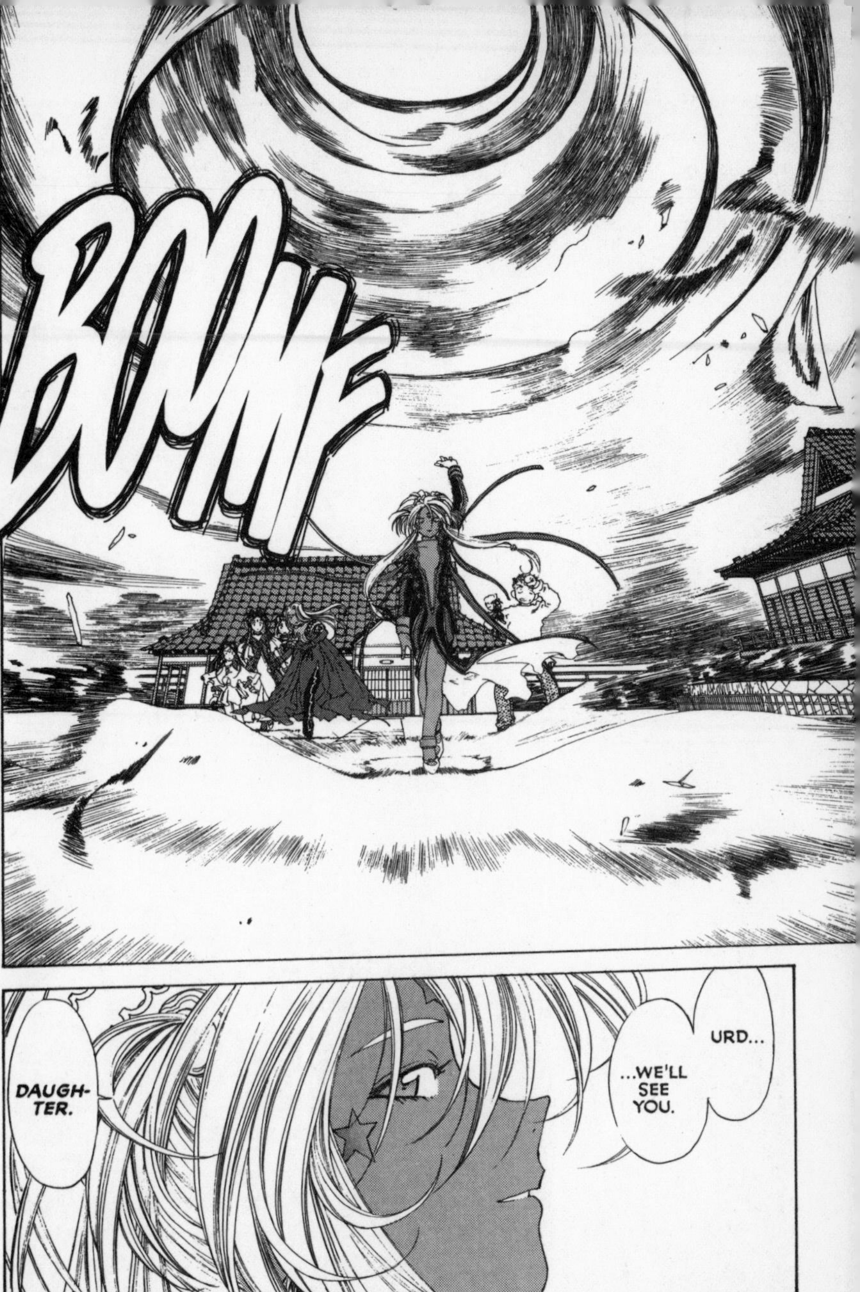
BOOM
URD...
...WE'LL SEE YOU.
DAUGHTER.

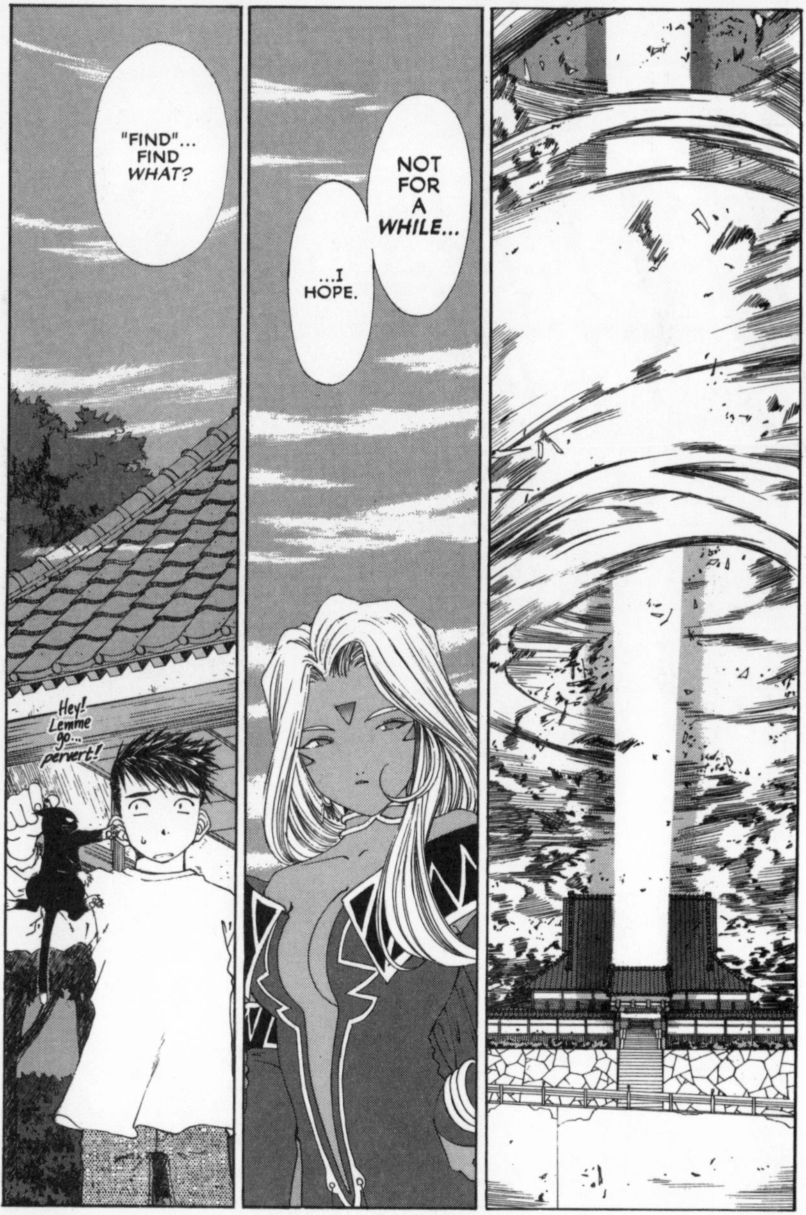
NOT FOR A WHILE...
...I HOPE.
"FIND"... FIND WHAT?
Hey! Lemme go... pervert!

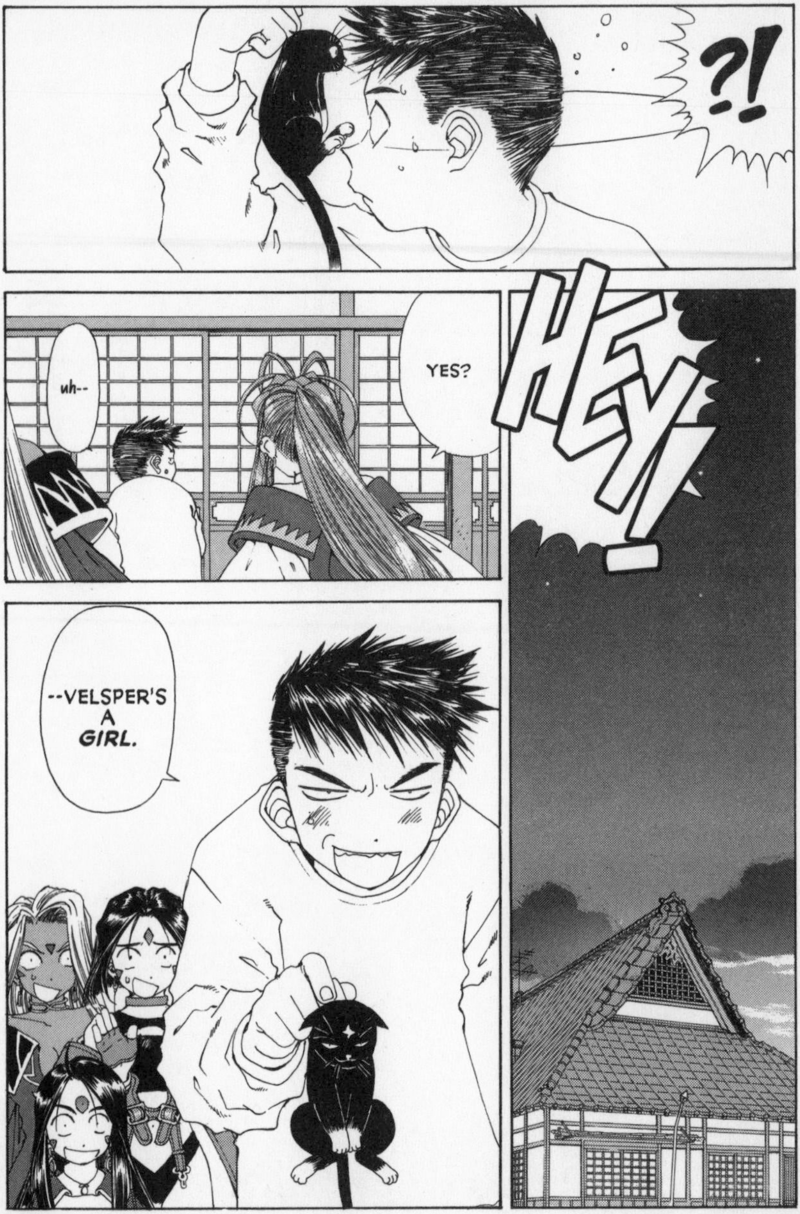
?!
HEY!
YES?
uh--
--VELSPER'S A GIRL.

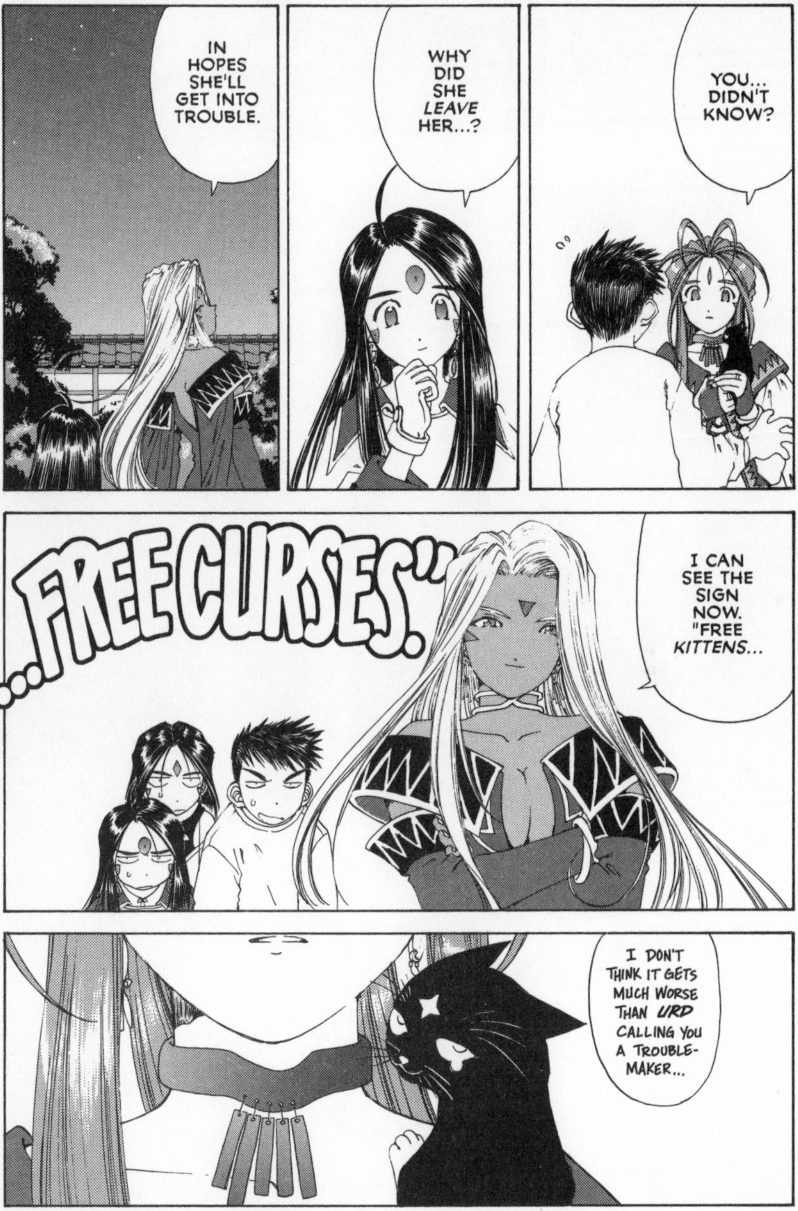
YOU... DIDN'T KNOW?
WHY DID SHE *LEAVE* HER...?
IN HOPES SHE'LL GET INTO TROUBLE.
I CAN SEE THE SIGN NOW. "FREE *KITTENS*...
...FREE CURSES."
I DON'T THINK IT GETS MUCH WORSE THAN *URD* CALLING YOU A TROUBLE-MAKER...

OH MY GODDESS!
U R D

CHAPTER 139
Wicked Game

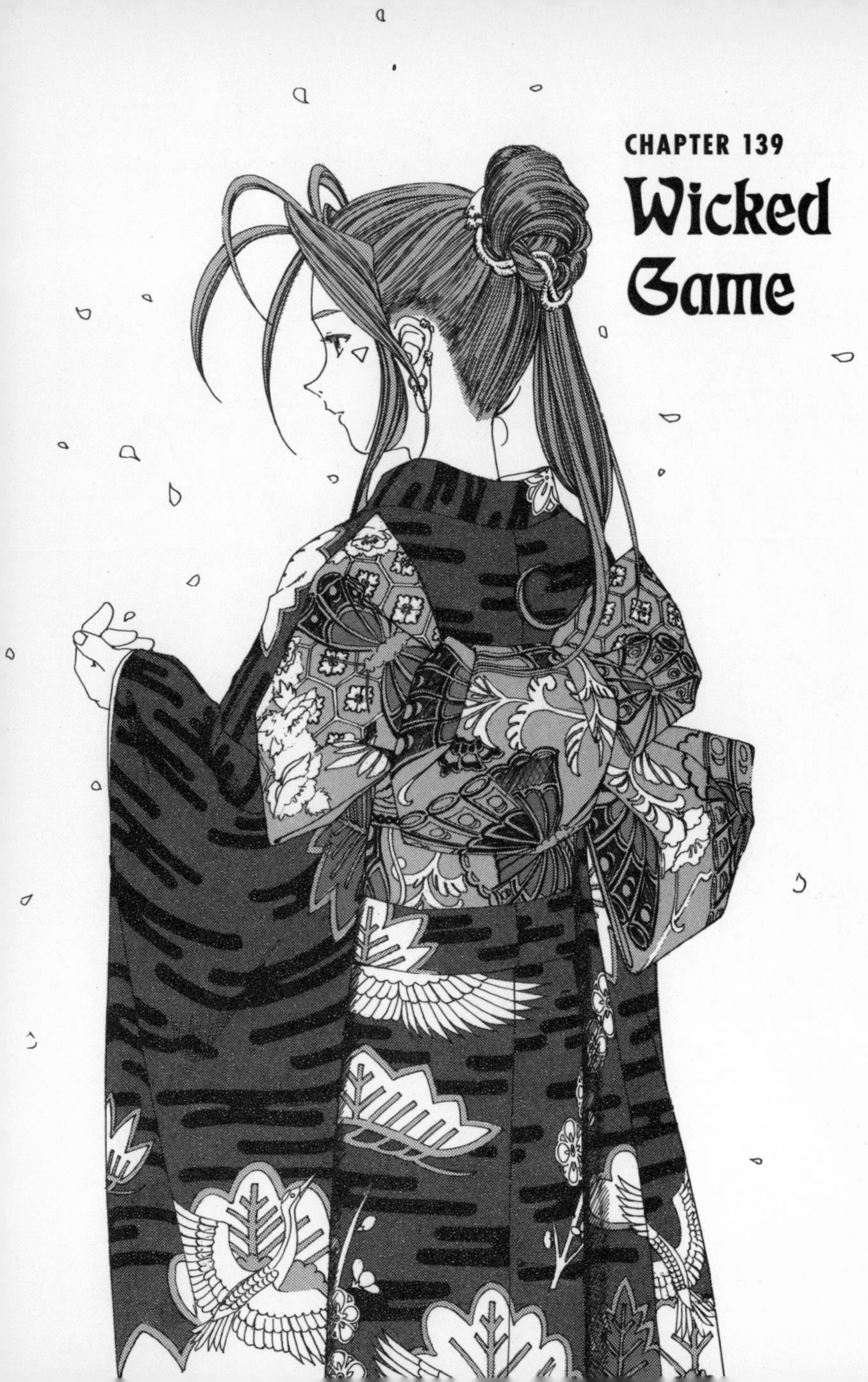

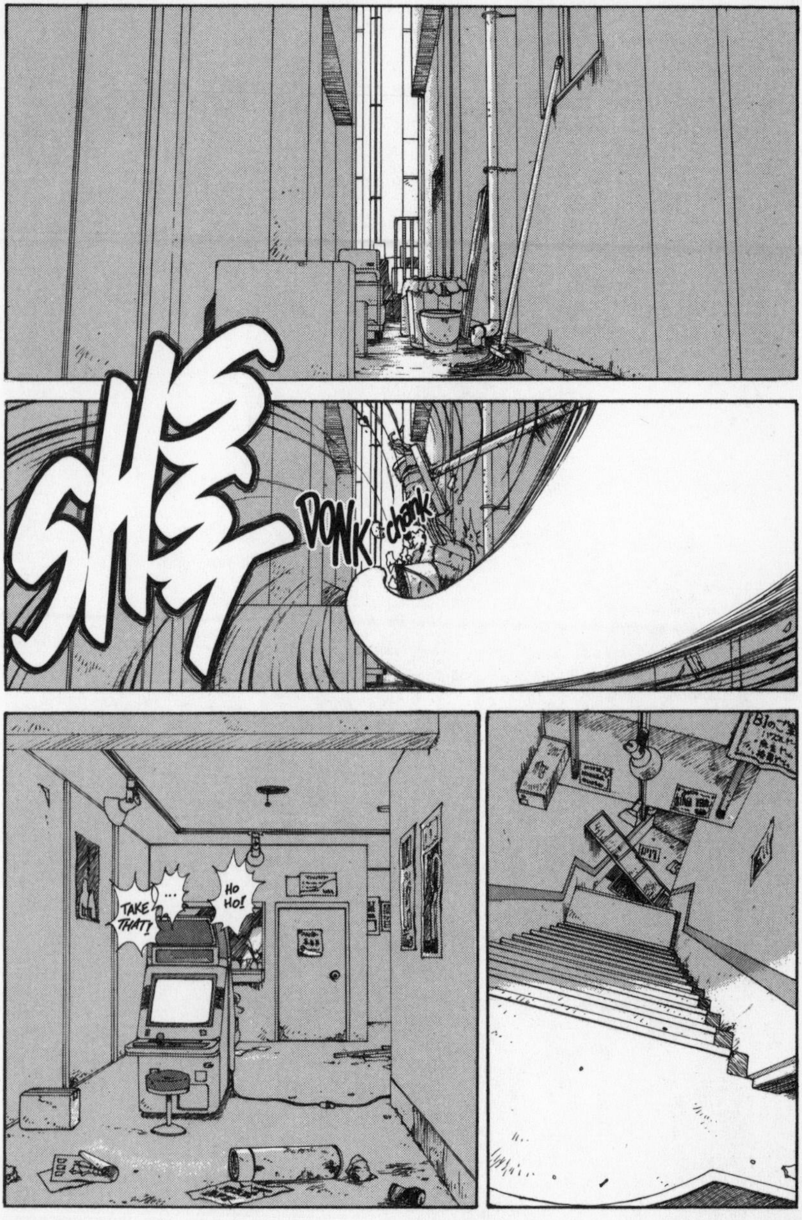
DONK
chank
HO HO!
...
TAKE THAT!

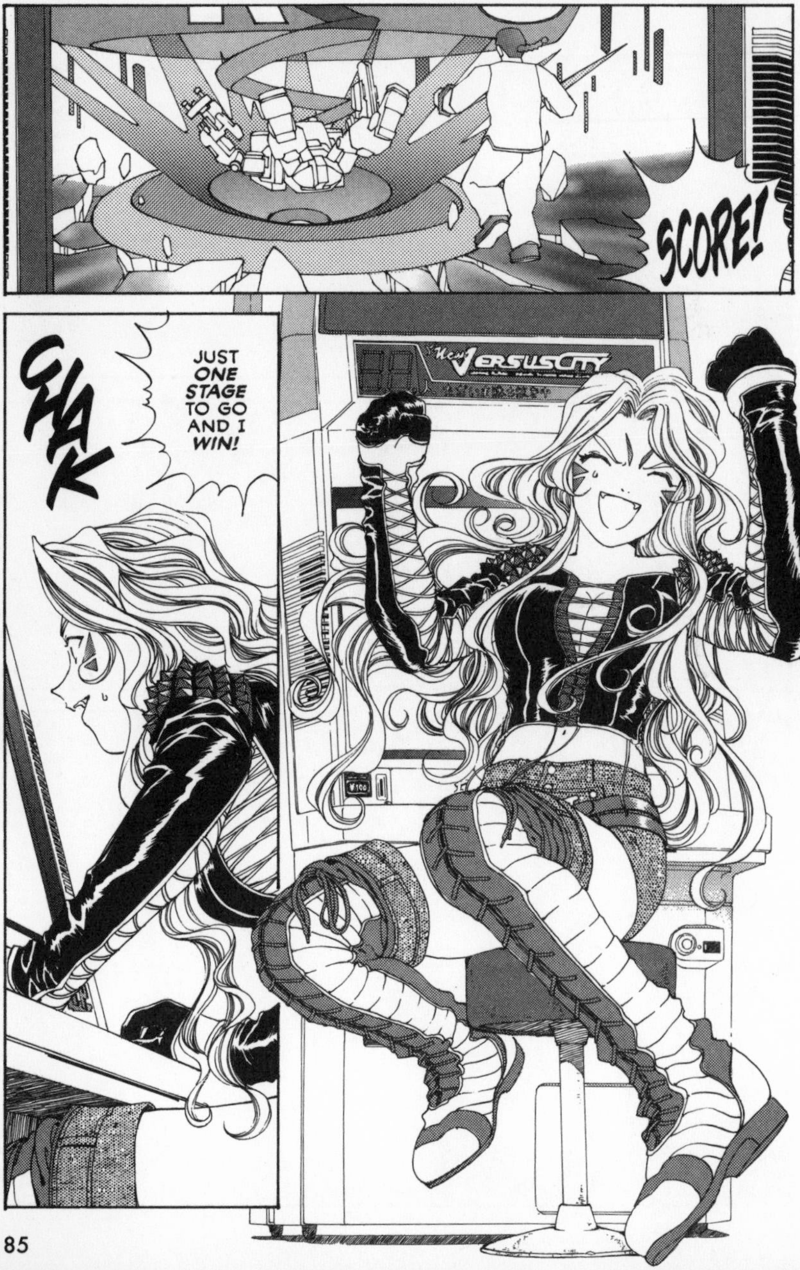
SCORE!
VERSUS CITY
JUST ONE STAGE TO GO AND I WIN!
CHAK

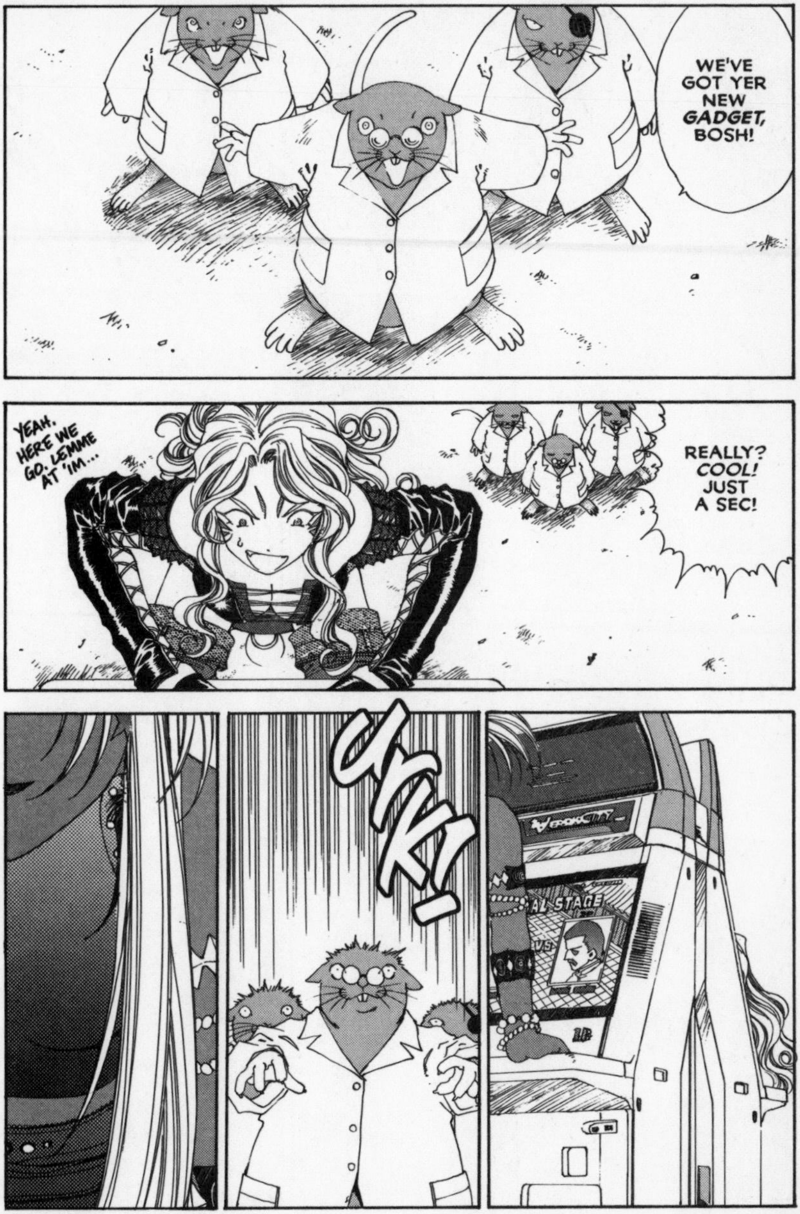
WE'VE GOT YER NEW GADGET, BOSH!
REALLY? COOL! JUST A SEC!
YEAH, HERE WE GO. LEMME AT 'IM...
AL STAGE
VS
UYK!

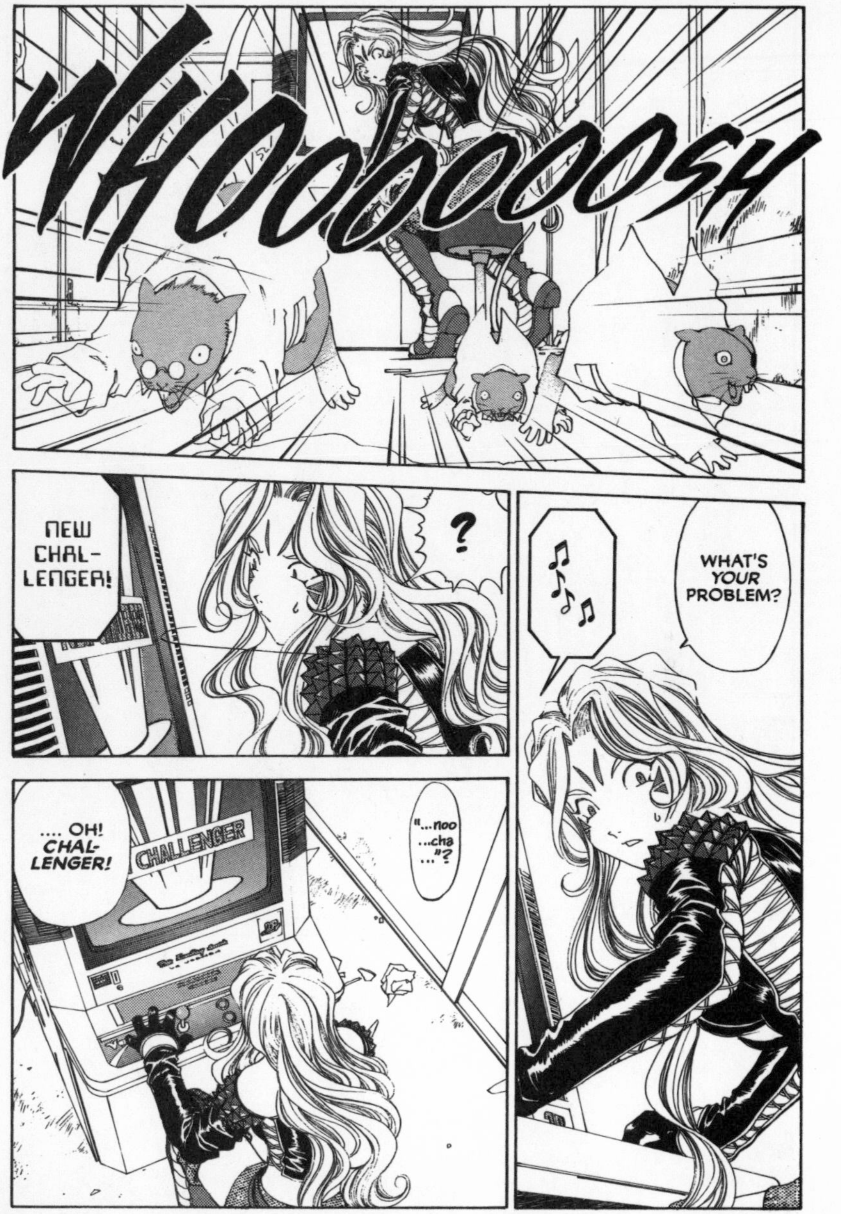
WHOOOOOOOSH
WHAT'S YOUR PROBLEM?
♪ ♪ ♪ ♪
?
NEW CHAL-LENGER!
"...noo ...cha ..."?
CHALLENGER
.... OH! CHAL-LENGER!

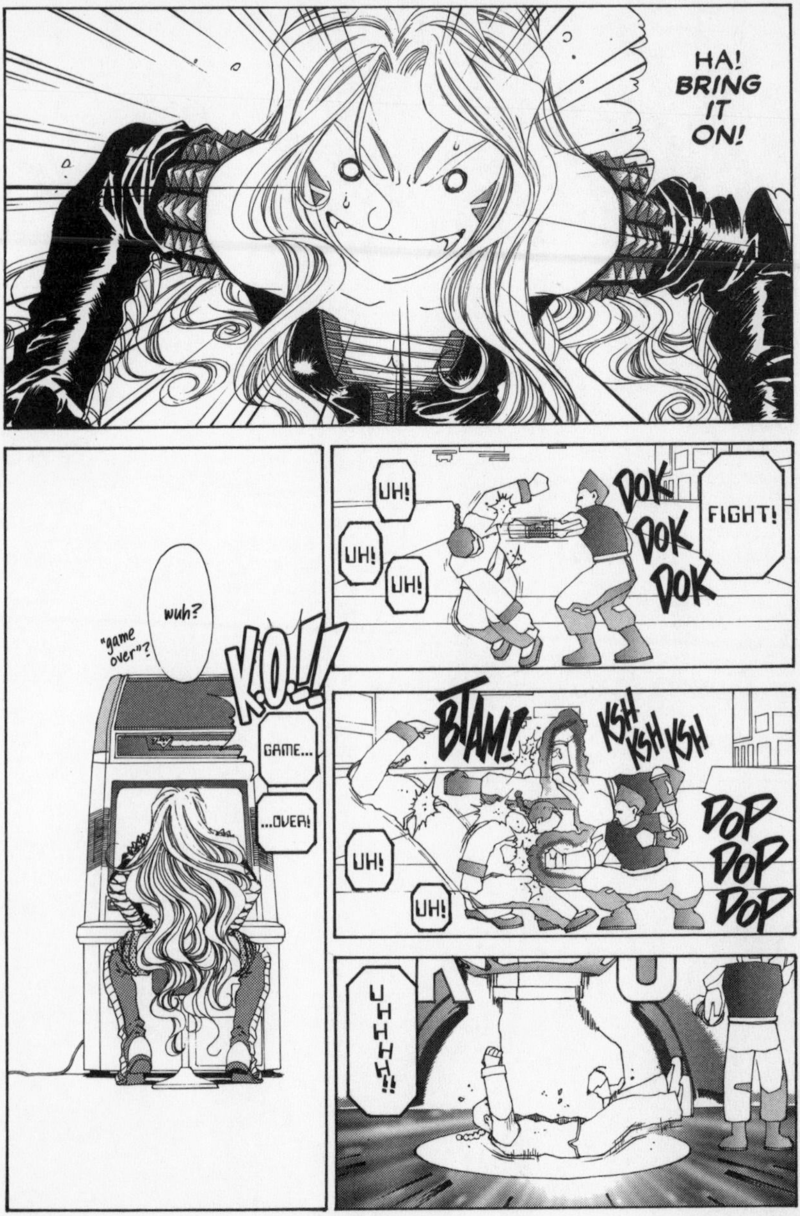
HA! BRING IT ON!
FIGHT!
DOK DOK DOK
UH!
UH!
UH!
BTAM!
KSH KSH KSH
DOP DOP DOP
UH!
UH!
UHHHHH!!
K.O.!!
GAME...
...OVER!
wuh?
"game over"?

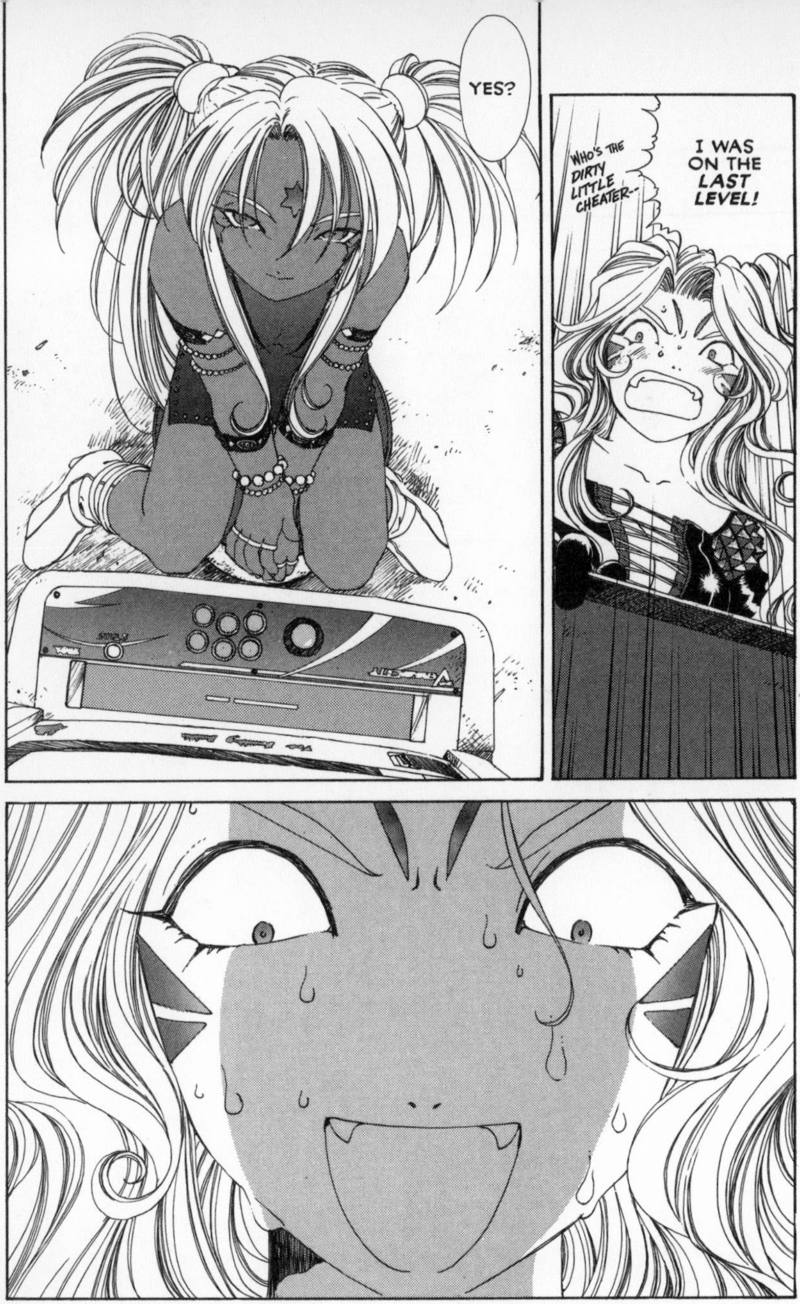
I WAS ON THE LAST LEVEL!
WHO'S THE DIRTY LITTLE CHEATER--
YES?

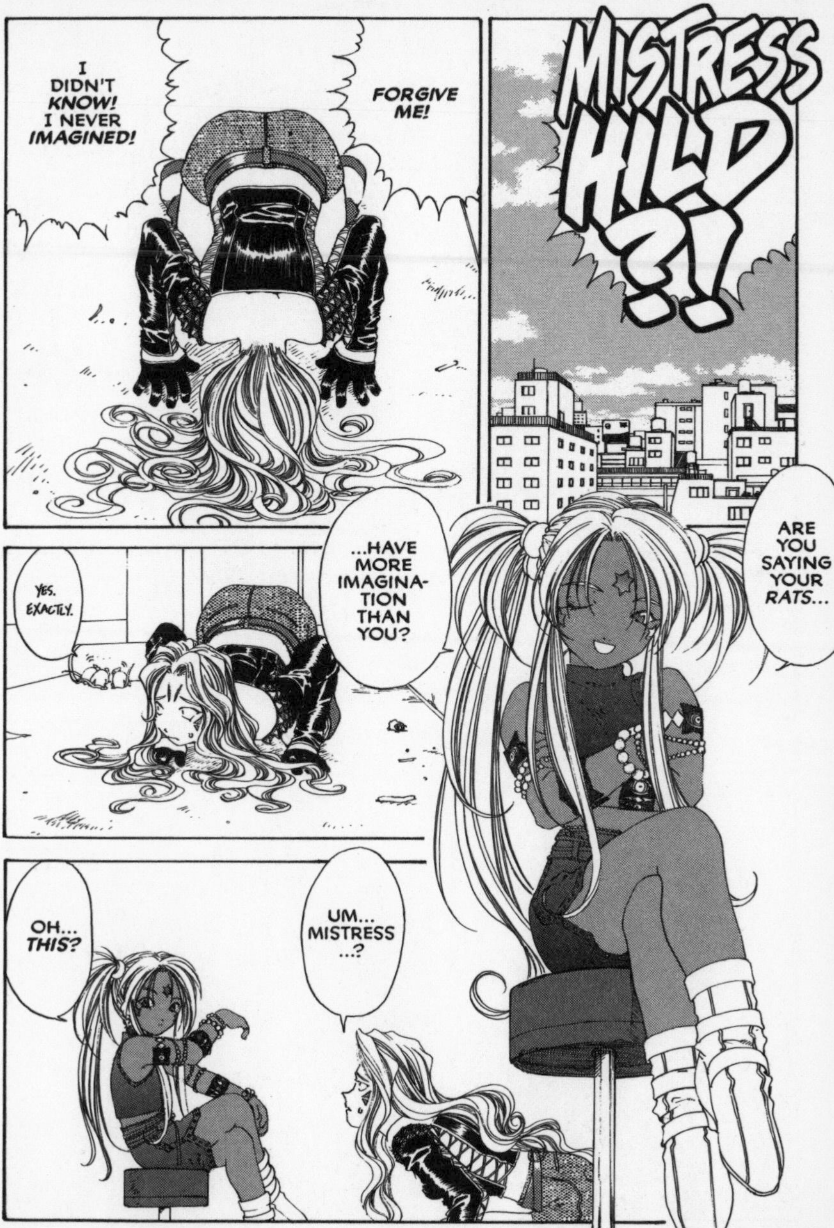
MISTRESS HILD ?!
FORGIVE ME!
I DIDN'T KNOW! I NEVER IMAGINED!
ARE YOU SAYING YOUR RATS...
...HAVE MORE IMAGINATION THAN YOU?
YES. EXACTLY.
UM... MISTRESS ...?
OH... THIS?

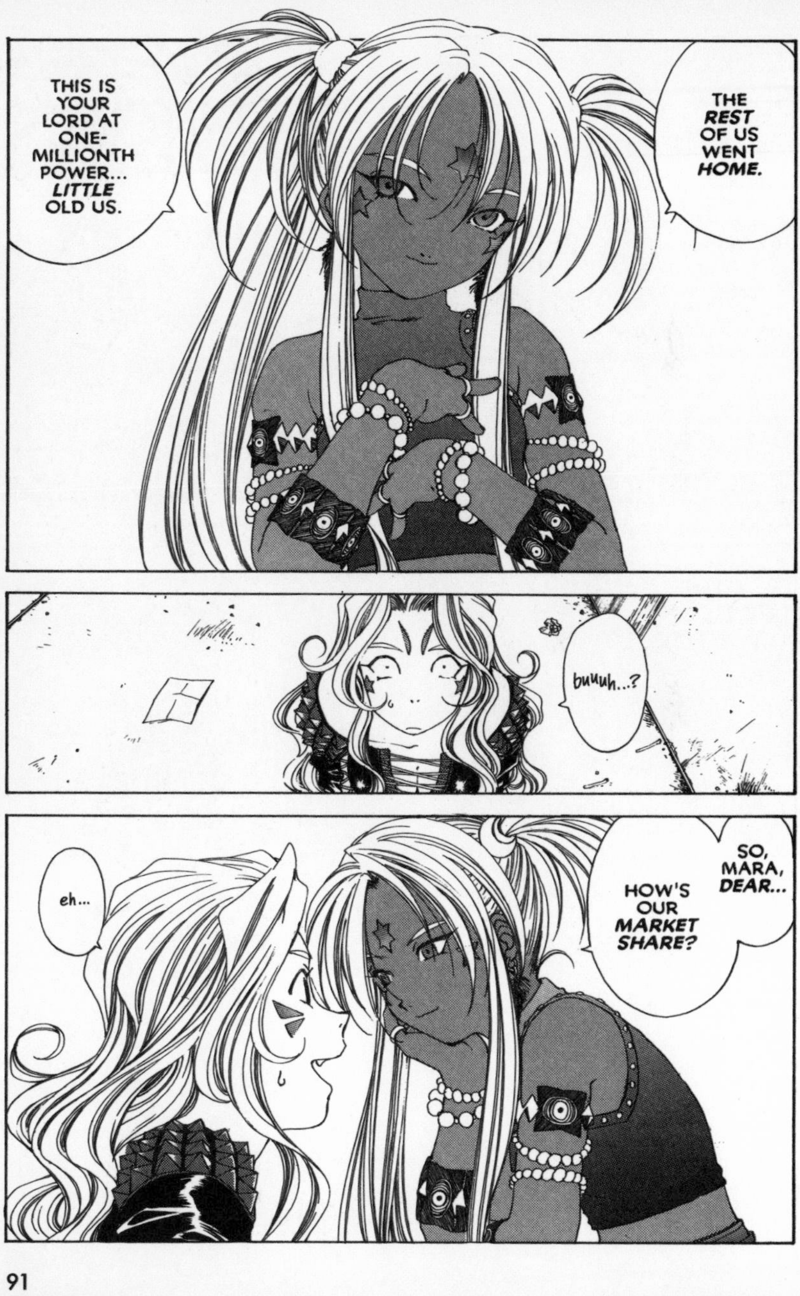
THE *REST* OF US WENT *HOME.*
THIS IS YOUR LORD AT ONE-MILLIONTH POWER... *LITTLE* OLD US.
buuuh...?
SO, MARA, *DEAR...*
HOW'S OUR *MARKET* SHARE?
eh...

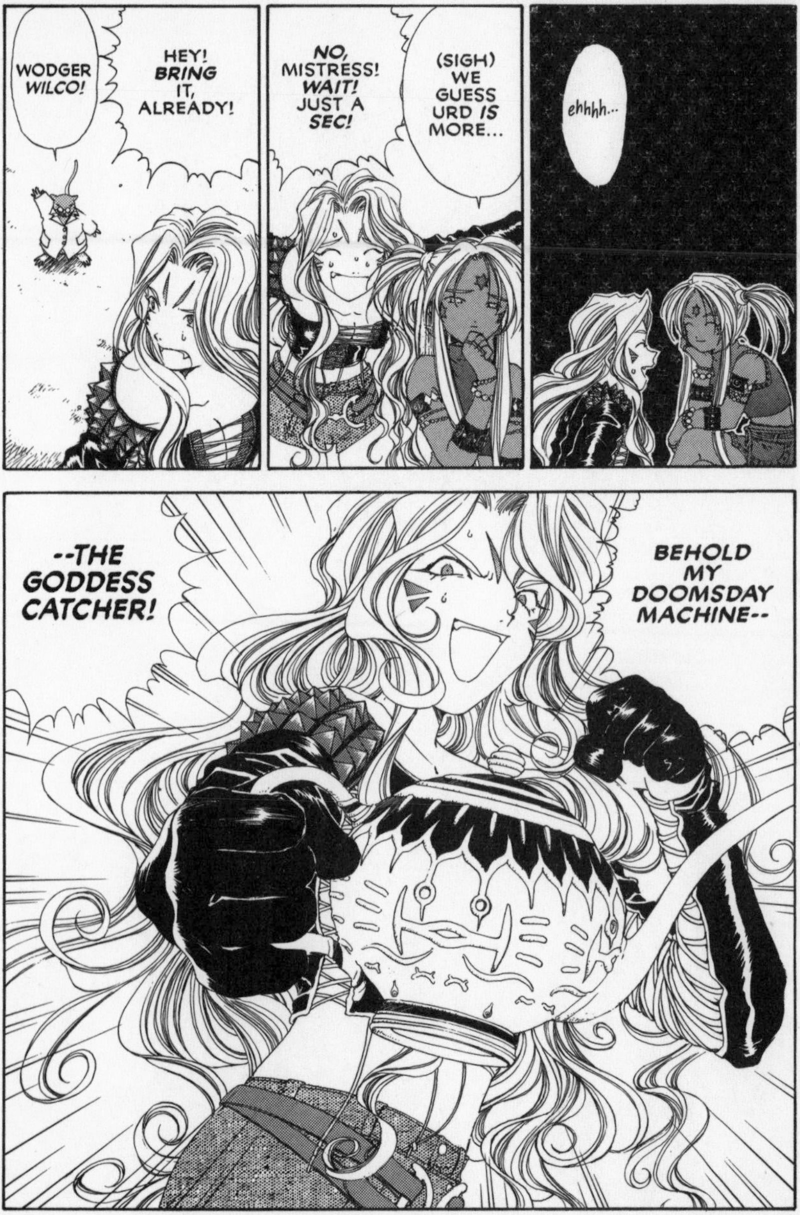
ehhhh...
(SIGH) WE GUESS URD IS MORE...
NO, MISTRESS! WAIT! JUST A SEC!
HEY! BRING IT, ALREADY!
WODGER WILCO!
BEHOLD MY DOOMSDAY MACHINE--
--THE GODDESS CATCHER!

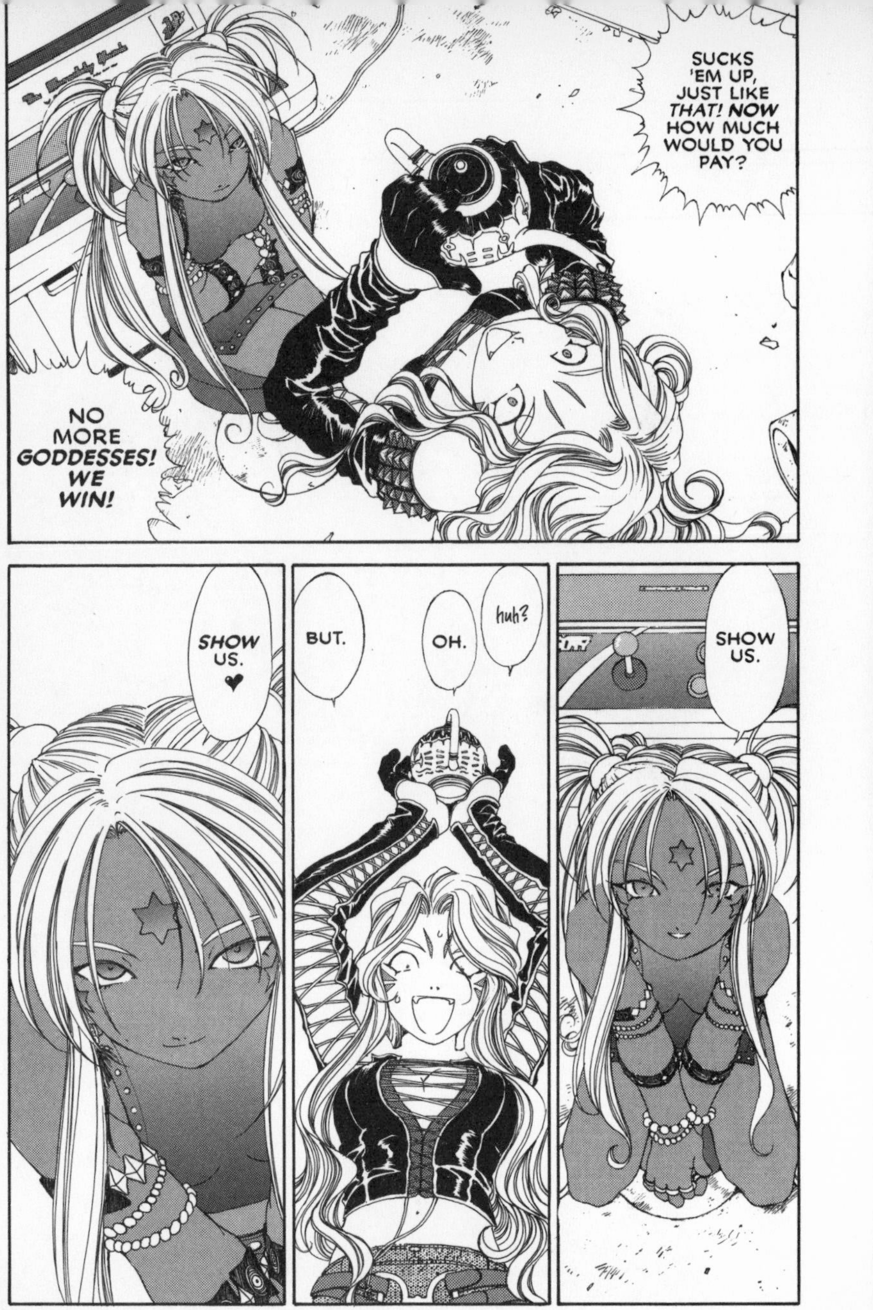
SUCKS 'EM UP, JUST LIKE *THAT! NOW* HOW MUCH WOULD YOU PAY?
NO MORE *GODDESSES!* WE WIN!
SHOW US.
huh?
OH.
BUT.
SHOW US. ♥

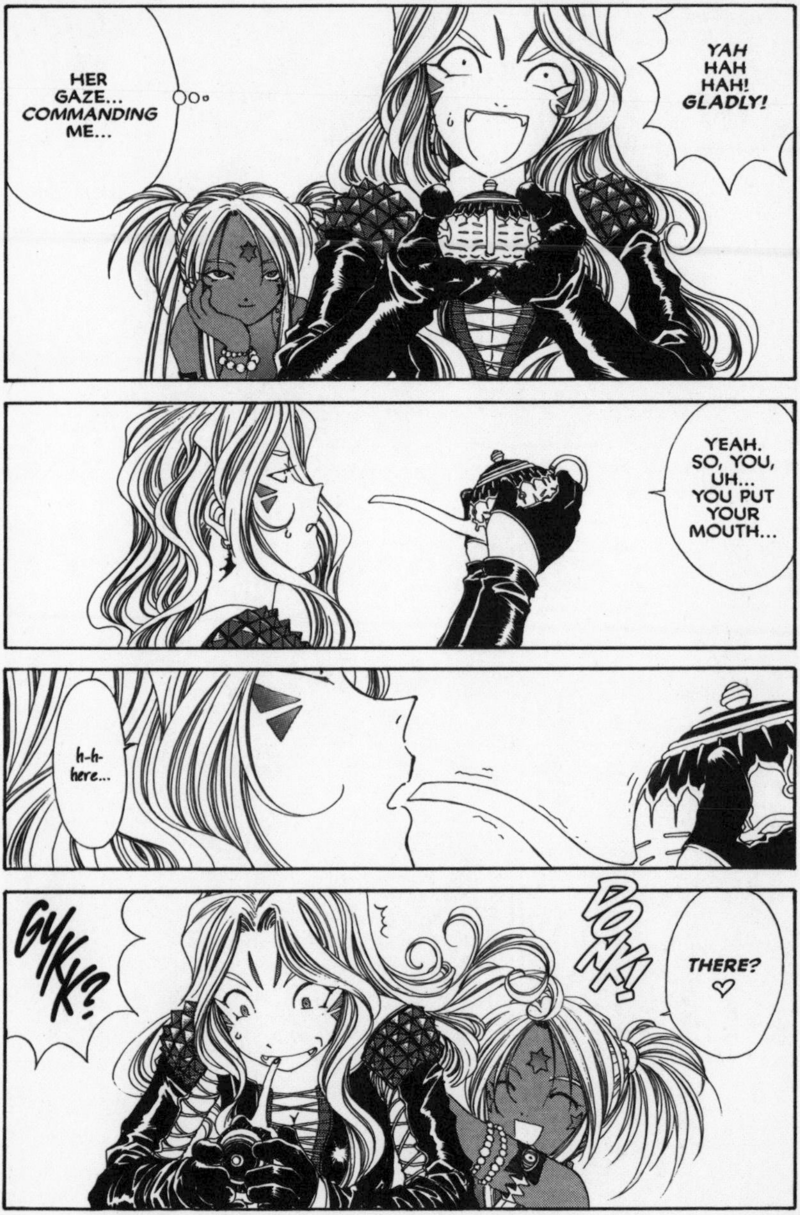
YAH HAH HAH! GLADLY!
HER GAZE... COMMANDING ME...
YEAH. SO, YOU, UH... YOU PUT YOUR MOUTH...
h-h-here...
THERE? ♡
DONK!
GYKK!?

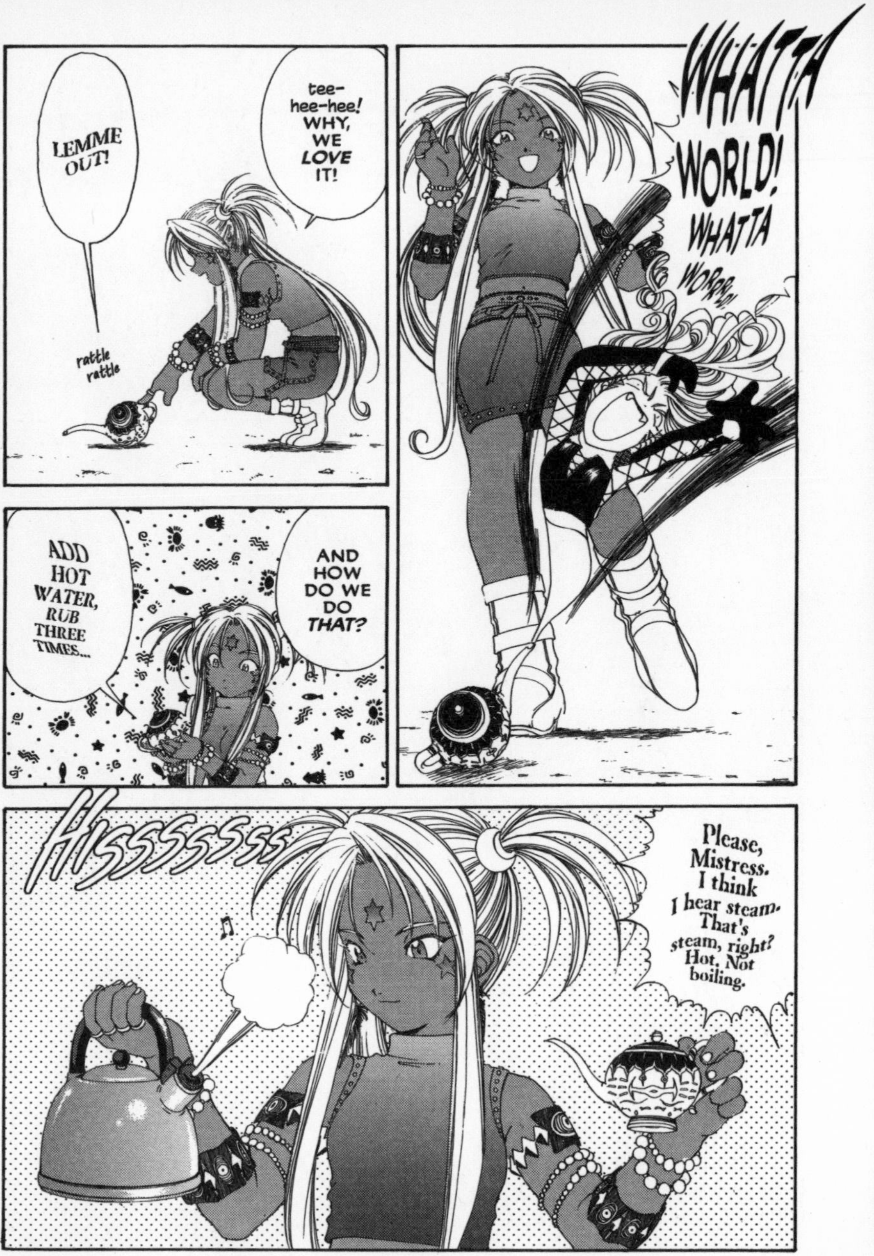
WHATTA WORLD!
WHATTA WORRRLD!
tee-hee-hee! WHY, WE *LOVE* IT!
LEMME OUT!
rattle rattle
AND HOW DO WE DO *THAT*?
ADD HOT WATER, *RUB* THREE TIMES...
Hissssssss
Please, Mistress. I think I hear steam. That's steam, right? Hot. Not boiling.

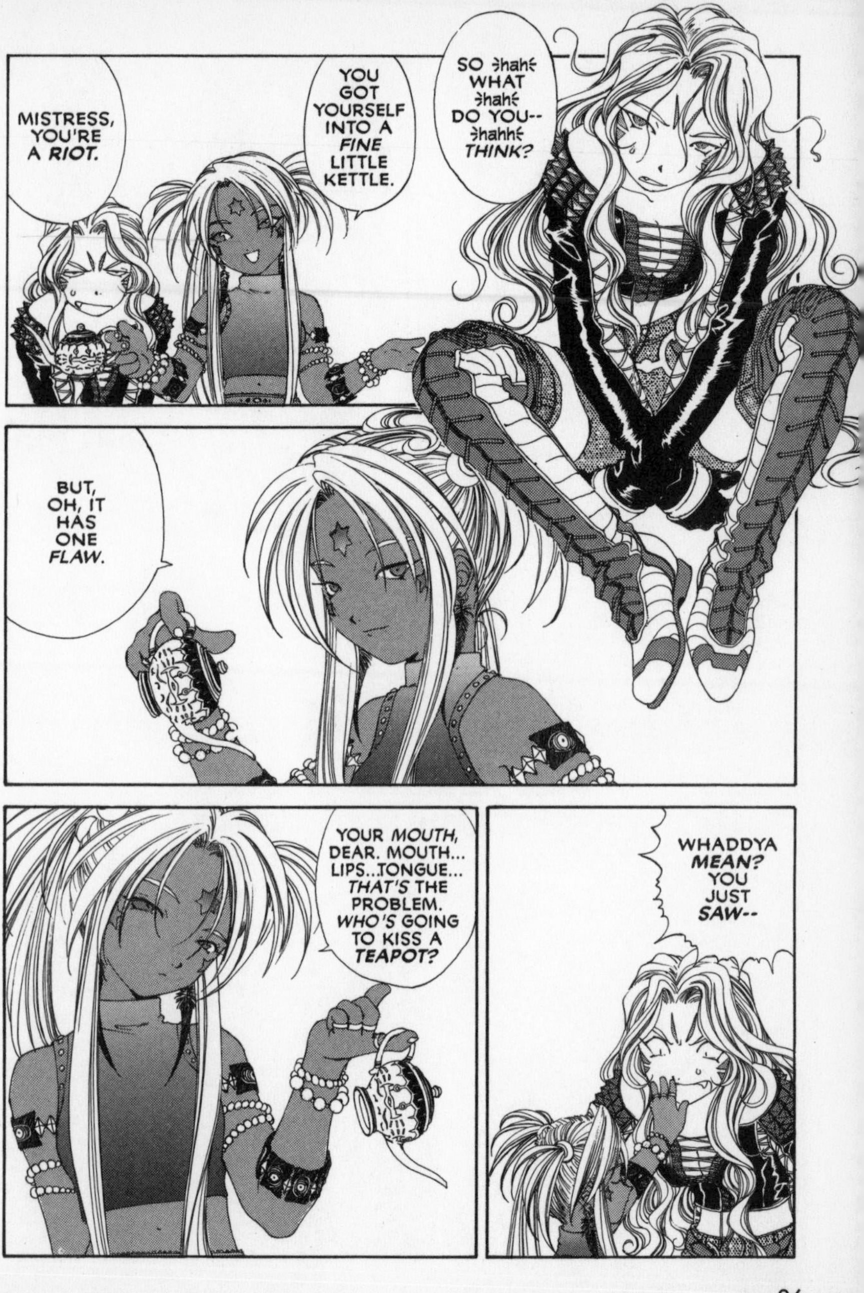
SO ∋hah∈ WHAT ∋hah∈ DO YOU-- ∋hahh∈ THINK?
YOU GOT YOURSELF INTO A FINE LITTLE KETTLE.
MISTRESS, YOU'RE A RIOT.
BUT, OH, IT HAS ONE FLAW.
WHADDYA MEAN? YOU JUST SAW--
YOUR MOUTH, DEAR. MOUTH... LIPS...TONGUE... THAT'S THE PROBLEM. WHO'S GOING TO KISS A TEAPOT?

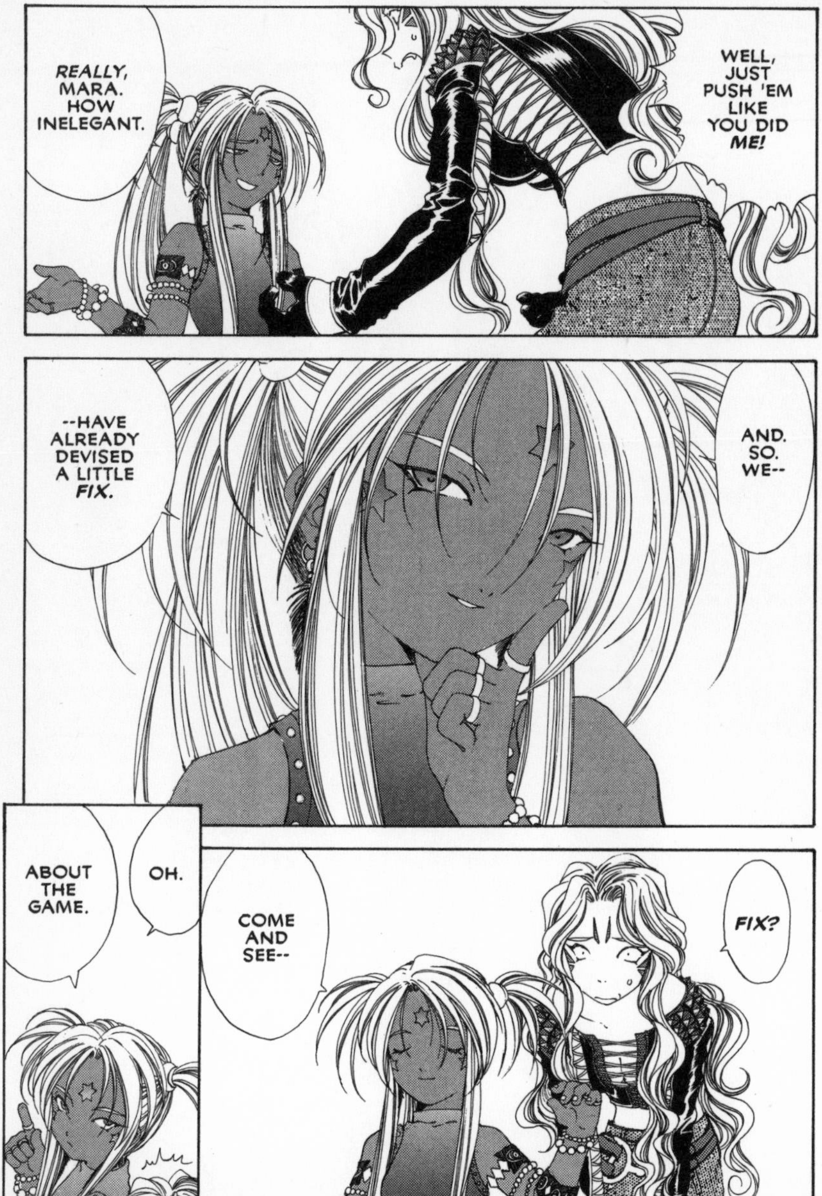
WELL, JUST PUSH 'EM LIKE YOU DID *ME!*
REALLY, MARA. HOW INELEGANT.
AND. SO. WE--
--HAVE ALREADY DEVISED A LITTLE *FIX.*
FIX?
COME AND SEE--
OH.
ABOUT THE GAME.

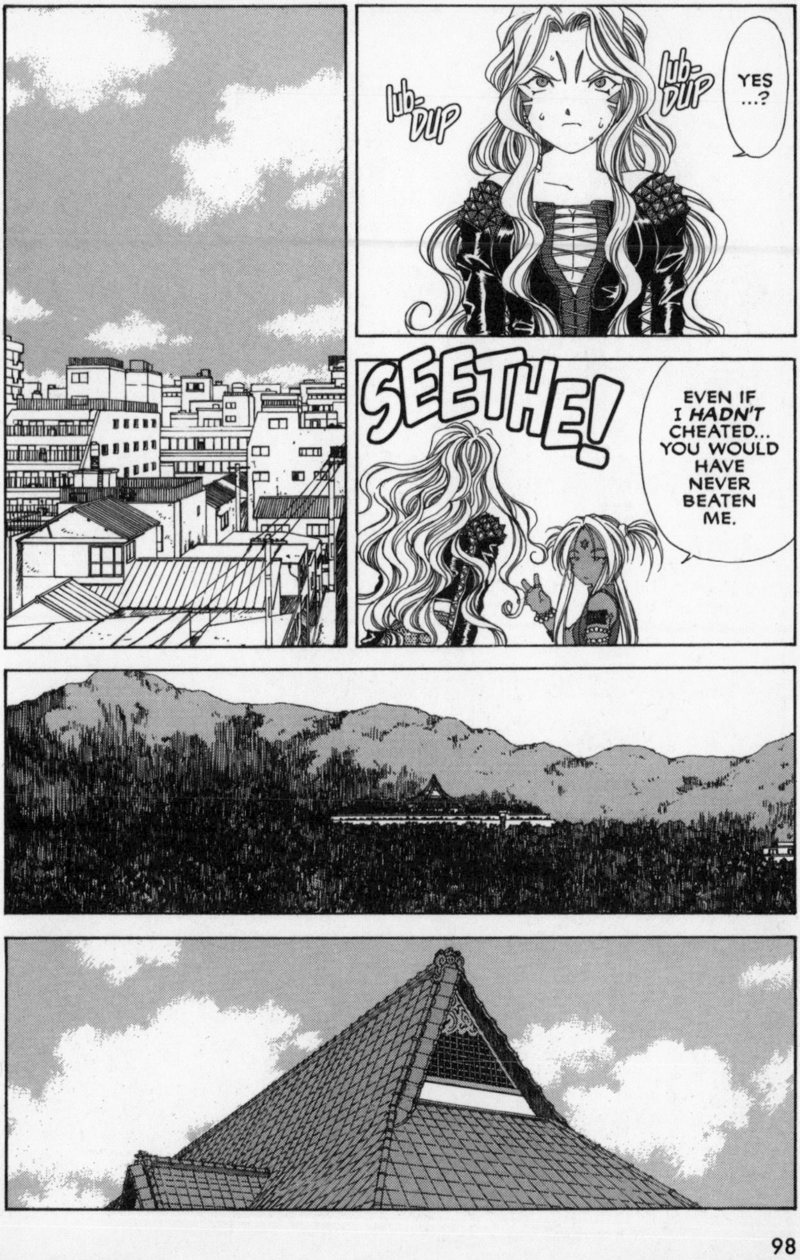
YES ...?
lub-DUP
lub-DUP
EVEN IF I HADN'T CHEATED... YOU WOULD HAVE NEVER BEATEN ME.
SEETHE!

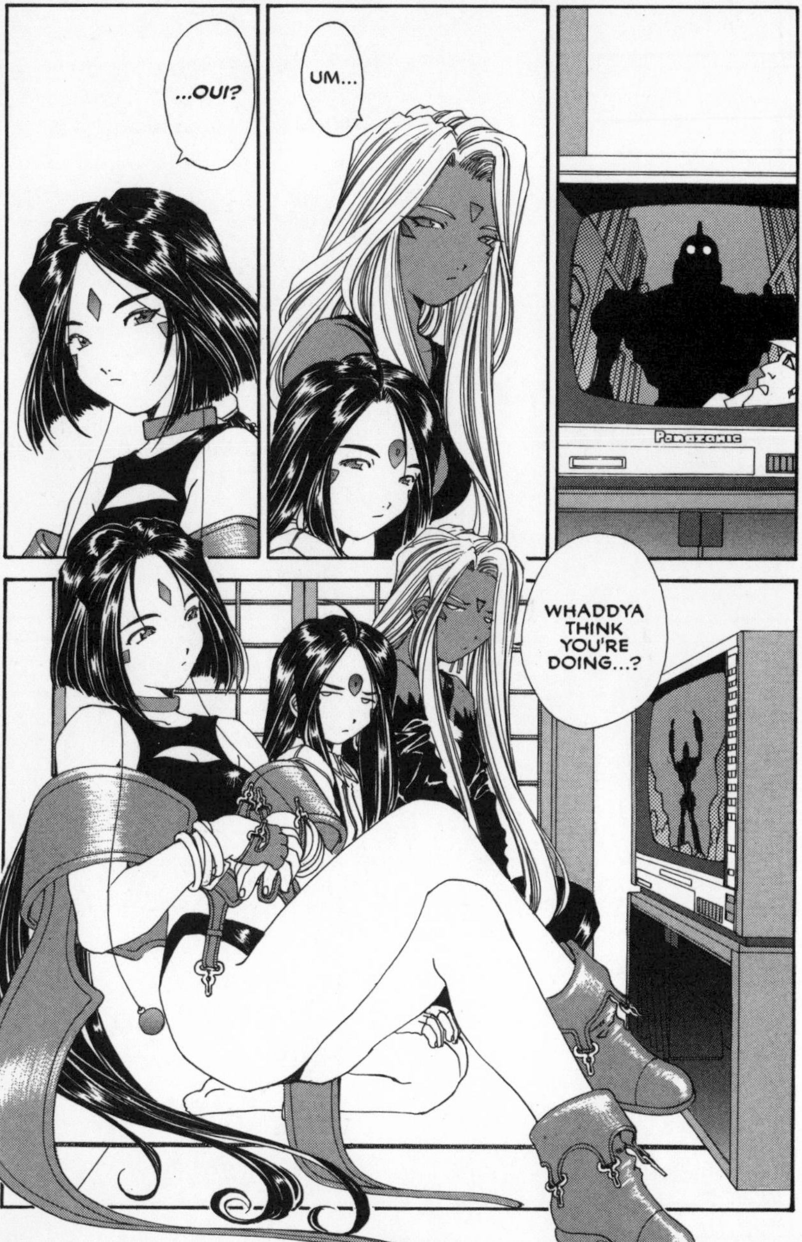
UM...
...OUI?
WHADDYA THINK YOU'RE DOING...?

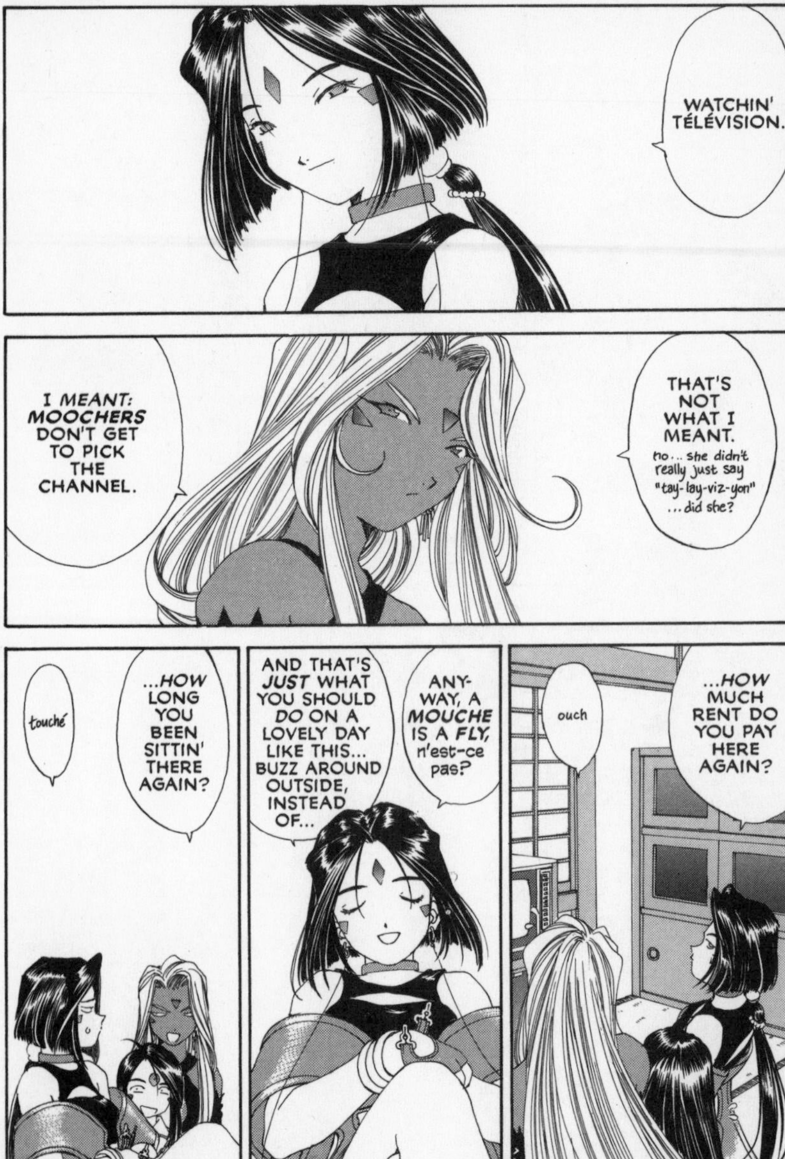
WATCHIN' TÉLÉVISION.
THAT'S NOT WHAT I MEANT.
no... she didn't really just say "tay-lay-viz-yon" ...did she?
I MEANT: MOOCHERS DON'T GET TO PICK THE CHANNEL.
...HOW MUCH RENT DO YOU PAY HERE AGAIN?
ouch
ANY-WAY, A MOUCHE IS A FLY, n'est-ce pas?
AND THAT'S JUST WHAT YOU SHOULD DO ON A LOVELY DAY LIKE THIS... BUZZ AROUND OUTSIDE, INSTEAD OF...
...HOW LONG YOU BEEN SITTIN' THERE AGAIN?
touché

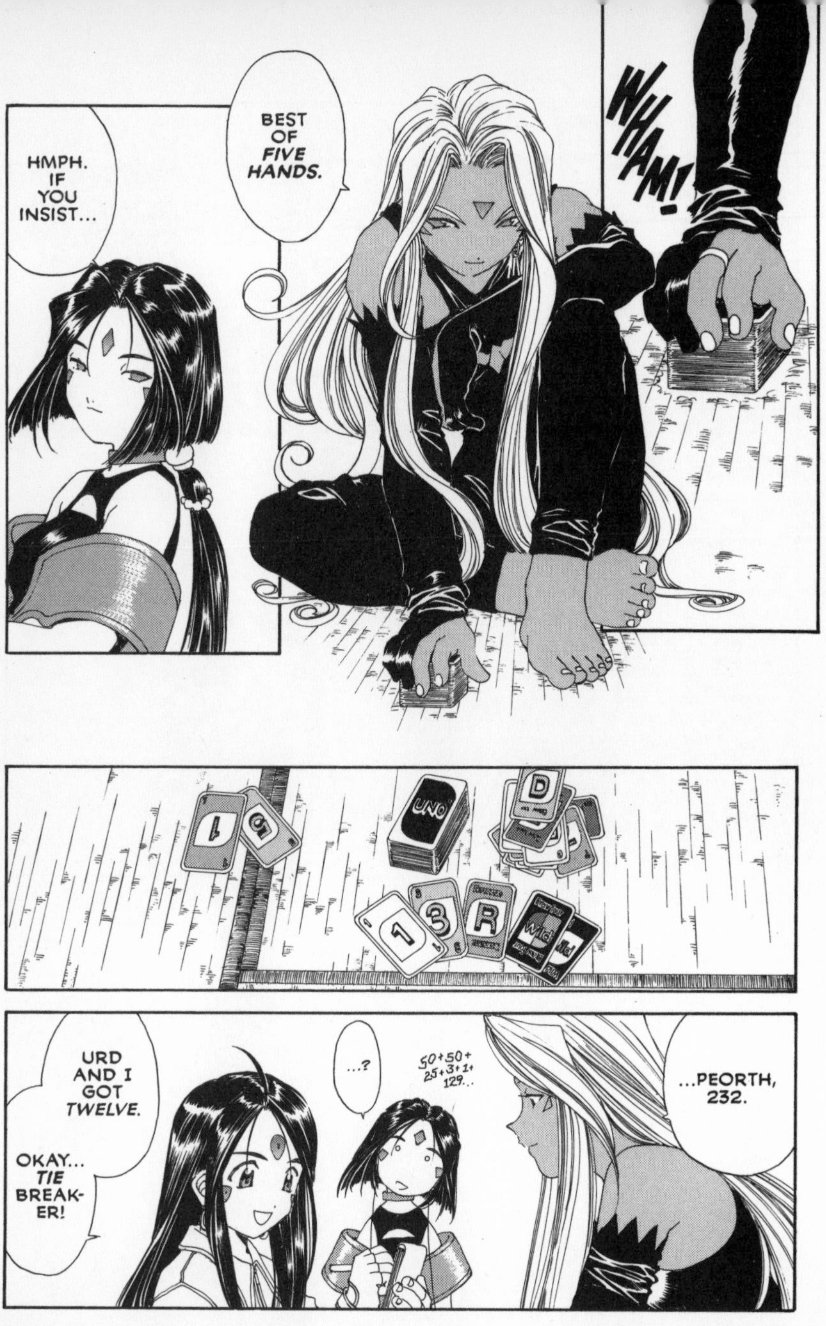
WHAM!
BEST OF FIVE HANDS.
HMPH. IF YOU INSIST...
UNO
...PEORTH, 232.
50+50+25+3+1+ 129...
...?
URD AND I GOT TWELVE.
OKAY... TIE BREAKER!

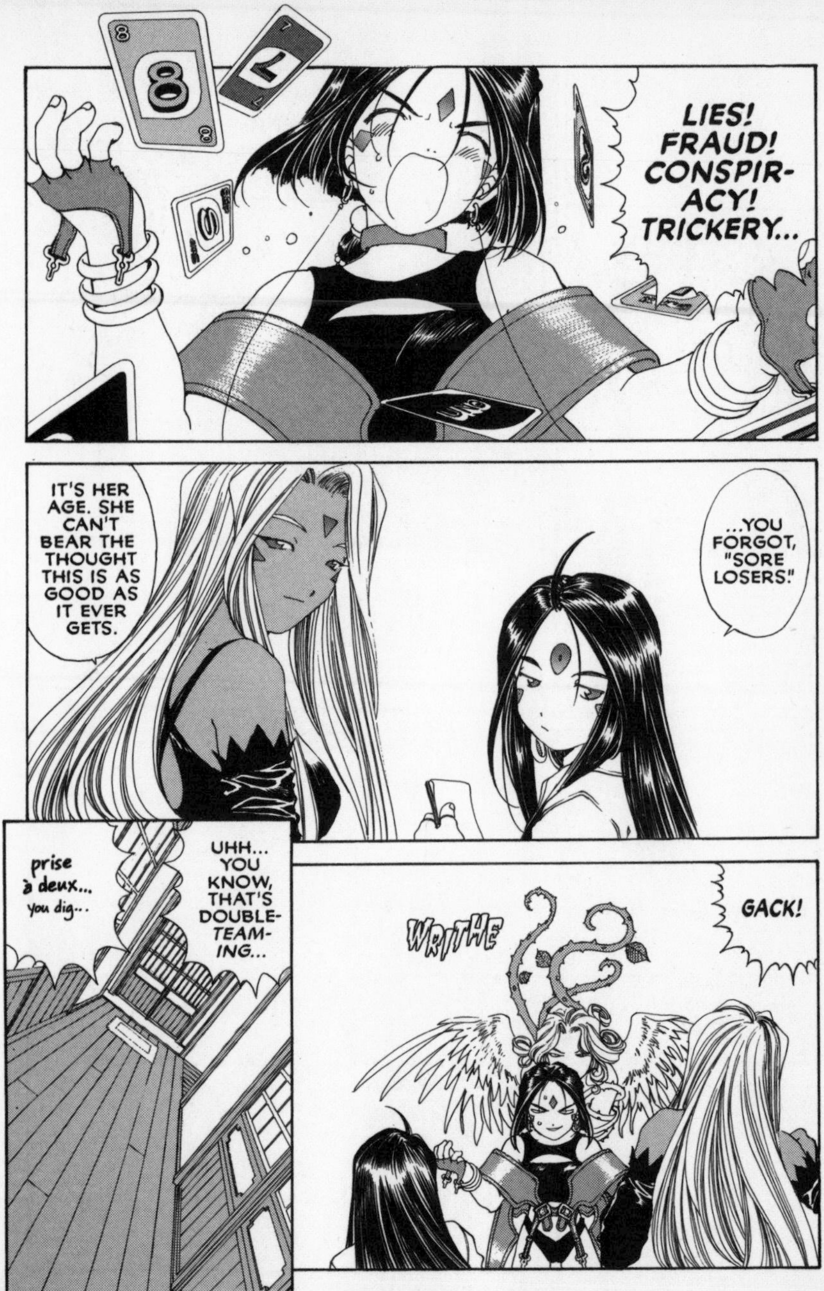
LIES! FRAUD! CONSPIR-ACY! TRICKERY...
...YOU FORGOT, "SORE LOSERS."
IT'S HER AGE. SHE CAN'T BEAR THE THOUGHT THIS IS AS GOOD AS IT EVER GETS.
GACK!
WRITHE
UHH... YOU KNOW, THAT'S DOUBLE-TEAM-ING...
prise à deux... you dig...

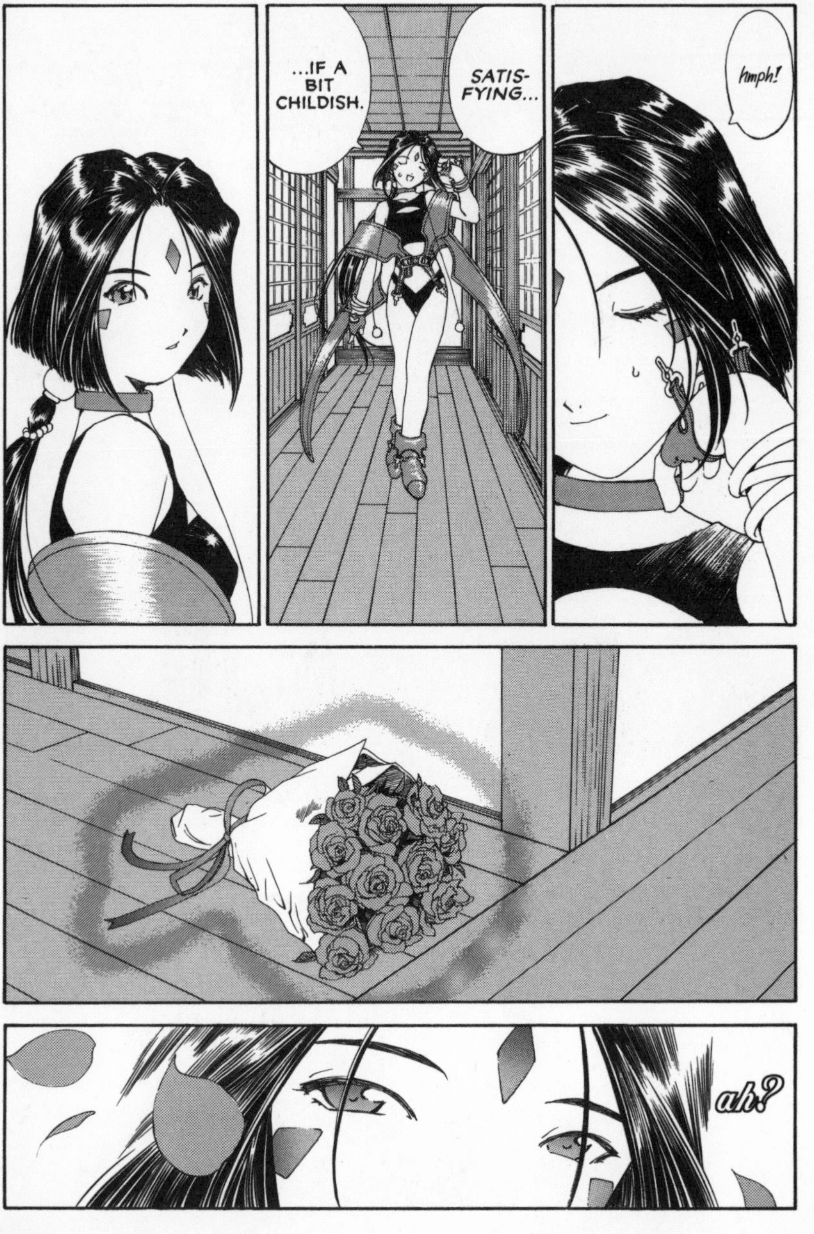
hmph!
SATIS-FYING...
...IF A BIT CHILDISH.
ah?

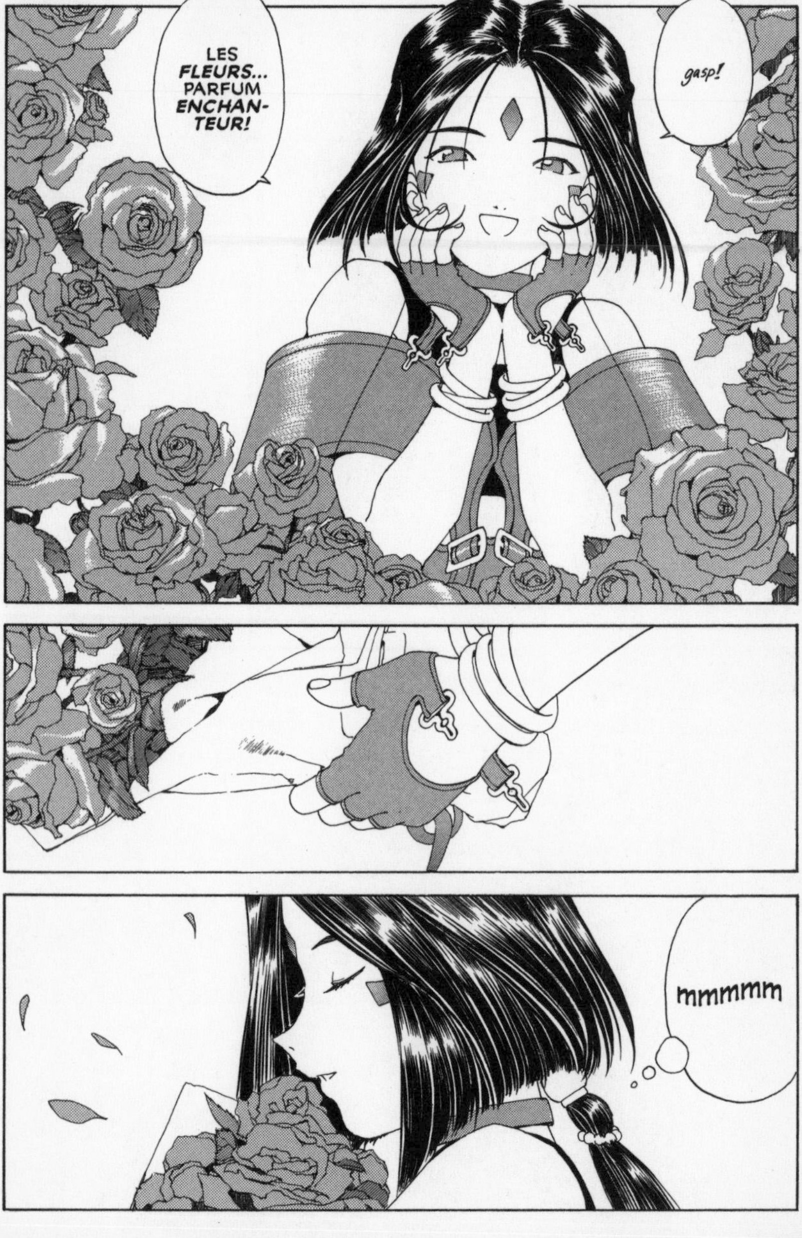
gasp!
LES FLEURS... PARFUM ENCHANTEUR!
mmmmm

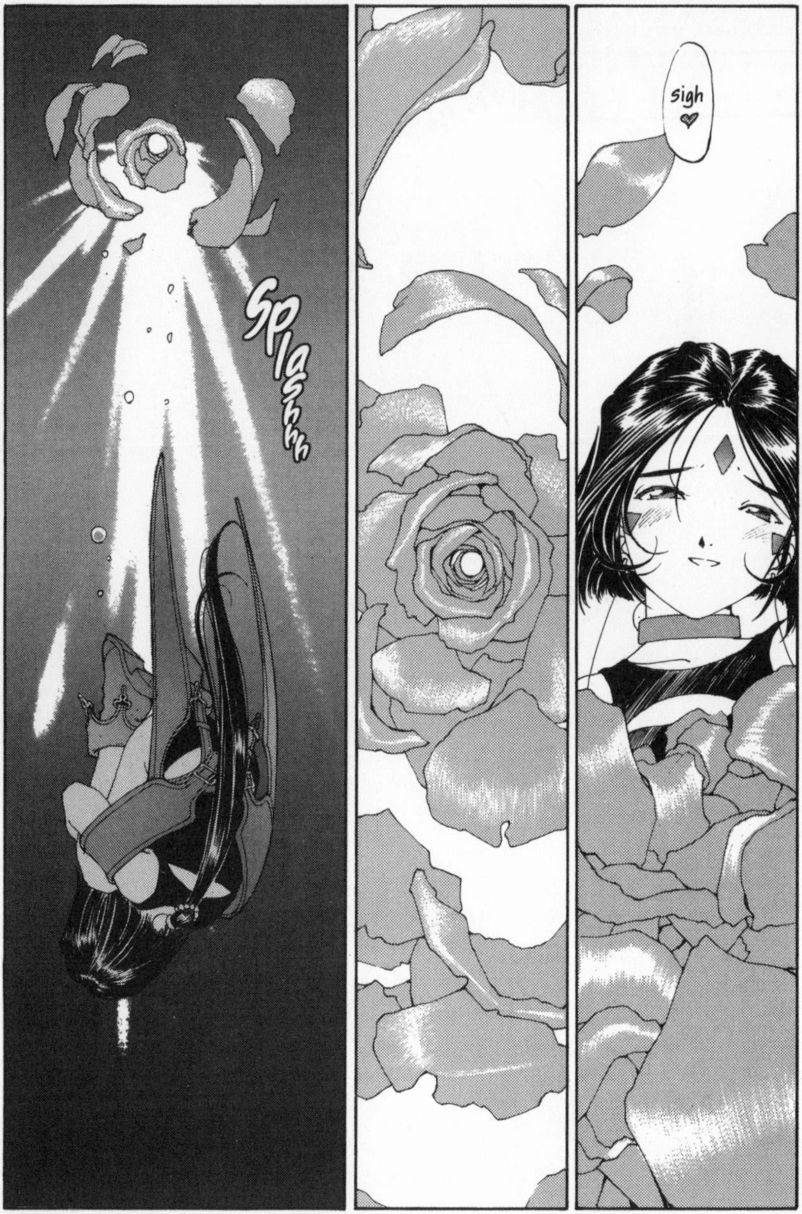
sigh ♥
Splashhh

OH MY GODDESS!
NIGHTINGALE

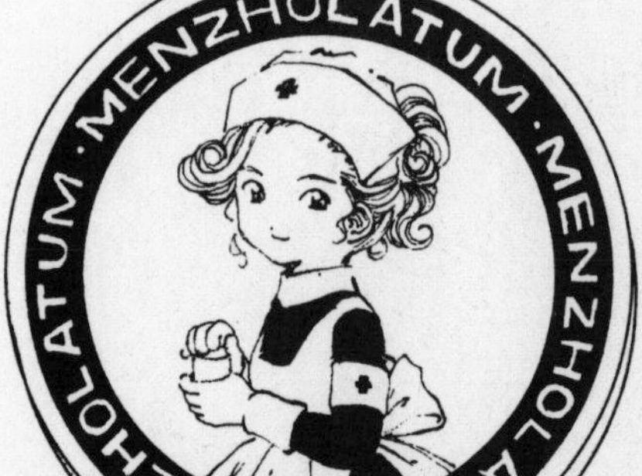
MENZHOLATUM · MENZHOLATUM · MENZHOLATUM · MENZHOLATUM

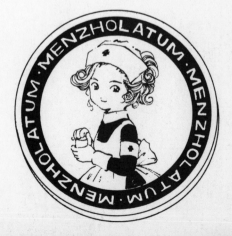

CHAPTER 140

Morisato Residence, Rooms to Let

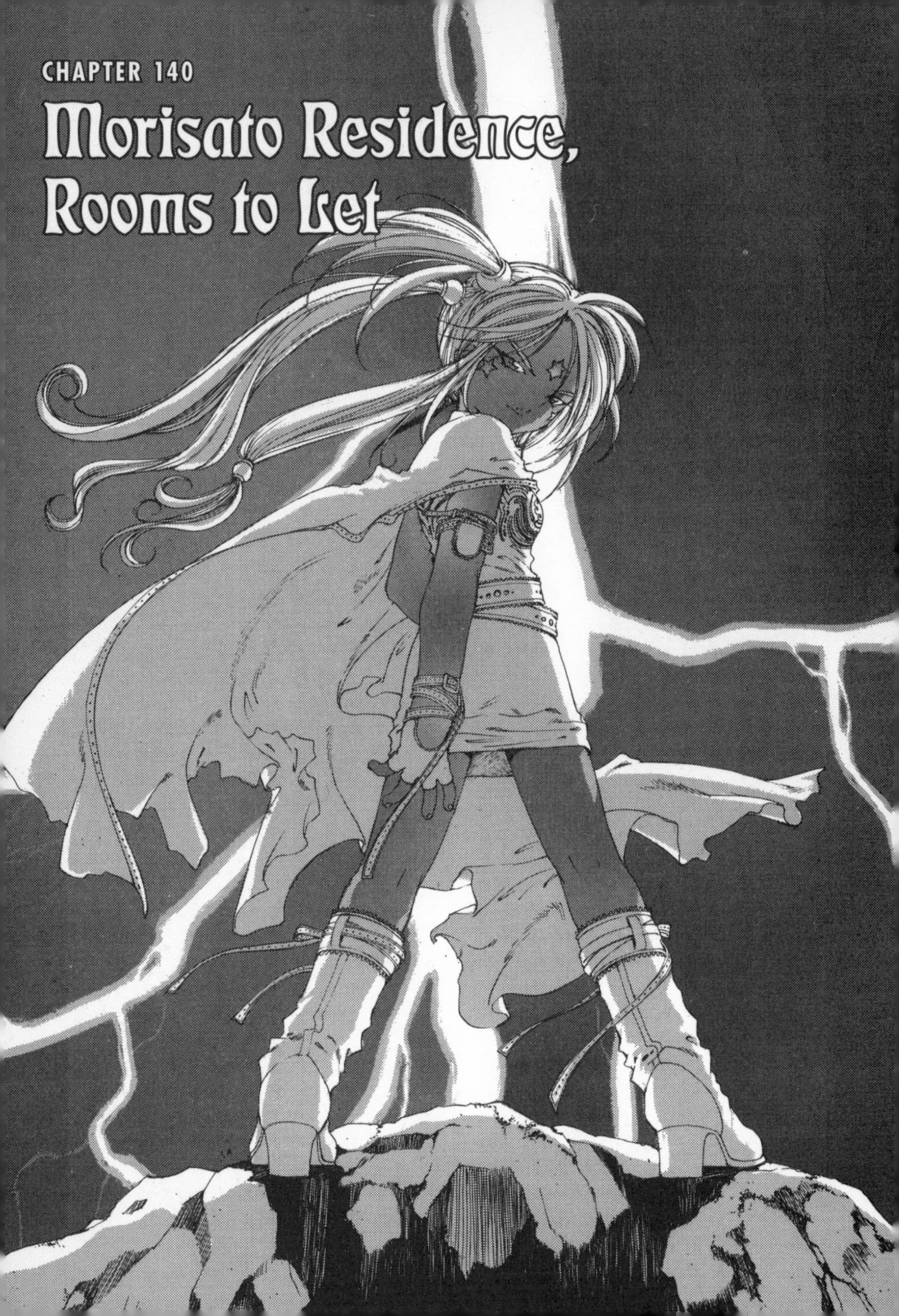

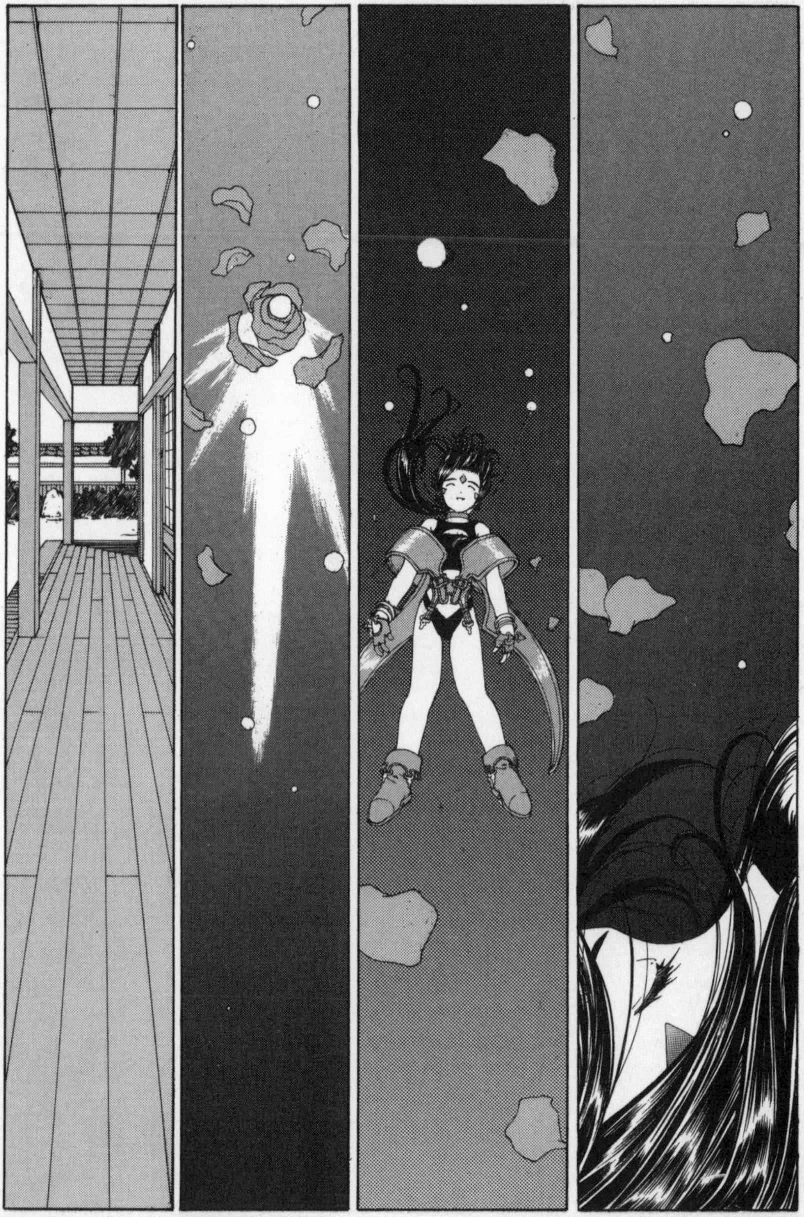

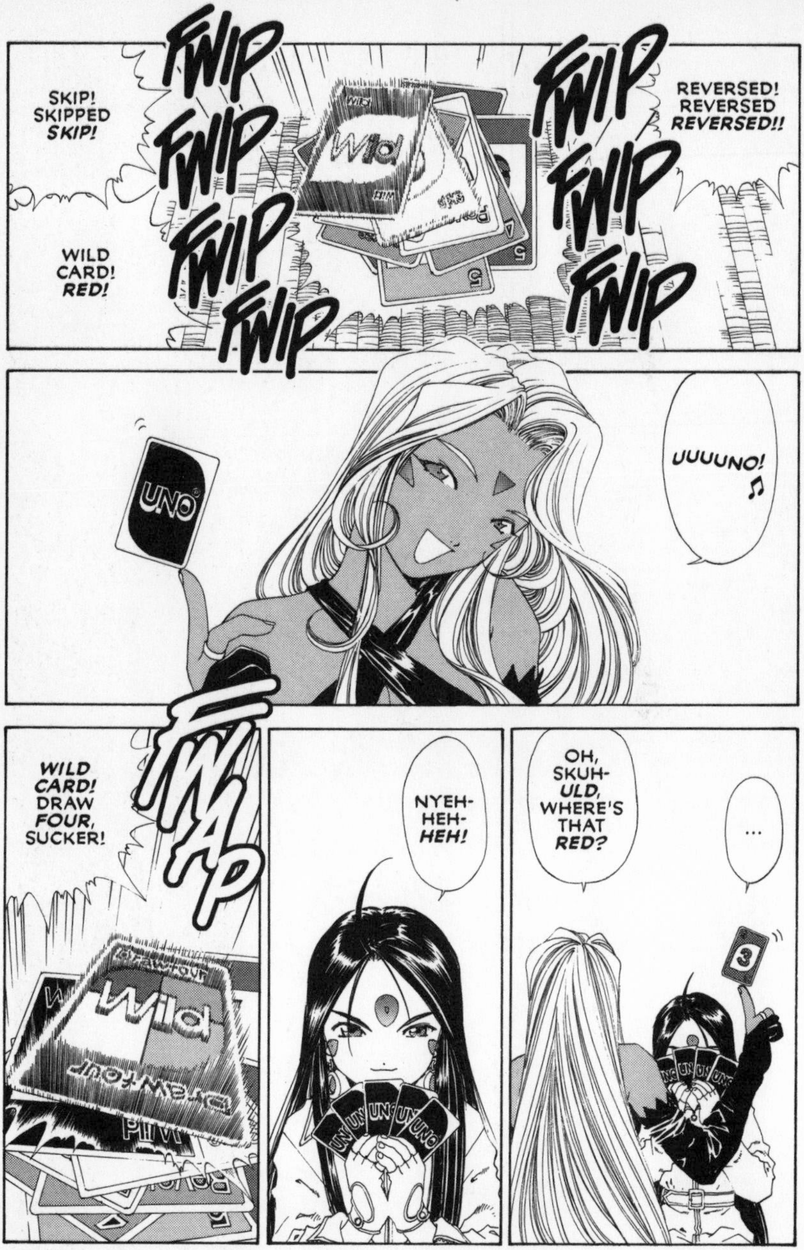
FWIP
FWIP
FWIP
REVERSED! REVERSED REVERSED!!
FWIP
FWIP
FWIP
FWIP
SKIP! SKIPPED SKIP!
WILD CARD! RED!
UUUUNO! ♫
...
OH, SKUH-ULD, WHERE'S THAT RED?
NYEH-HEH-HEH!
WILD CARD! DRAW FOUR, SUCKER!
FWAP

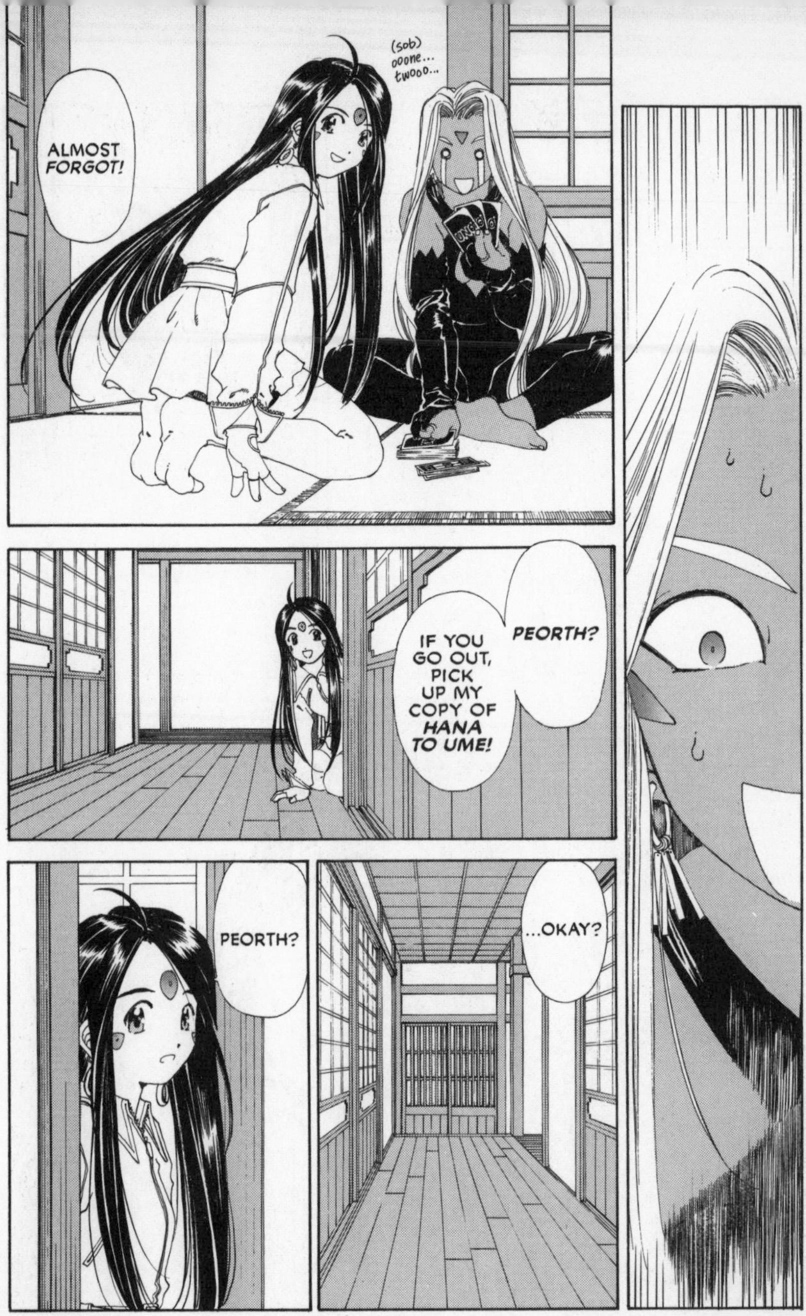
(sob) ooone... twooo...
ALMOST FORGOT!
PEORTH?
IF YOU GO OUT, PICK UP MY COPY OF HANA TO UME!
...OKAY?
PEORTH?

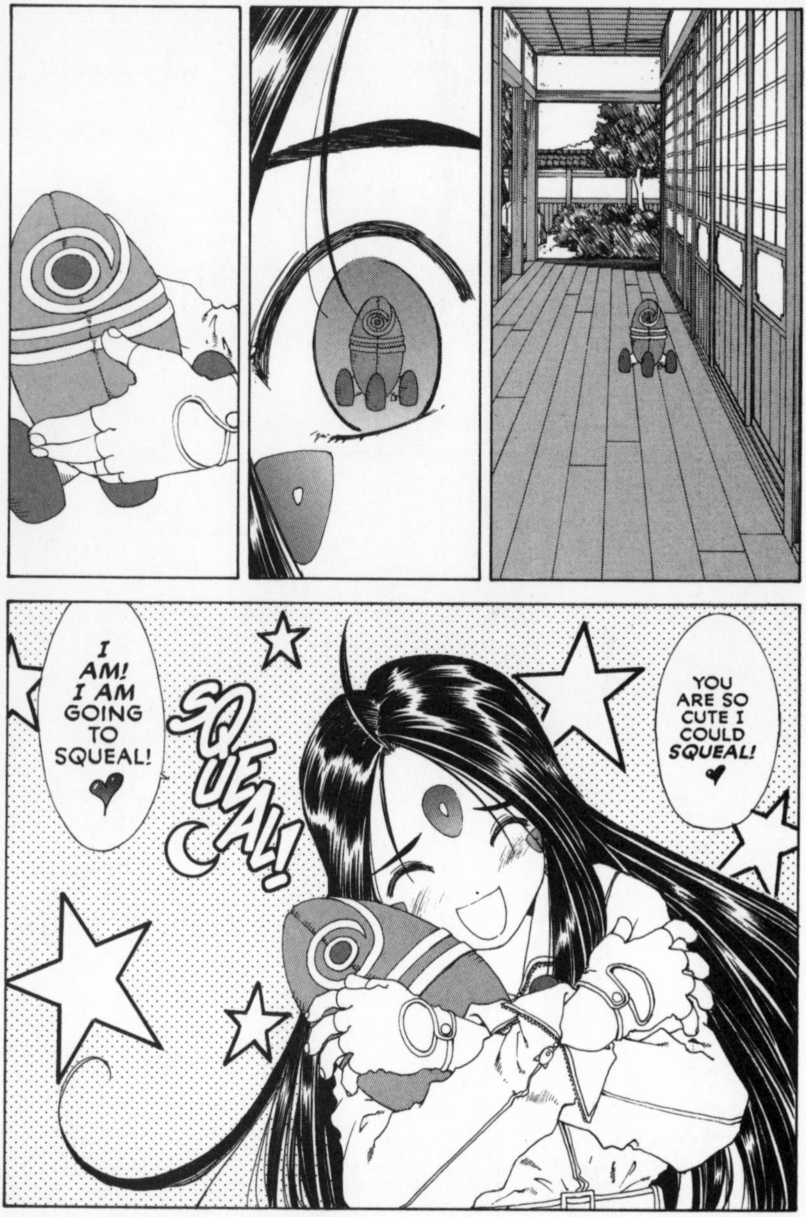
YOU ARE SO CUTE I COULD SQUEAL! ♥
I AM! I AM GOING TO SQUEAL! ♥
SQUEAL!

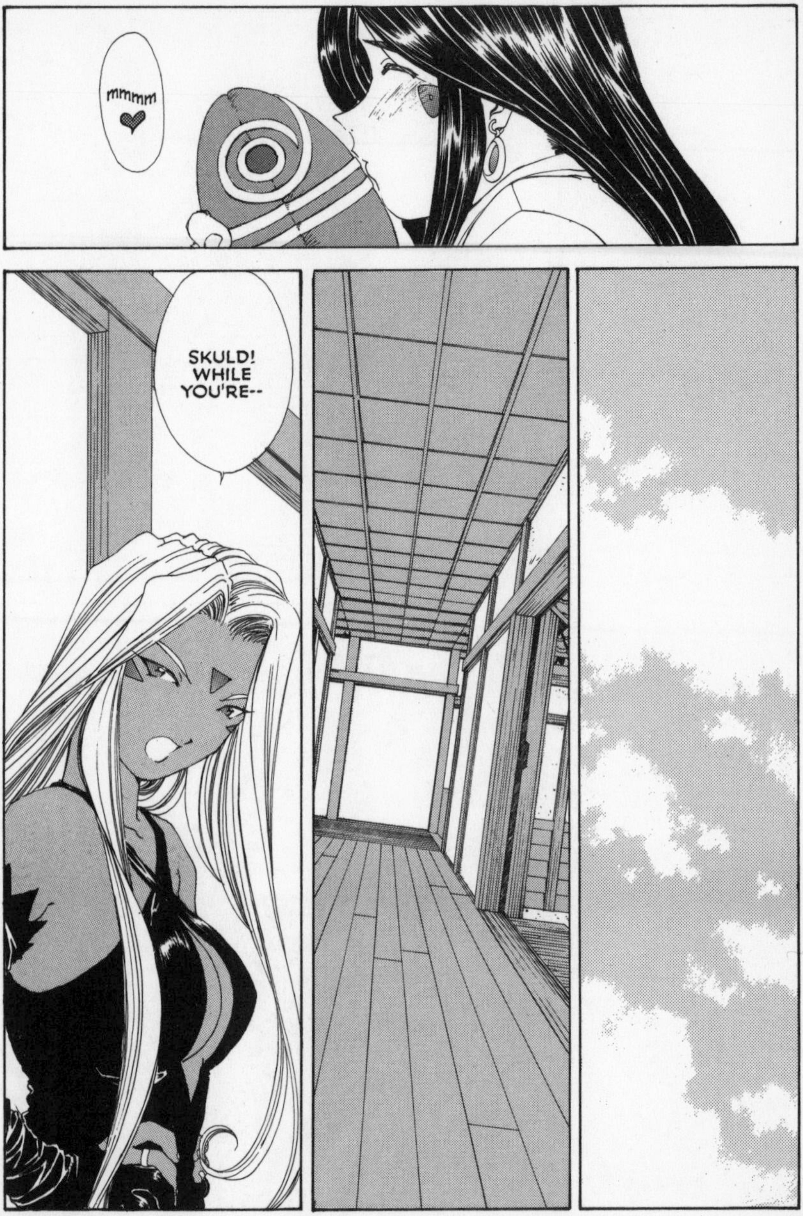
mmmm ♥
SKULD! WHILE YOU'RE--

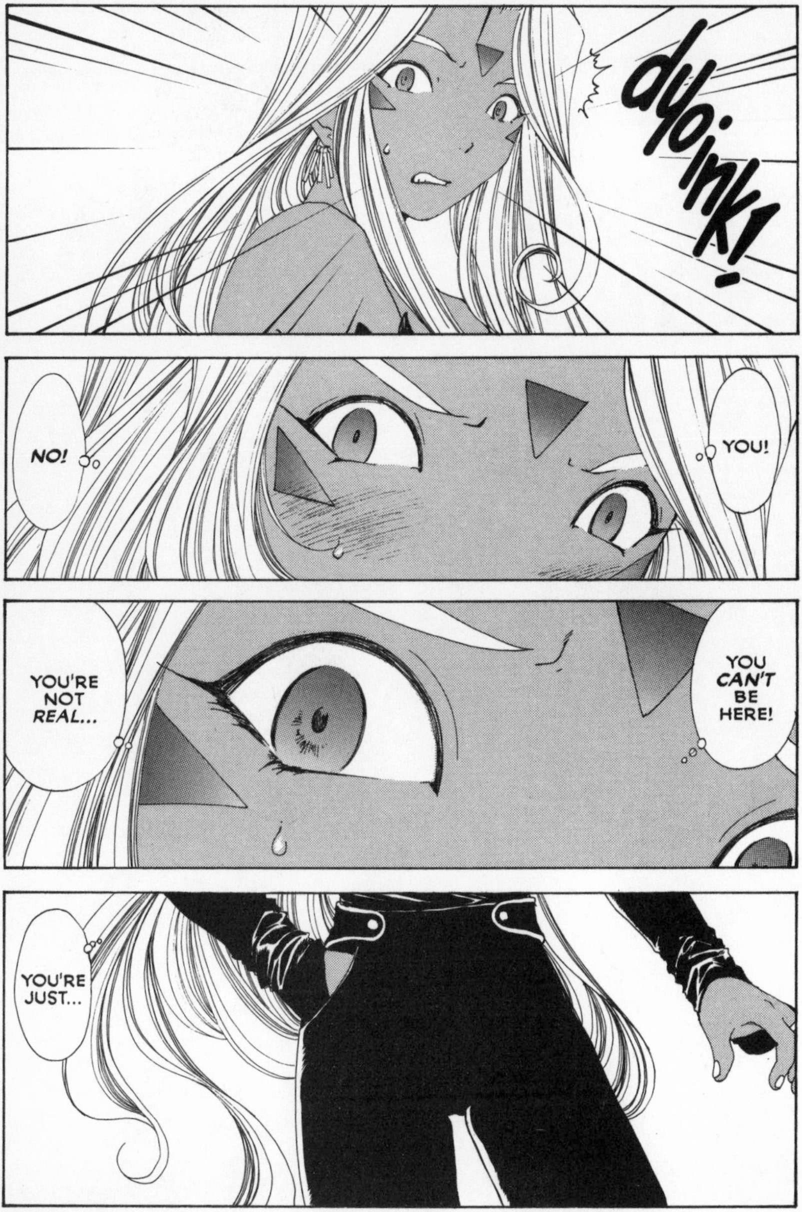
dyoink!
YOU!
NO!
YOU CAN'T BE HERE!
YOU'RE NOT REAL...
YOU'RE JUST...

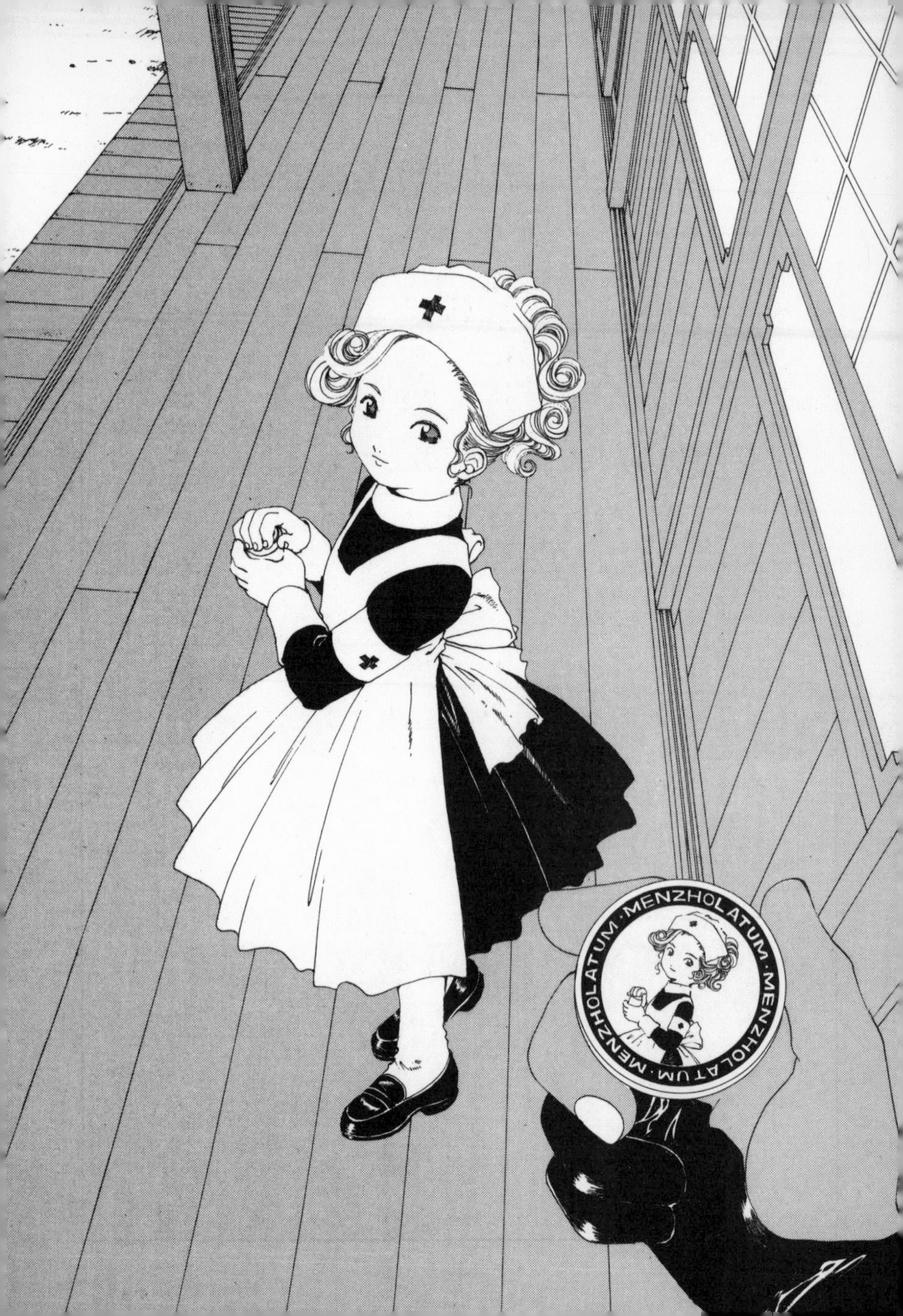
MENZHOLATUM · MENZHOLATUM · MENZHOLATUM

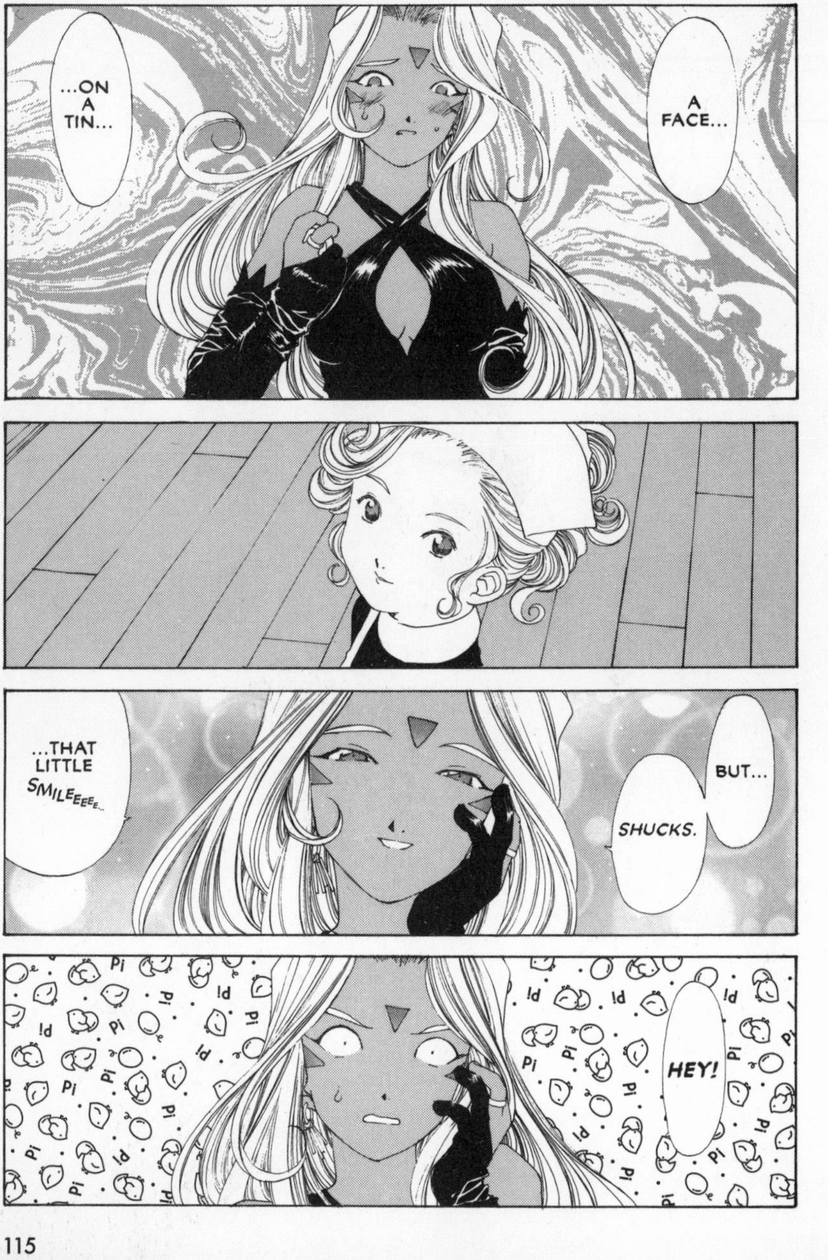
A FACE...
...ON A TIN...
BUT...
SHUCKS.
...THAT LITTLE SMILEEEEE...
HEY!
Pi Pi Pi

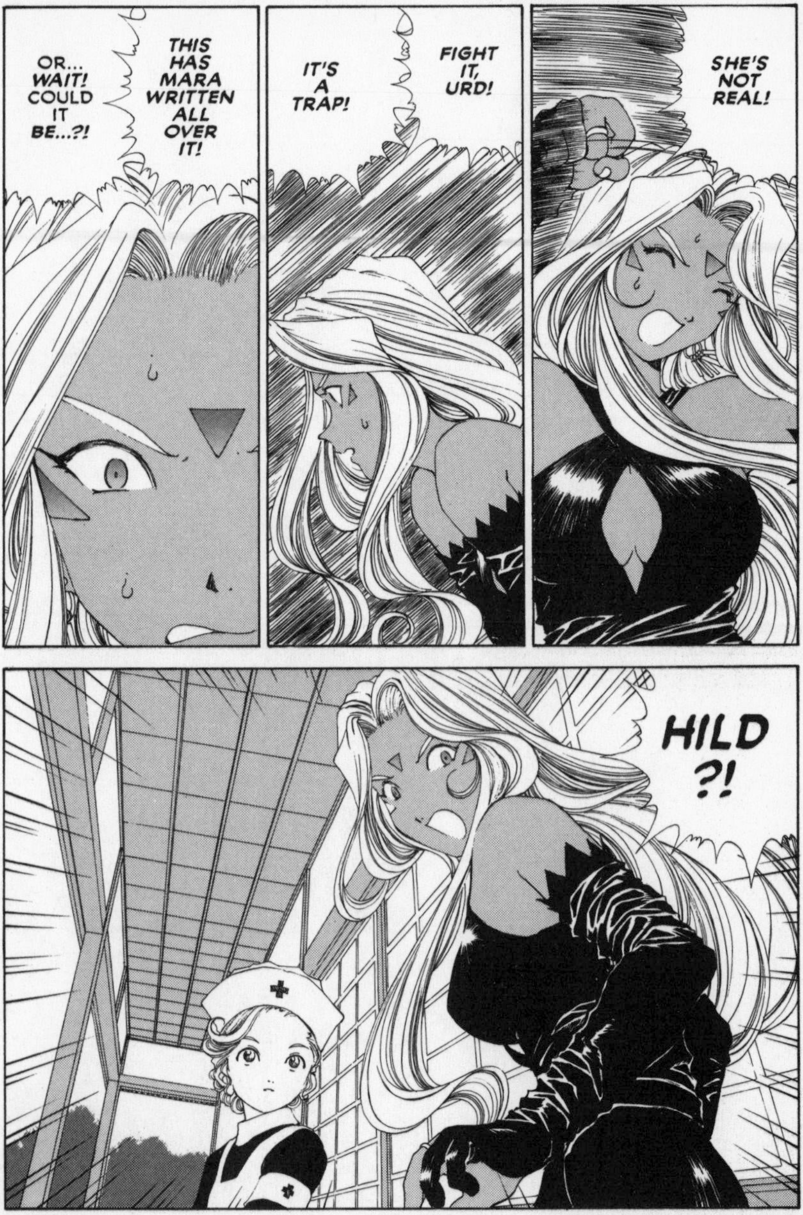

SHE'S NOT REAL!
FIGHT IT, URD!
IT'S A TRAP!
THIS HAS MARA WRITTEN ALL OVER IT!
OR... WAIT! COULD IT BE...?!
HILD ?!

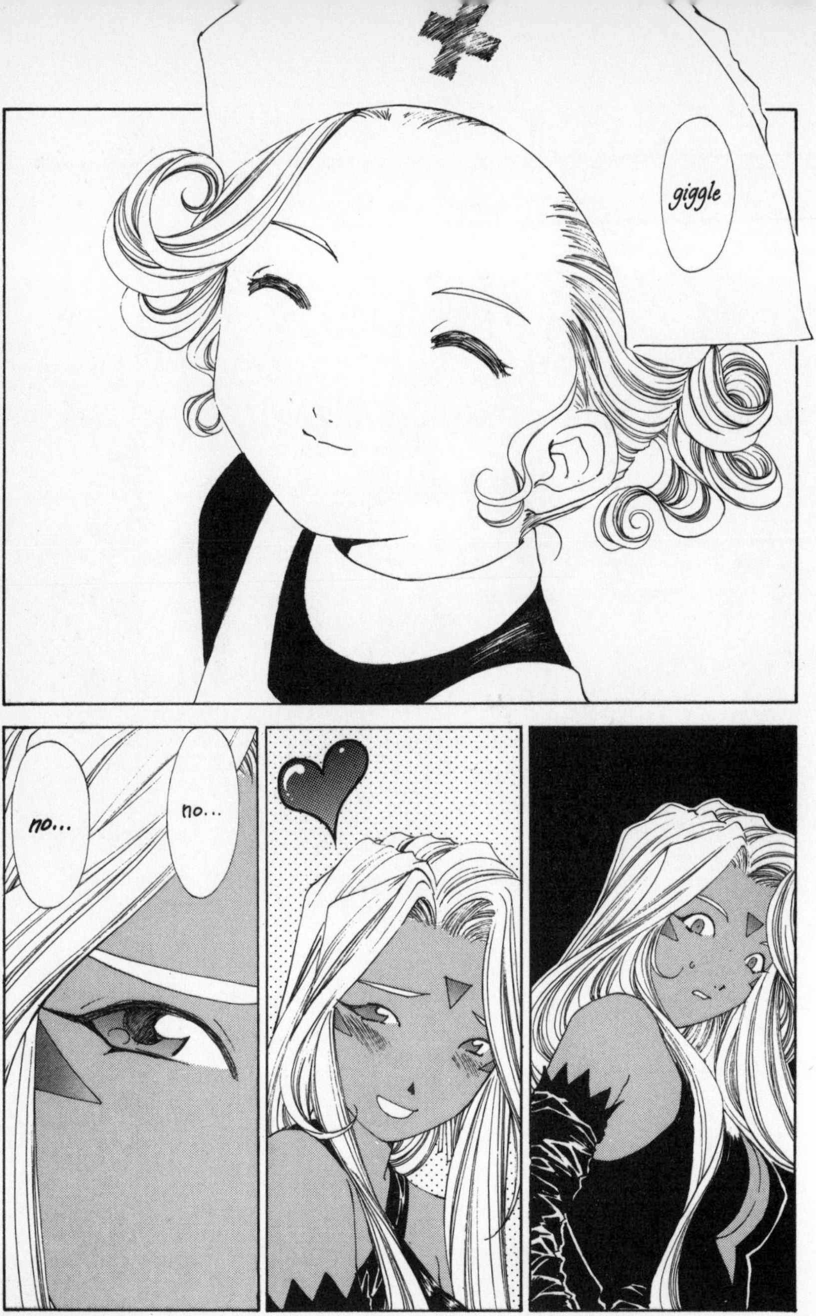
giggle
no...
no...

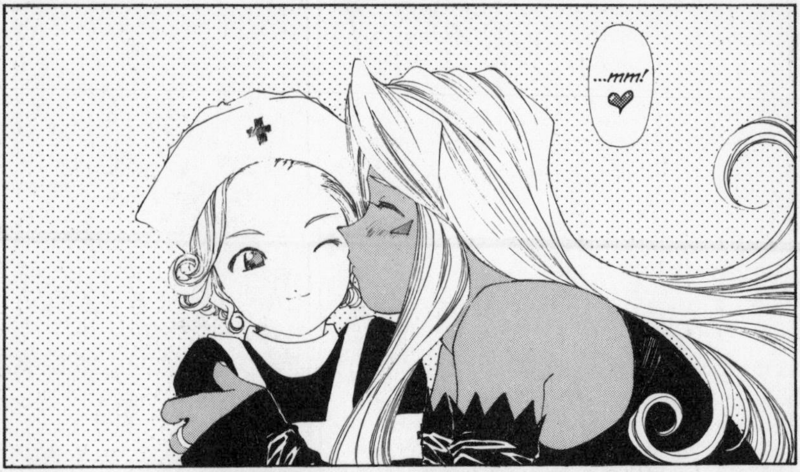
...mm!

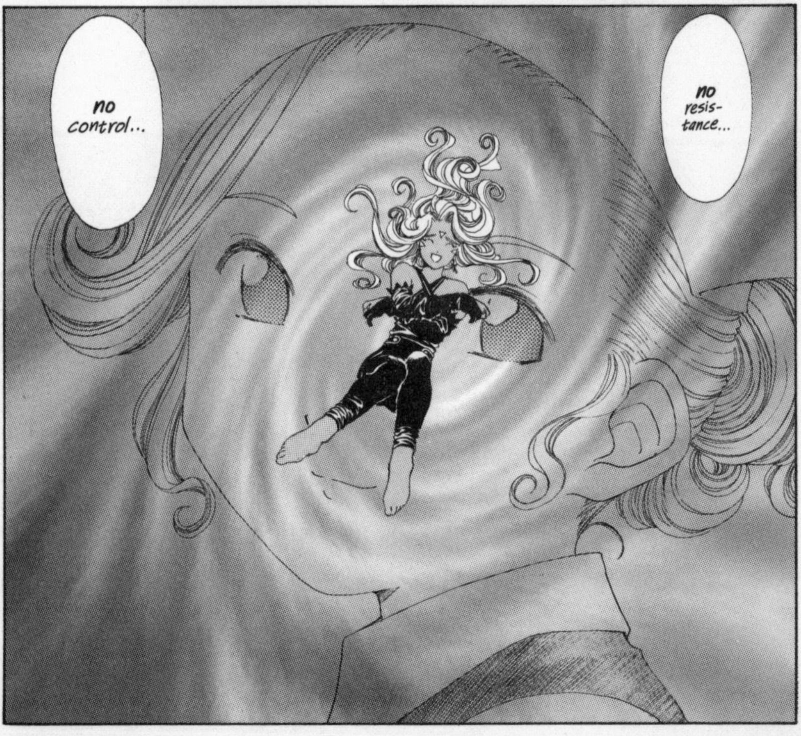
no resis-tance...
no control...

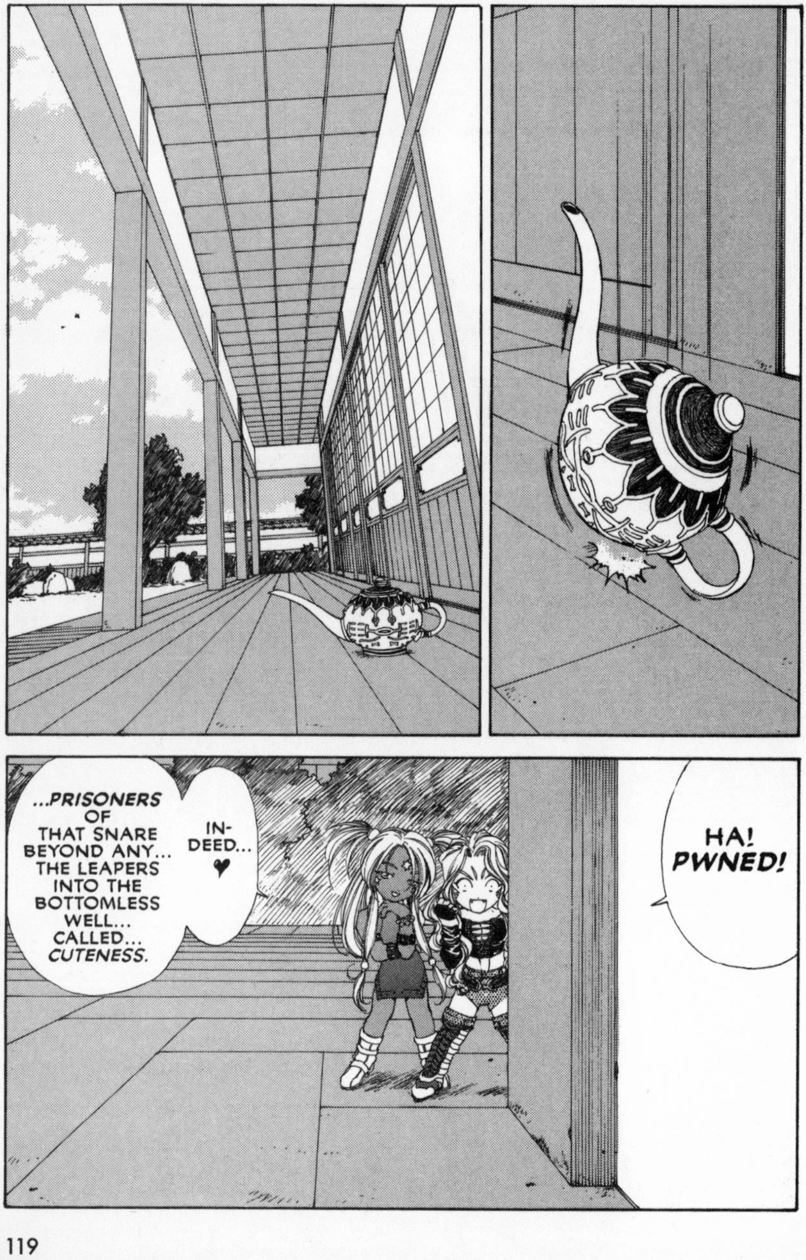
HA! PWNED!
IN-DEED... ♥
...PRISONERS OF THAT SNARE BEYOND ANY... THE LEAPERS INTO THE BOTTOMLESS WELL... CALLED... CUTENESS.

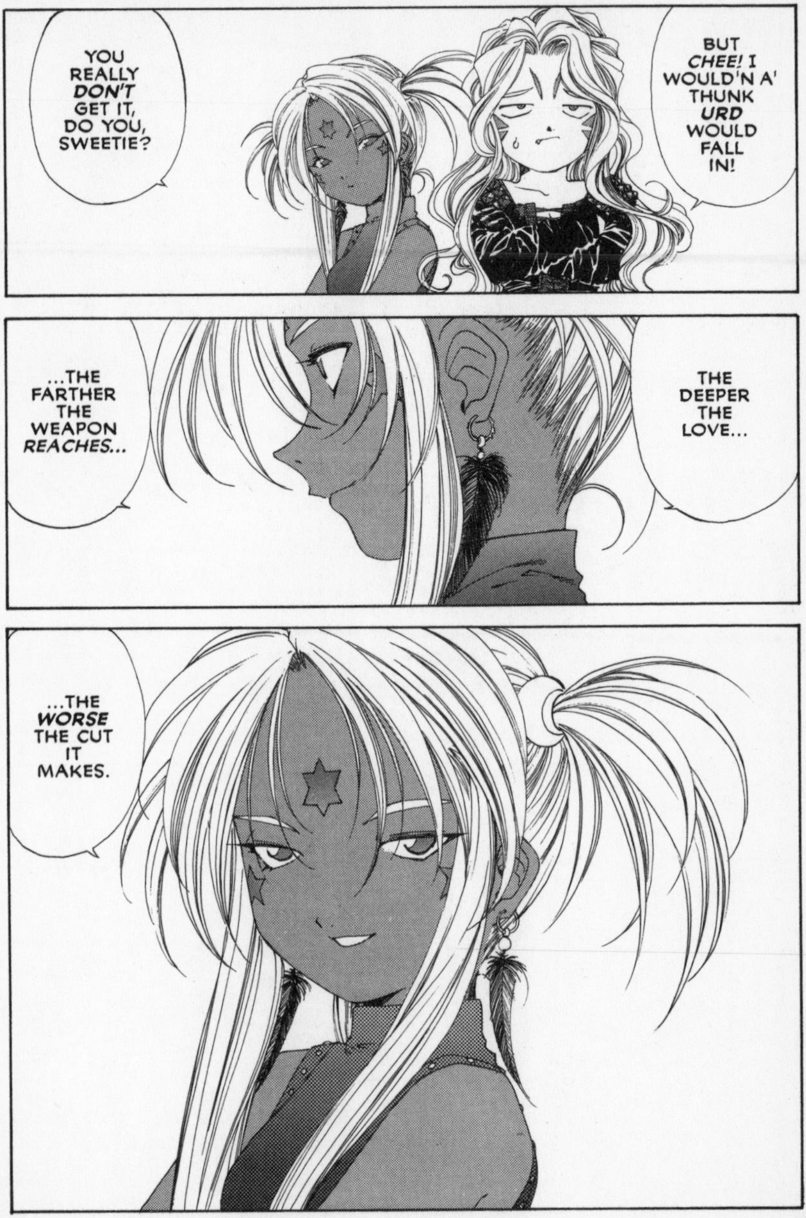
BUT *CHEE!* I WOULD'N A' THUNK **URD** WOULD FALL IN!
YOU REALLY ***DON'T*** GET IT, DO YOU, SWEETIE?
THE DEEPER THE LOVE...
...THE FARTHER THE WEAPON *REACHES...*
...THE ***WORSE*** THE CUT IT MAKES.

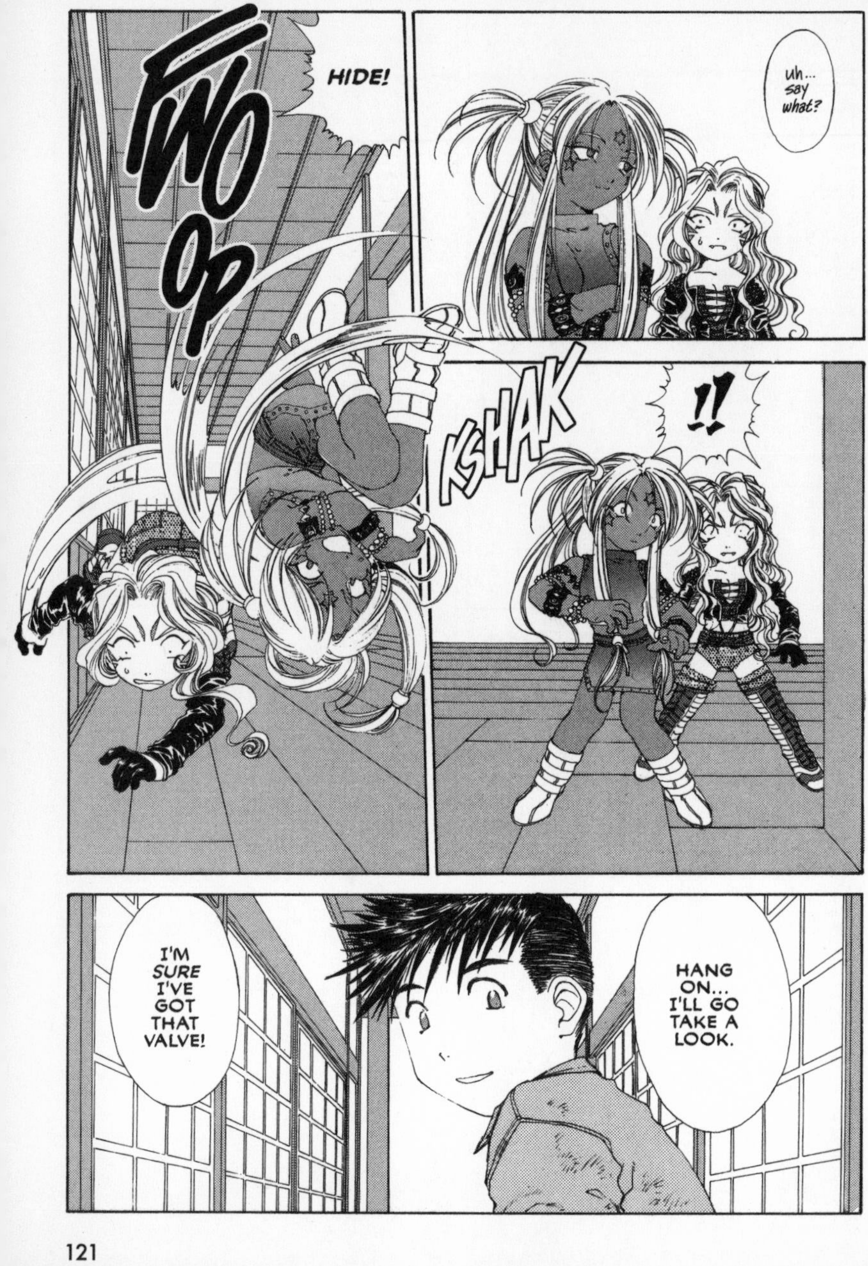
uh... say what?
KSHAK
!!
HIDE!
FWOOP
HANG ON... I'LL GO TAKE A LOOK.
I'M SURE I'VE GOT THAT VALVE!

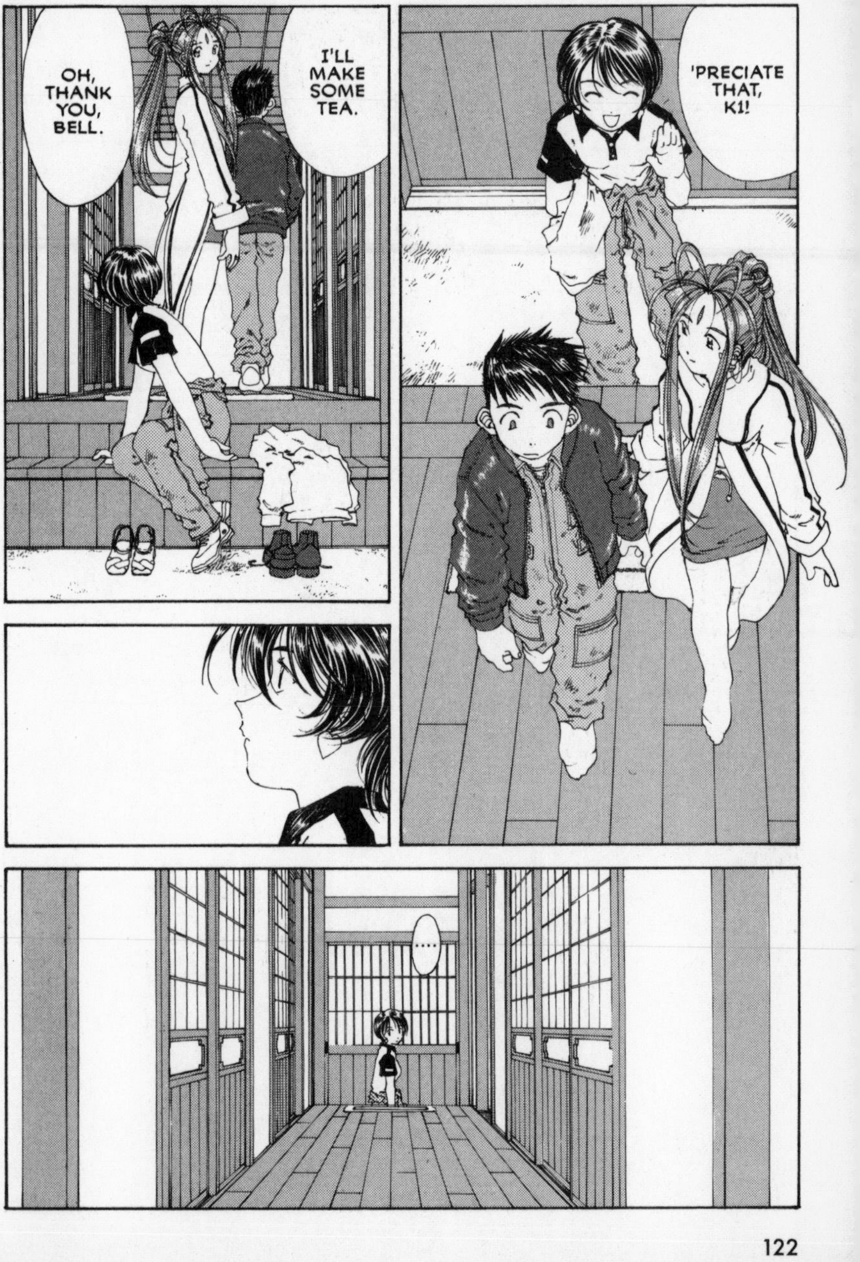
'PRECIATE THAT, K1!
I'LL MAKE SOME TEA.
OH, THANK YOU, BELL.
....

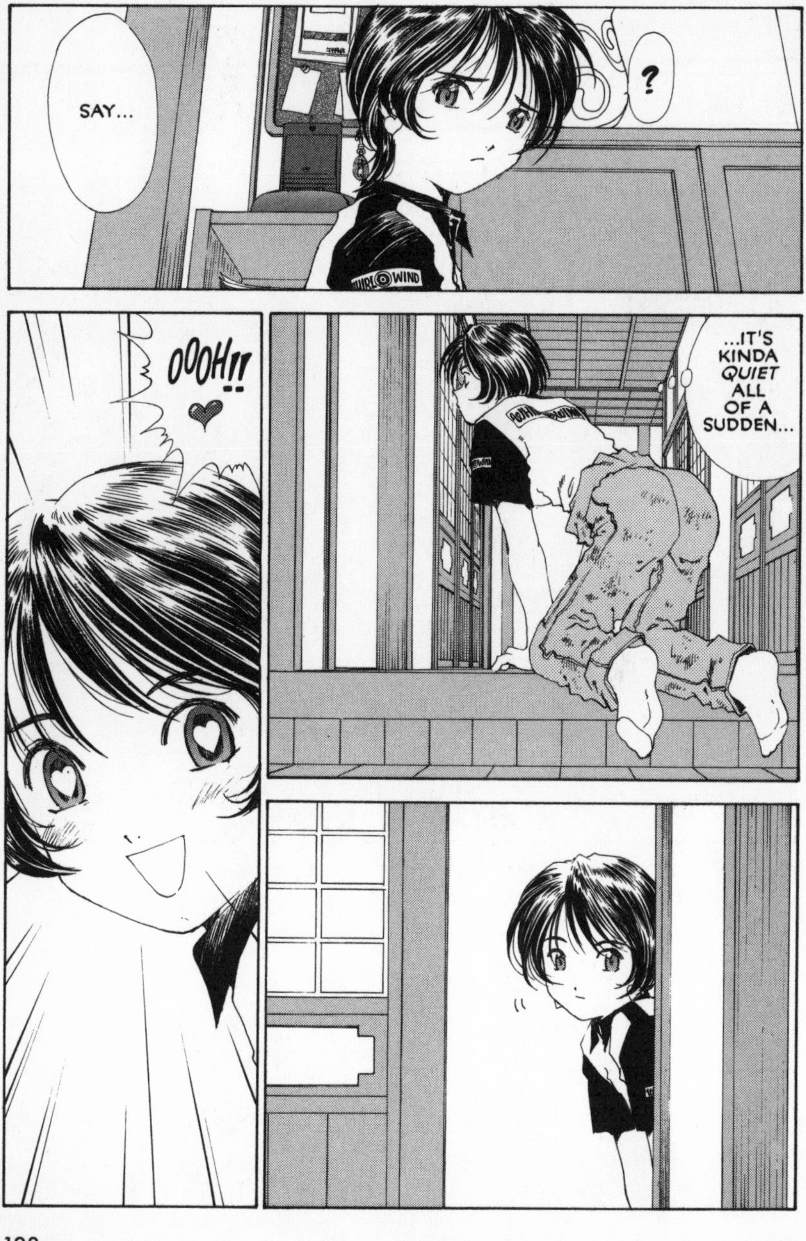
?
SAY...
...IT'S KINDA *QUIET* ALL OF A SUDDEN...
OOOH!!

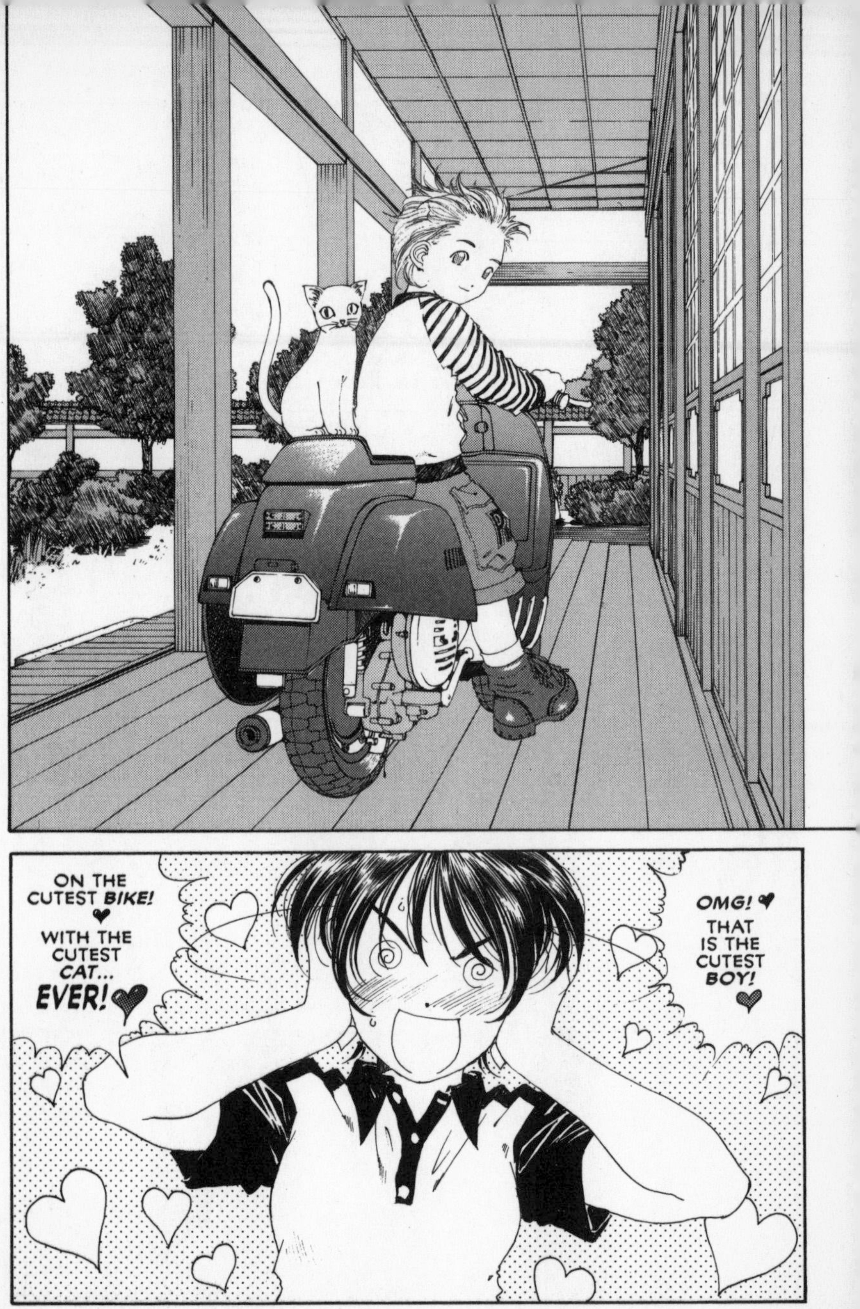
OMG! ♥ THAT IS THE CUTEST BOY! ♥
ON THE CUTEST BIKE! ♥ WITH THE CUTEST CAT... EVER! ♥

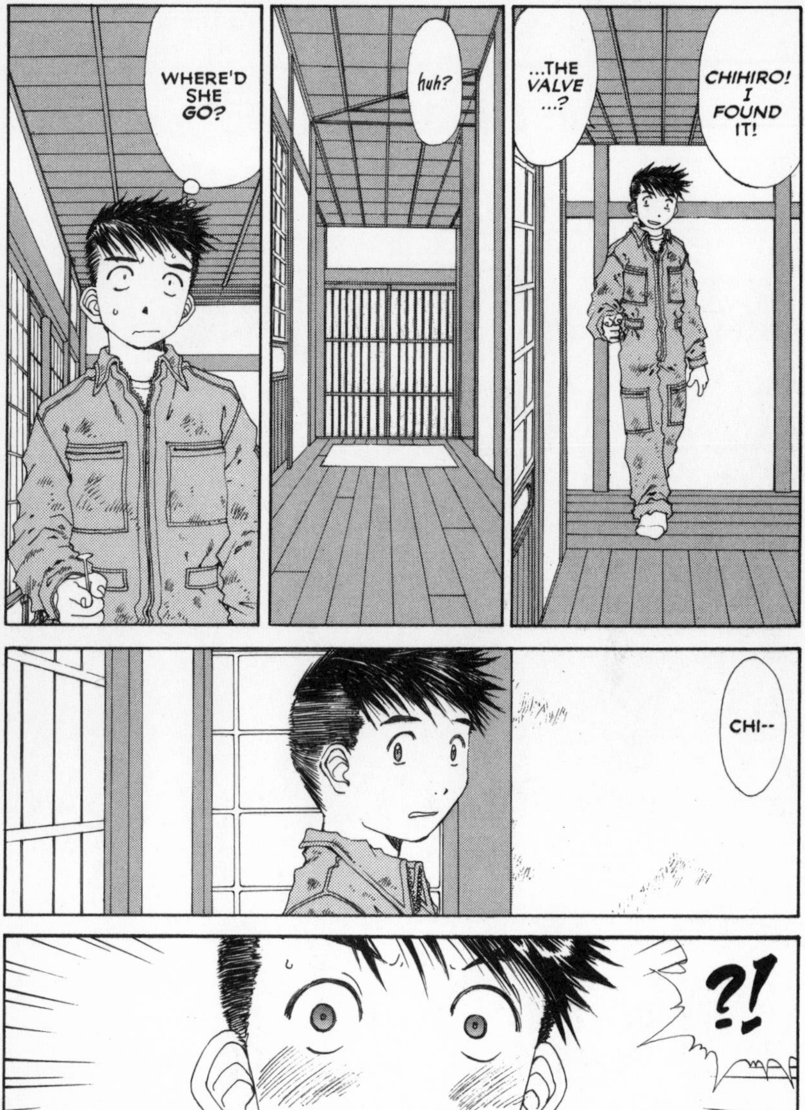
CHIHIRO! I FOUND IT!
...THE VALVE ...?
huh?
WHERE'D SHE GO?
CHI--
?!

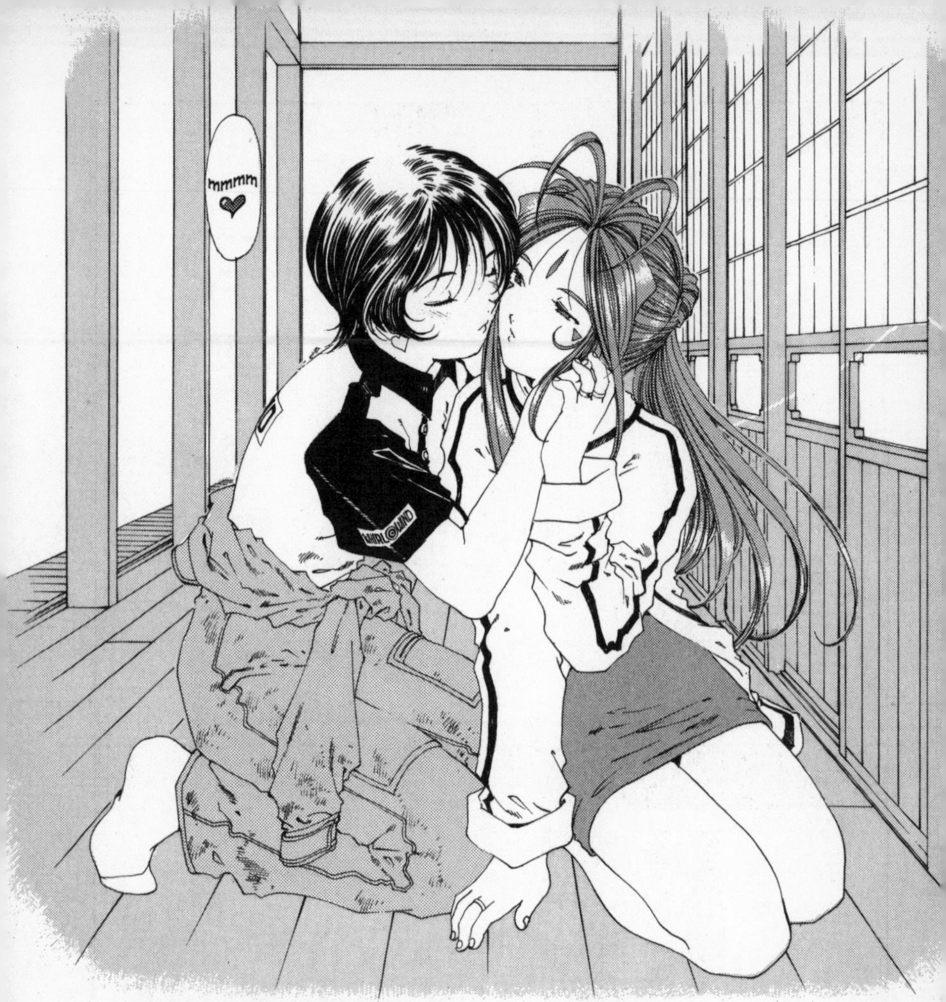
mmmm
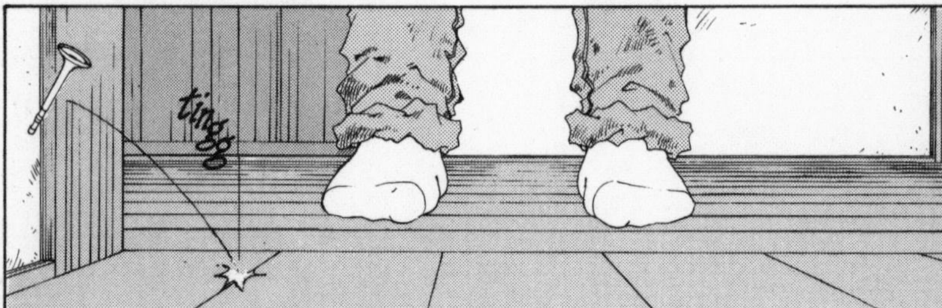
tingg

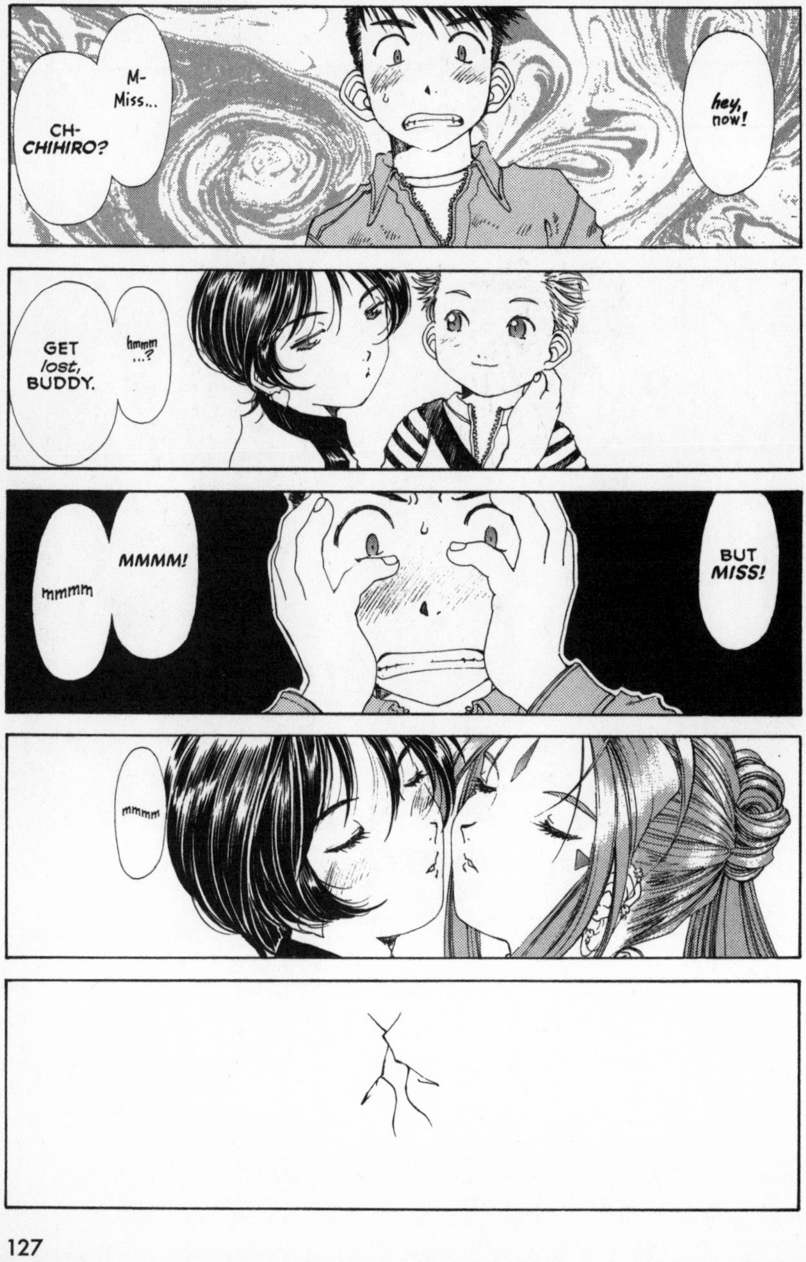
hey, now!
M- Miss... CH- CHIHIRO?
hmmm ...?
GET *lost,* BUDDY.
BUT *MISS!*
MMMM!
mmmm
mmmm

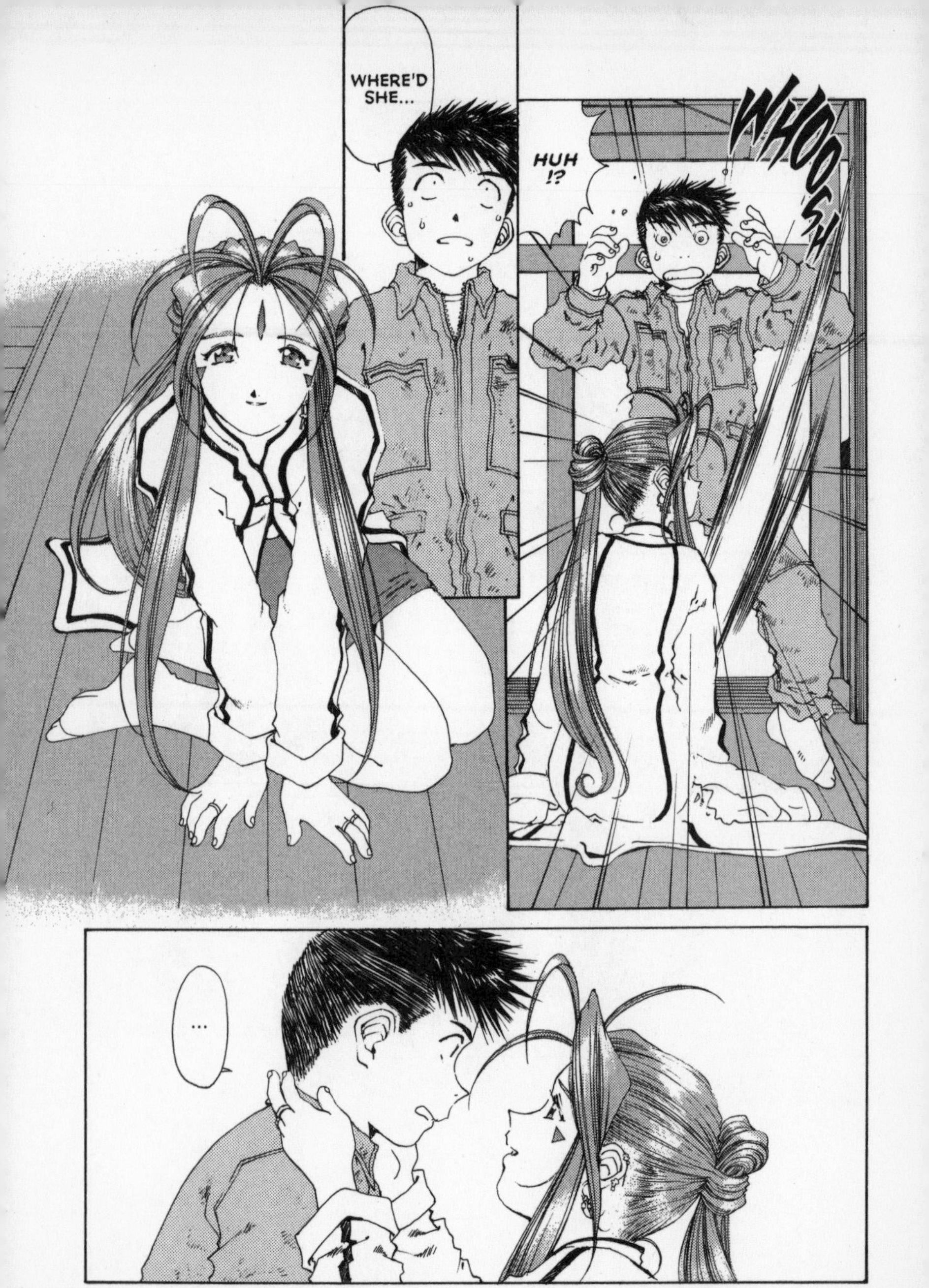
WHERE'D SHE...
WHOOSH
HUH !?
...

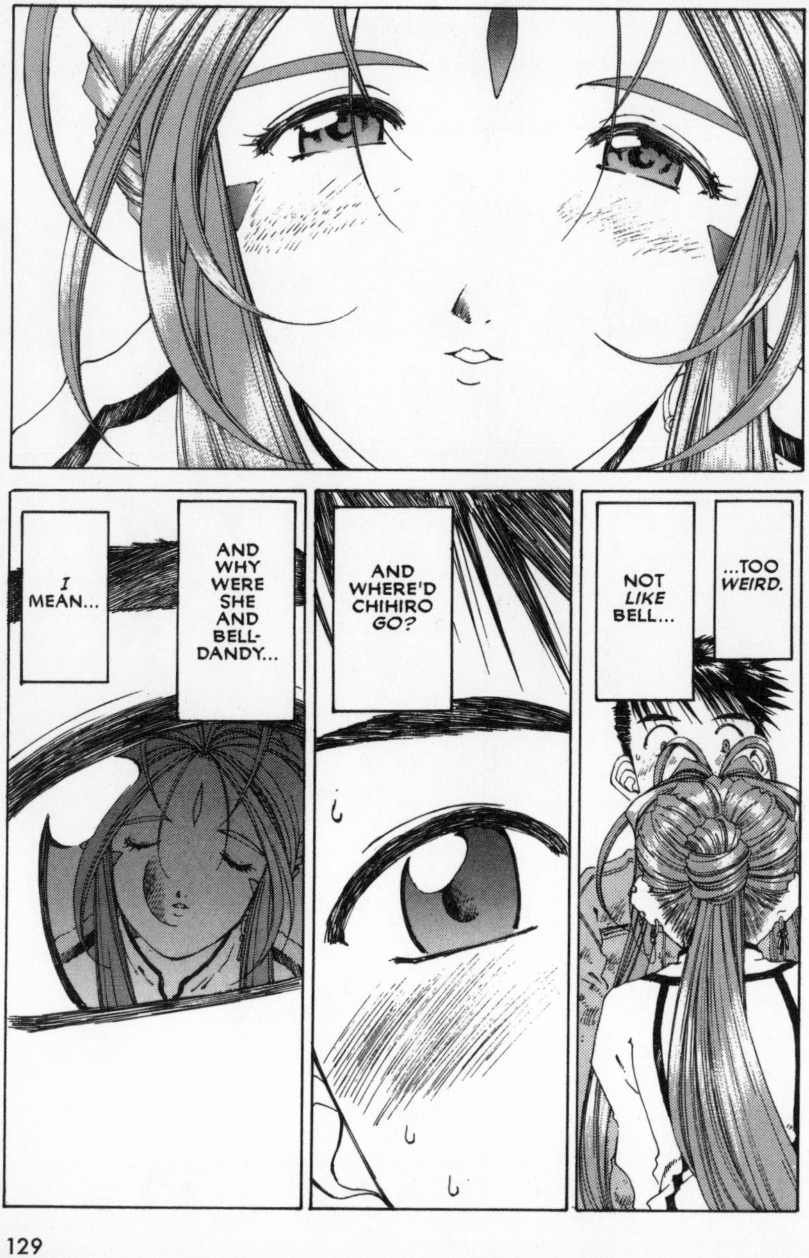
I MEAN...
AND WHY WERE SHE AND BELL-DANDY...
AND WHERE'D CHIHIRO *GO?*
NOT *LIKE* BELL...
...TOO *WEIRD.*

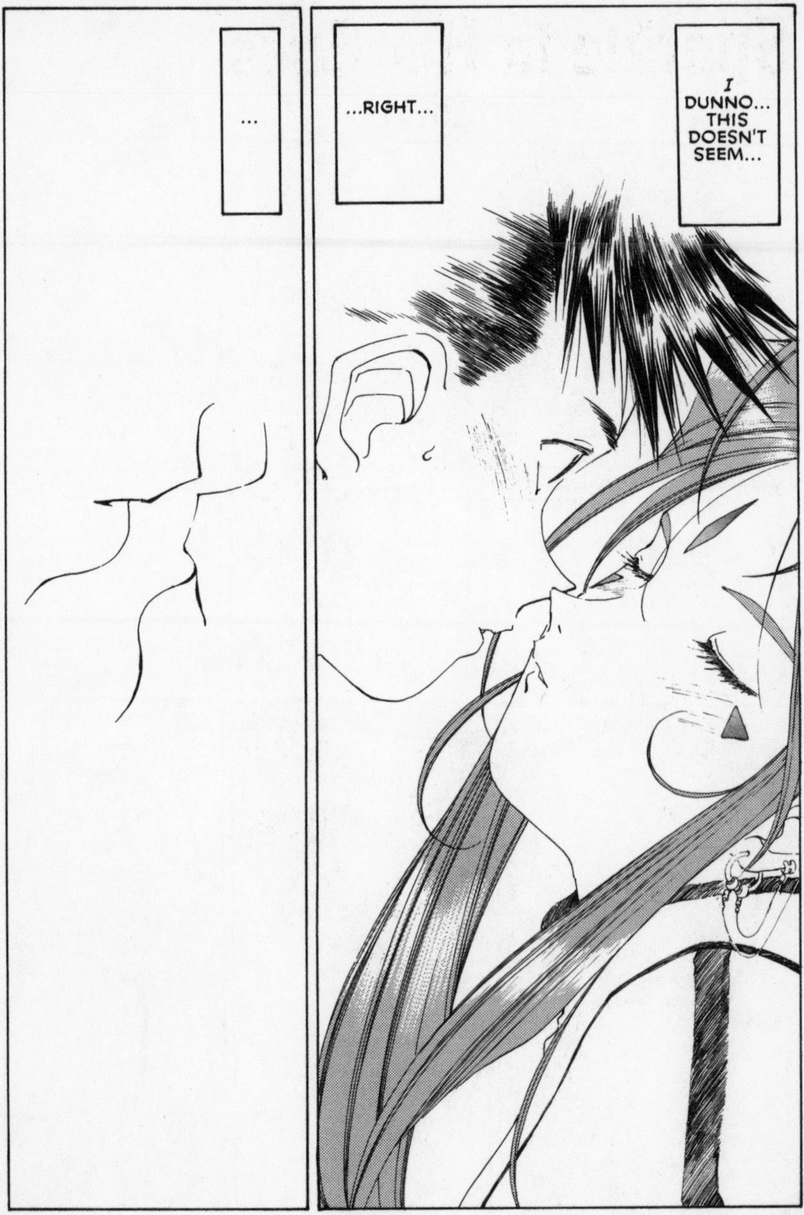
I DUNNO... THIS DOESN'T SEEM...
...RIGHT...
...

CHAPTER 141

Sparkle in Her Eyes

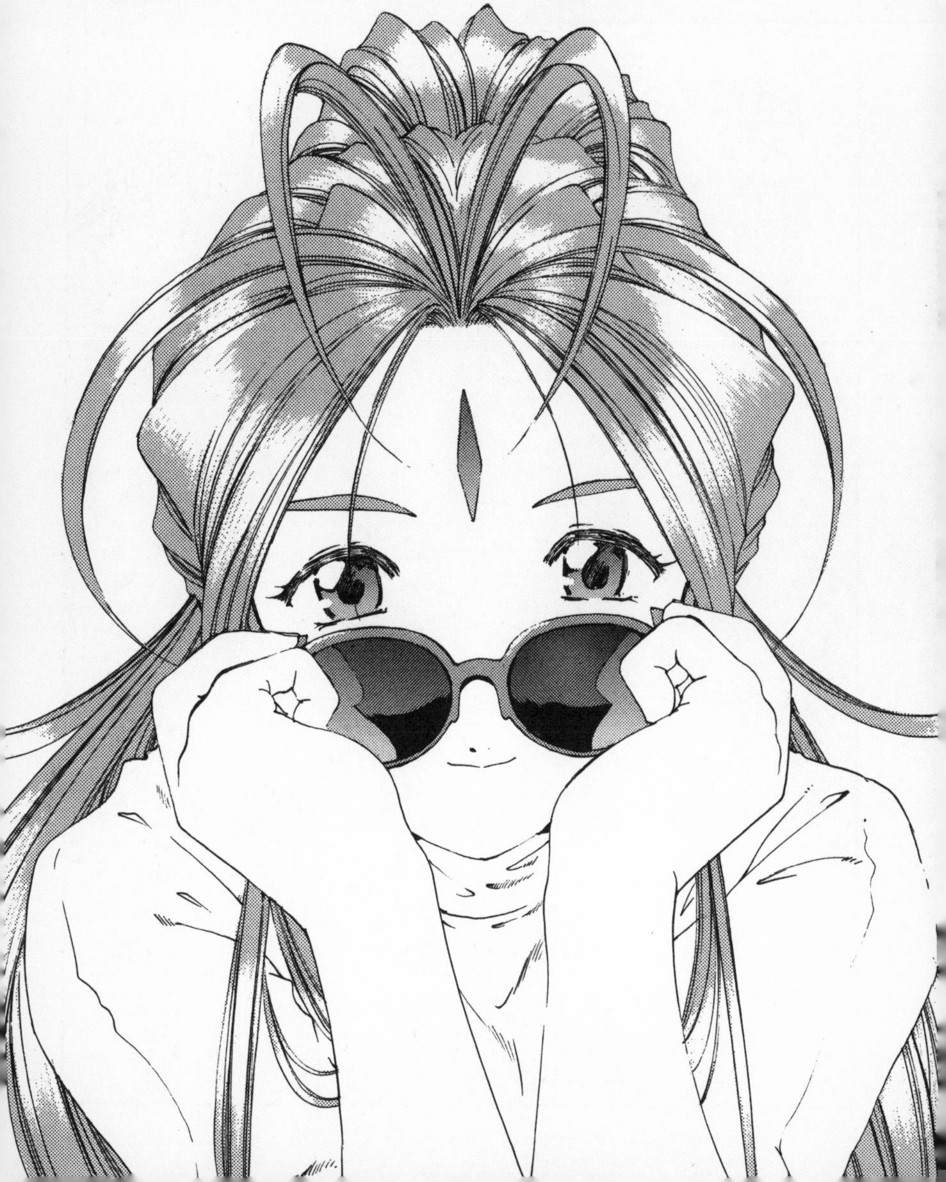

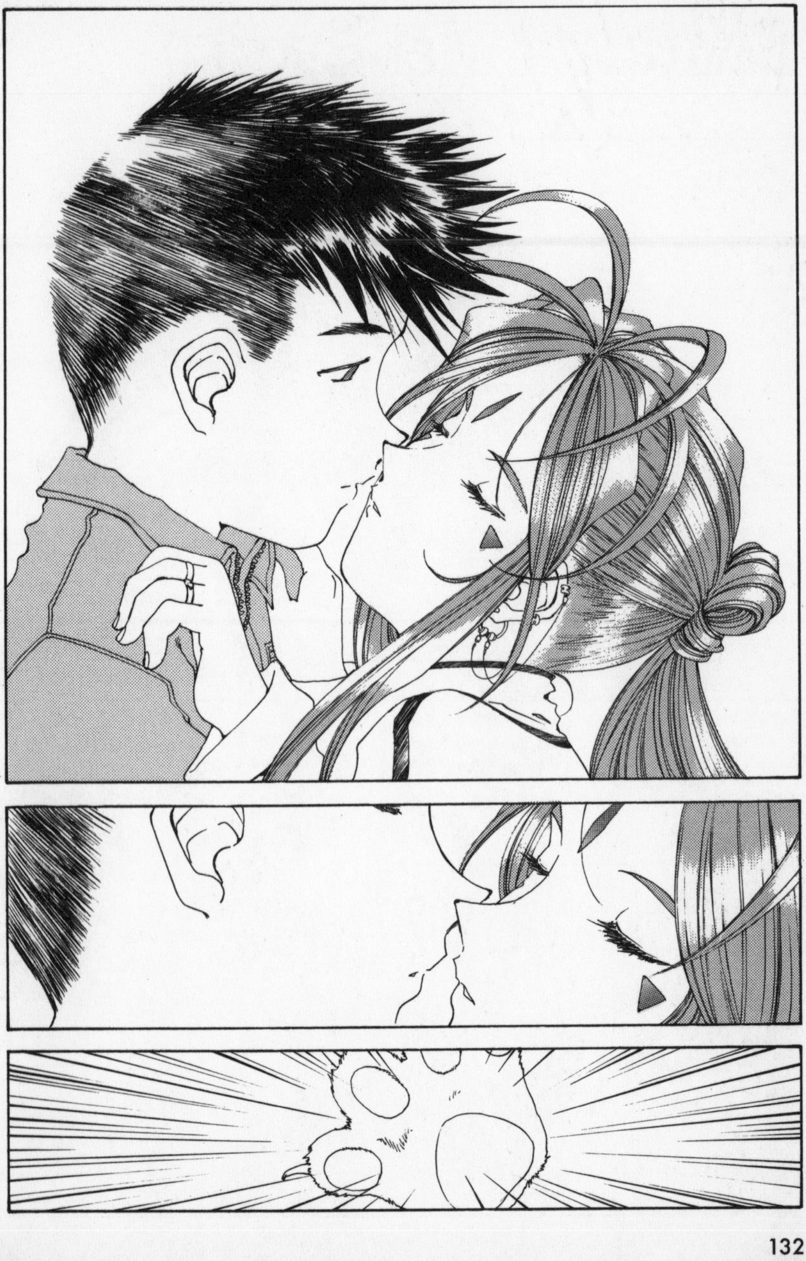

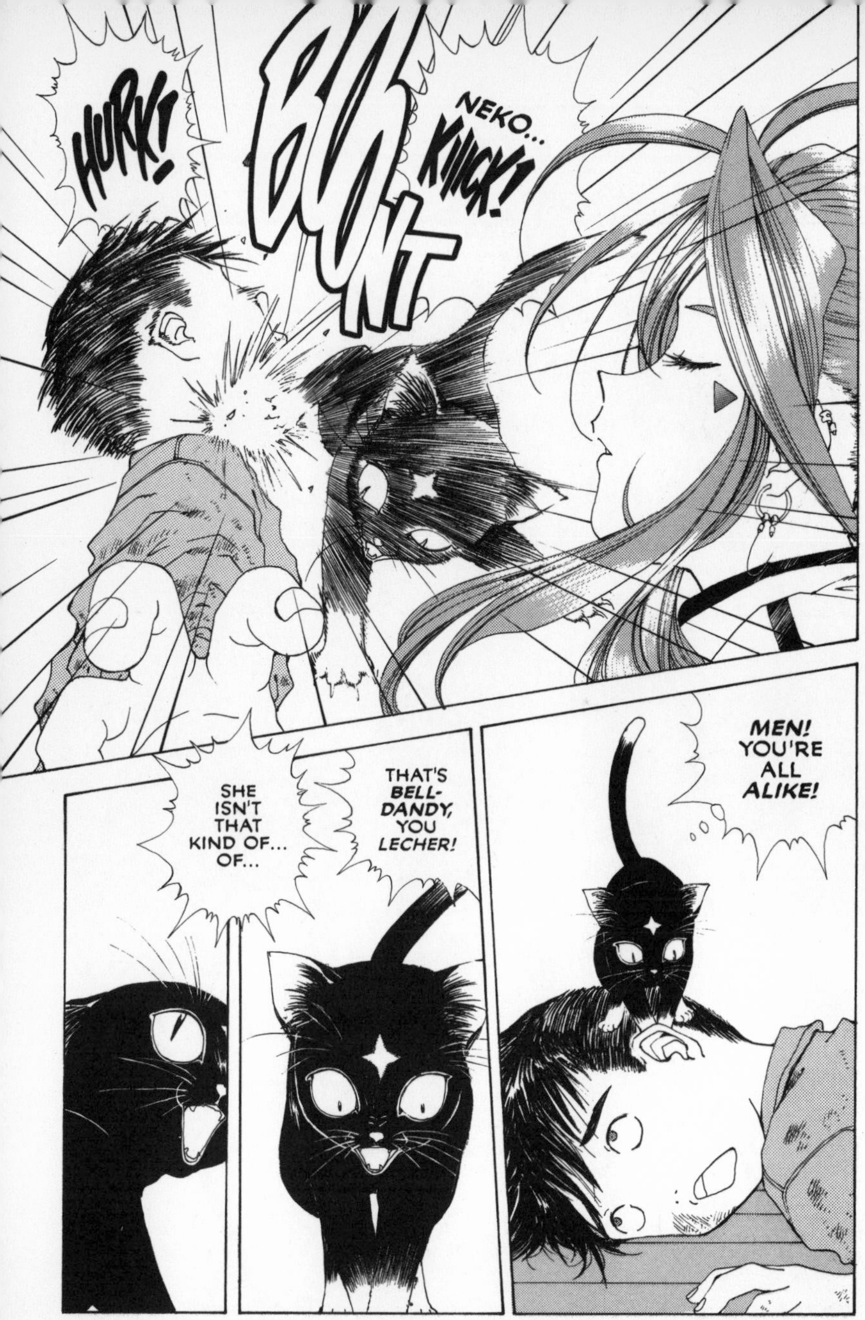
NEKO... KIIICK!
HURK!
MEN! YOU'RE ALL ALIKE!
THAT'S BELL-DANDY, YOU LECHER!
SHE ISN'T THAT KIND OF... OF...

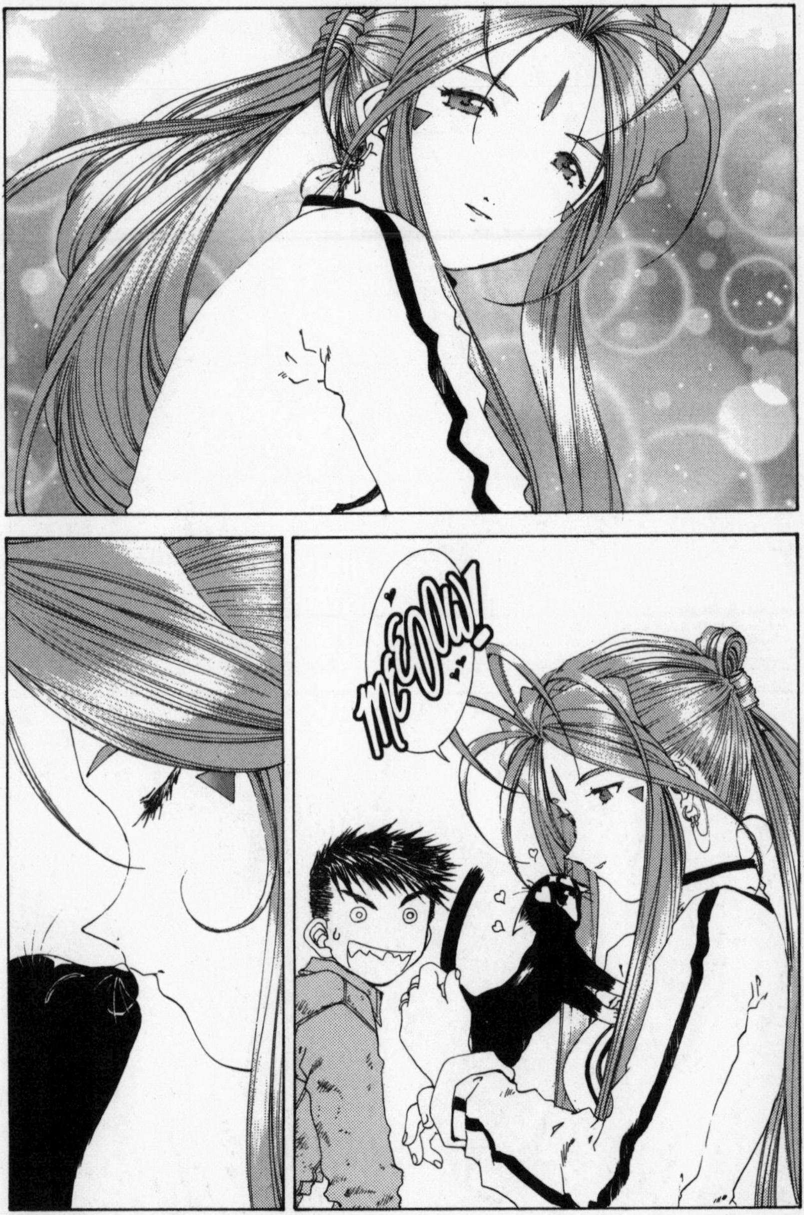
MEOOW!

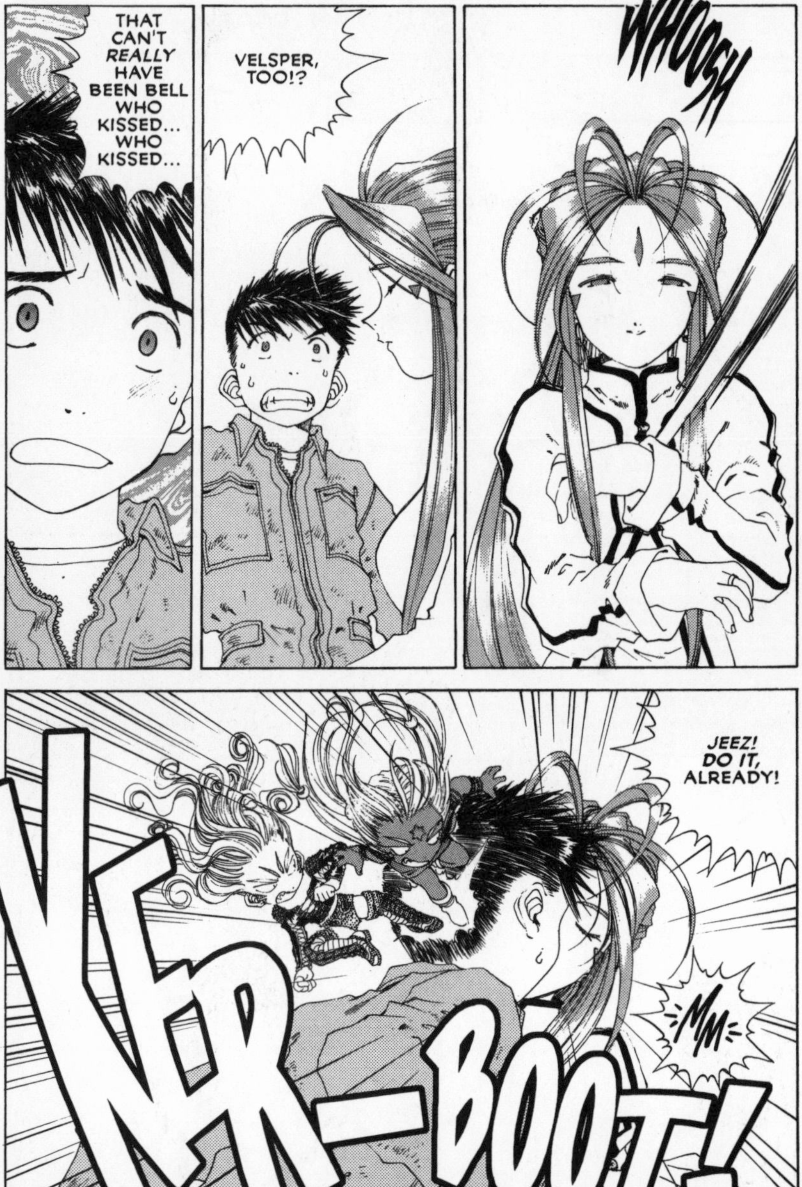
WHOOSH
VELSPER, TOO!?
THAT CAN'T REALLY HAVE BEEN BELL WHO KISSED... WHO KISSED...
JEEZ! DO IT, ALREADY!
MM
KER-BOOT!

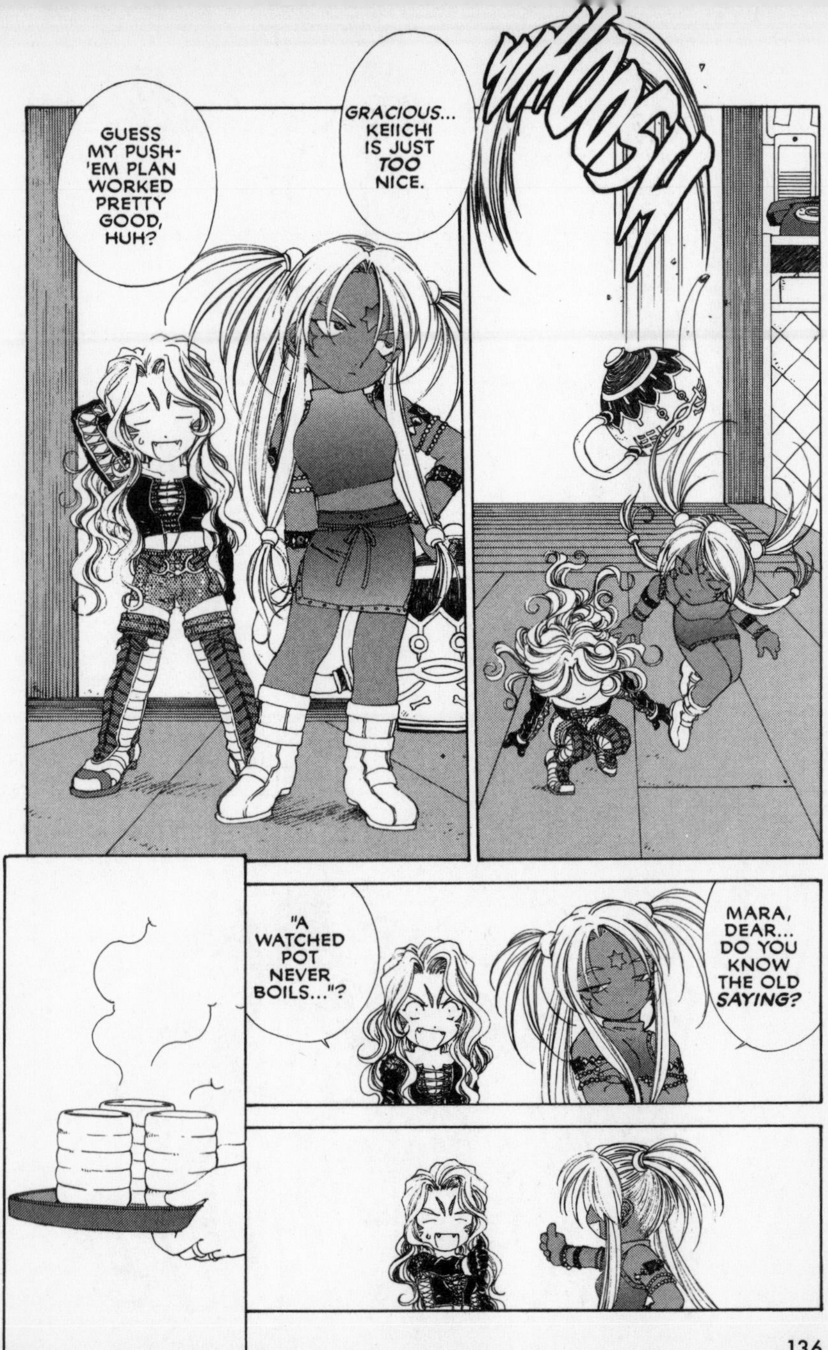
WHOOSH
GRACIOUS... KEIICHI IS JUST *TOO* NICE.
GUESS MY PUSH-'EM PLAN WORKED PRETTY GOOD, HUH?
MARA, DEAR... DO YOU KNOW THE OLD *SAYING?*
"A WATCHED POT NEVER BOILS..."?

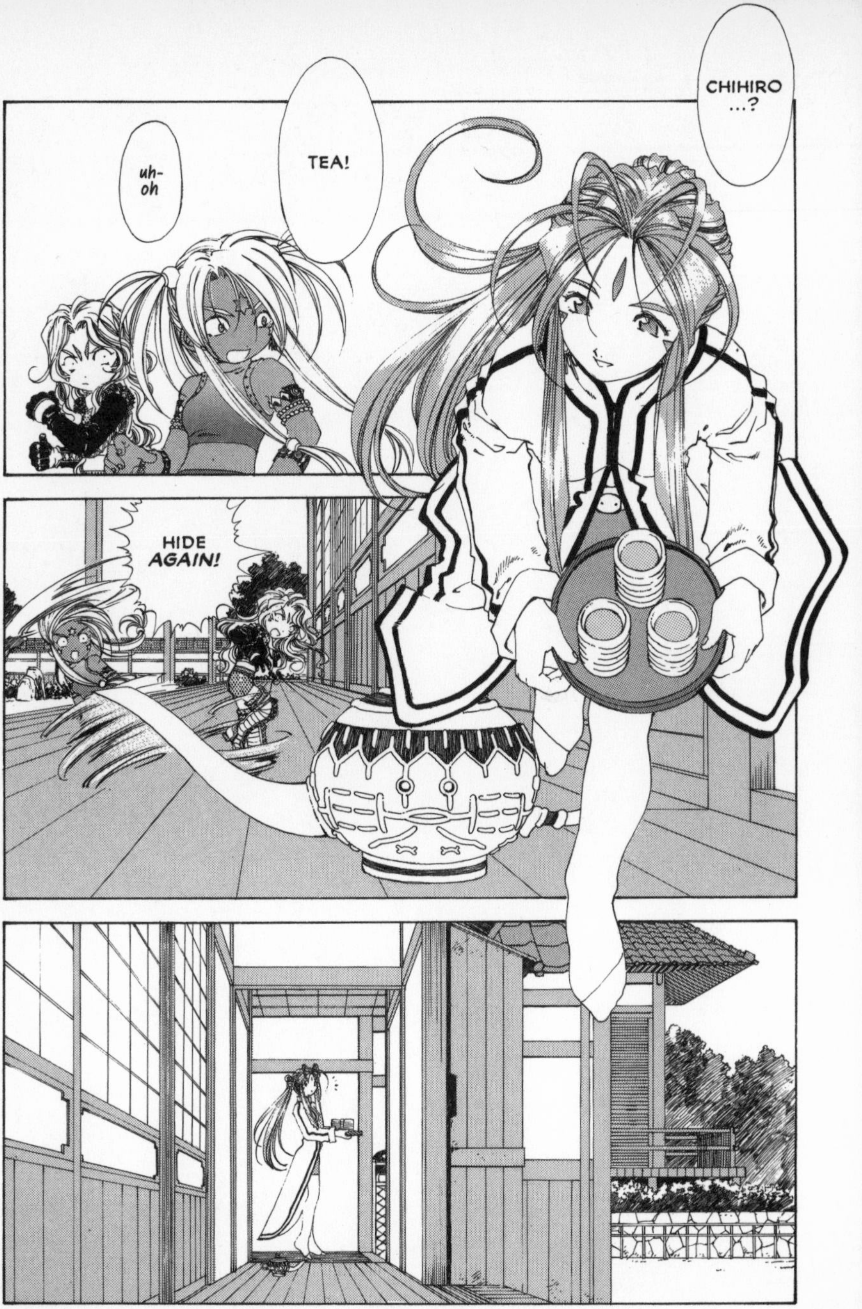
CHIHIRO ...?
TEA!
uh-oh
HIDE AGAIN!

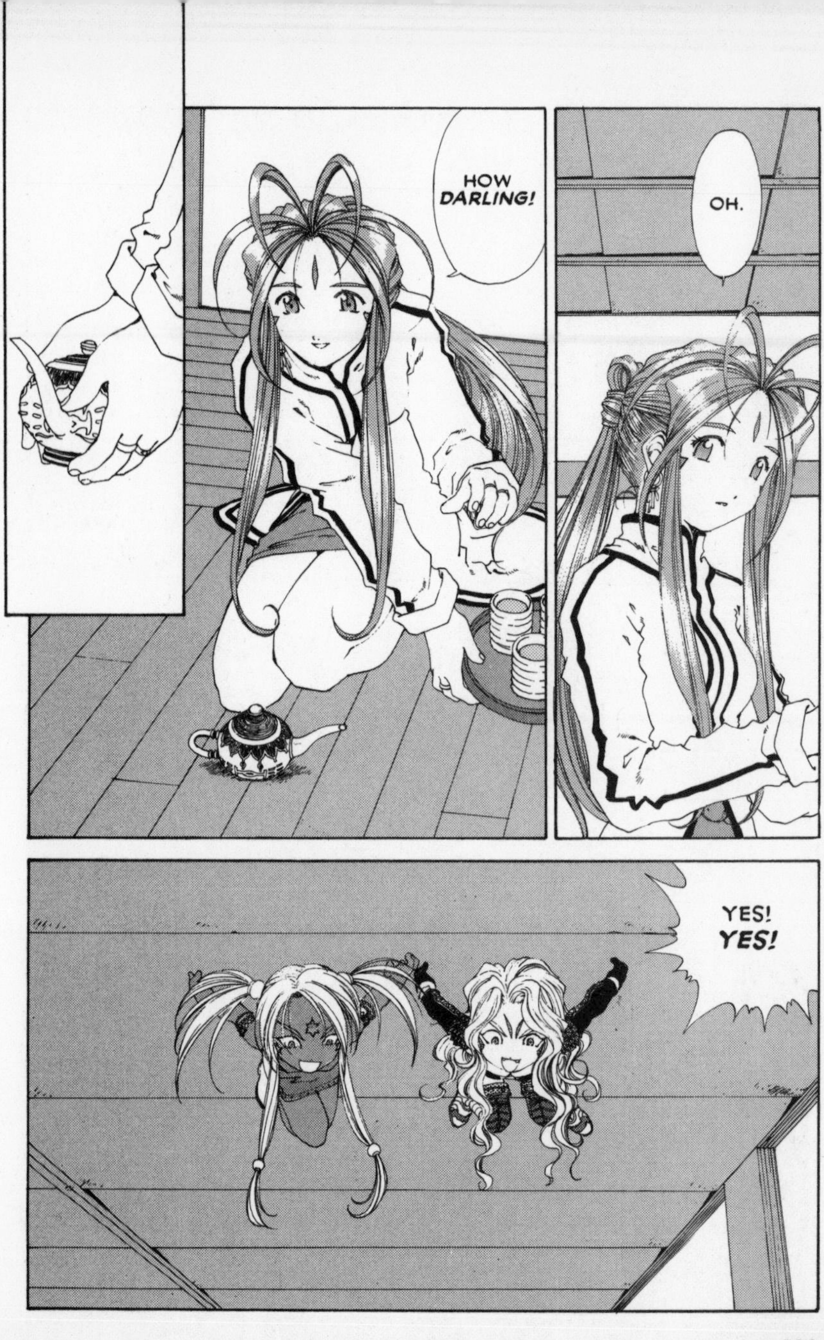
OH.
HOW DARLING!
YES! YES!

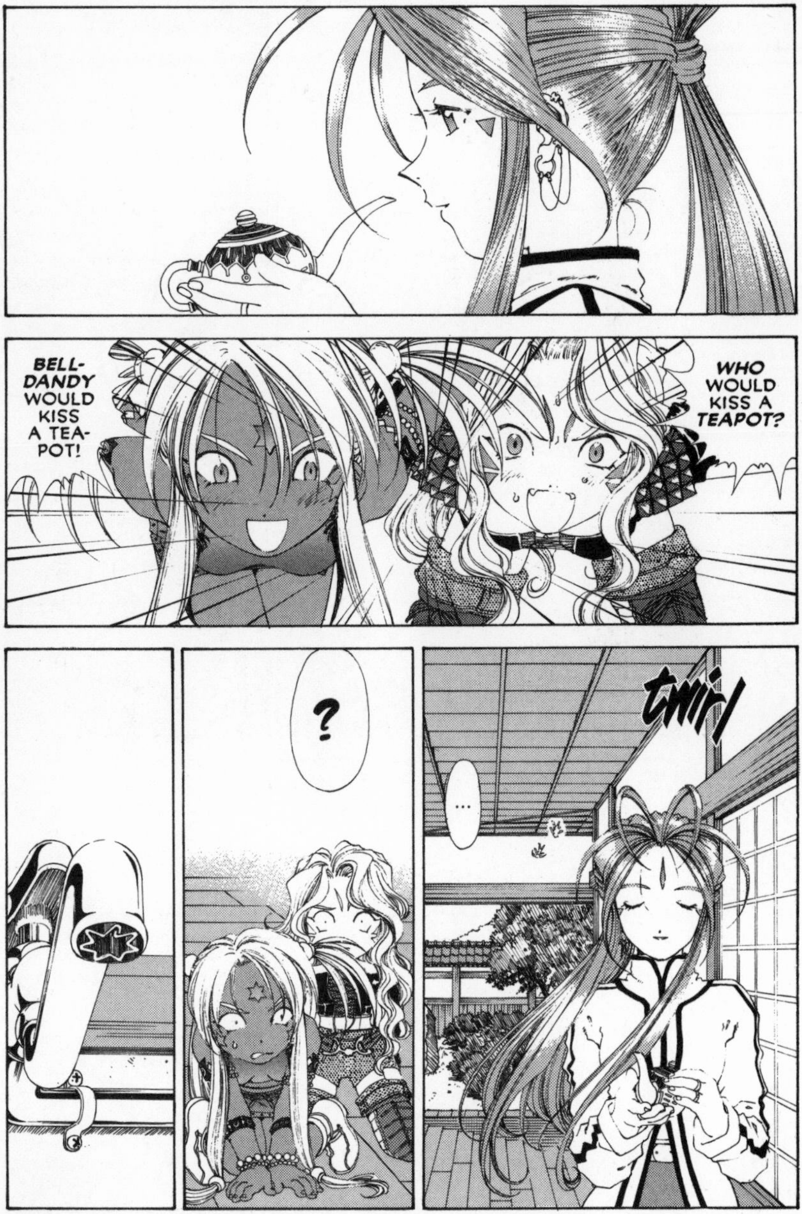
WHO WOULD KISS A TEAPOT?
BELL-DANDY WOULD KISS A TEA-POT!
twirl
...
?

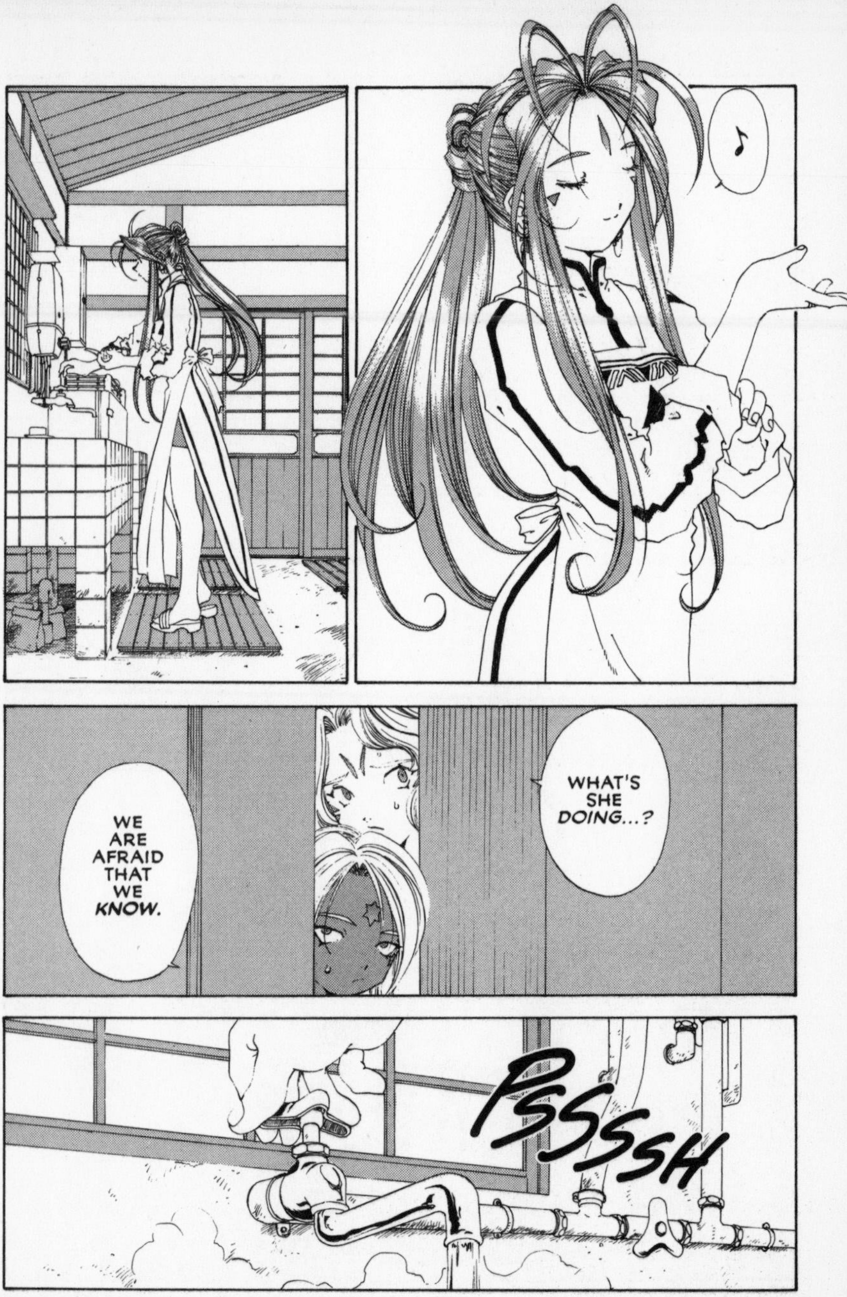
♪
WHAT'S SHE DOING...?
WE ARE AFRAID THAT WE KNOW.
PSSSH

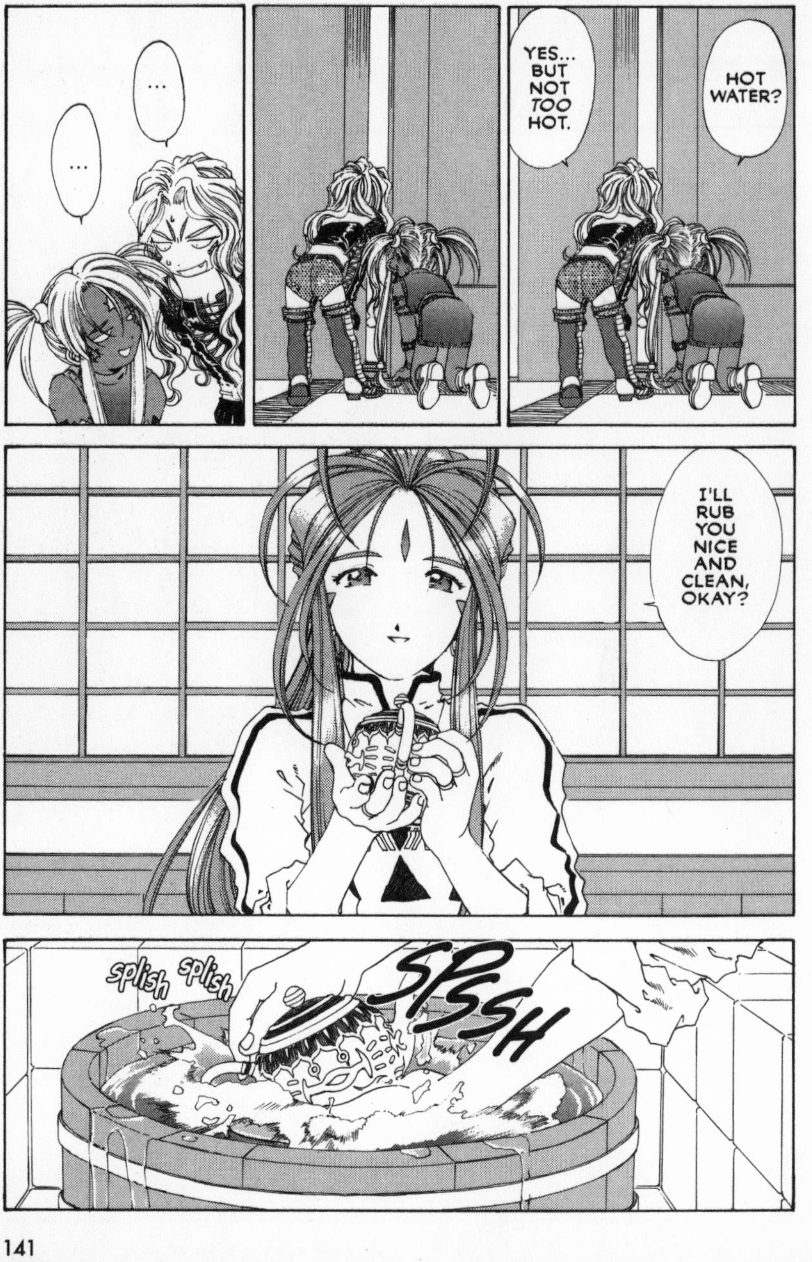
HOT WATER?
YES... BUT NOT *TOO* HOT.
...
...
I'LL RUB YOU NICE AND CLEAN, OKAY?
SPSSH
splish splish

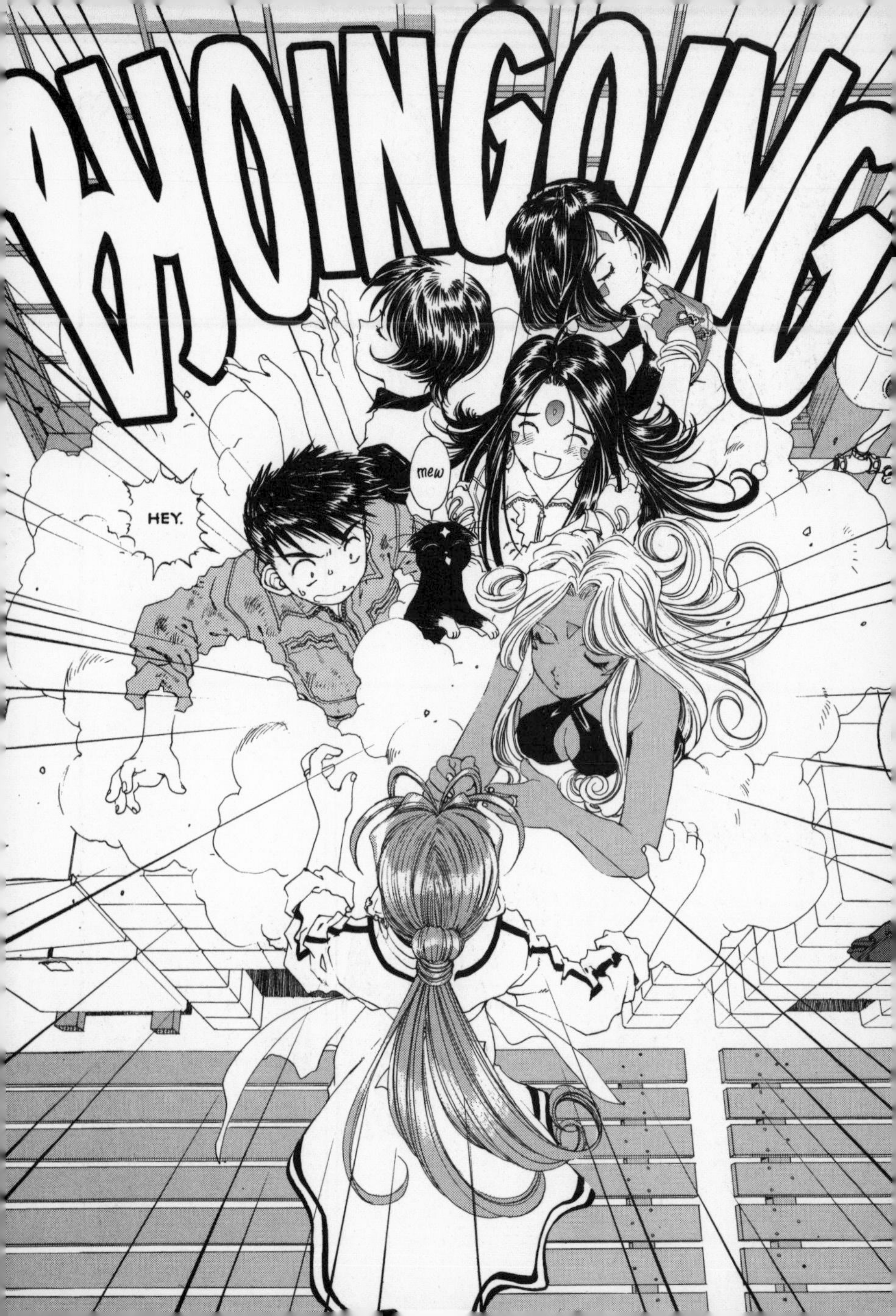
BWOINGOING
mew
HEY.

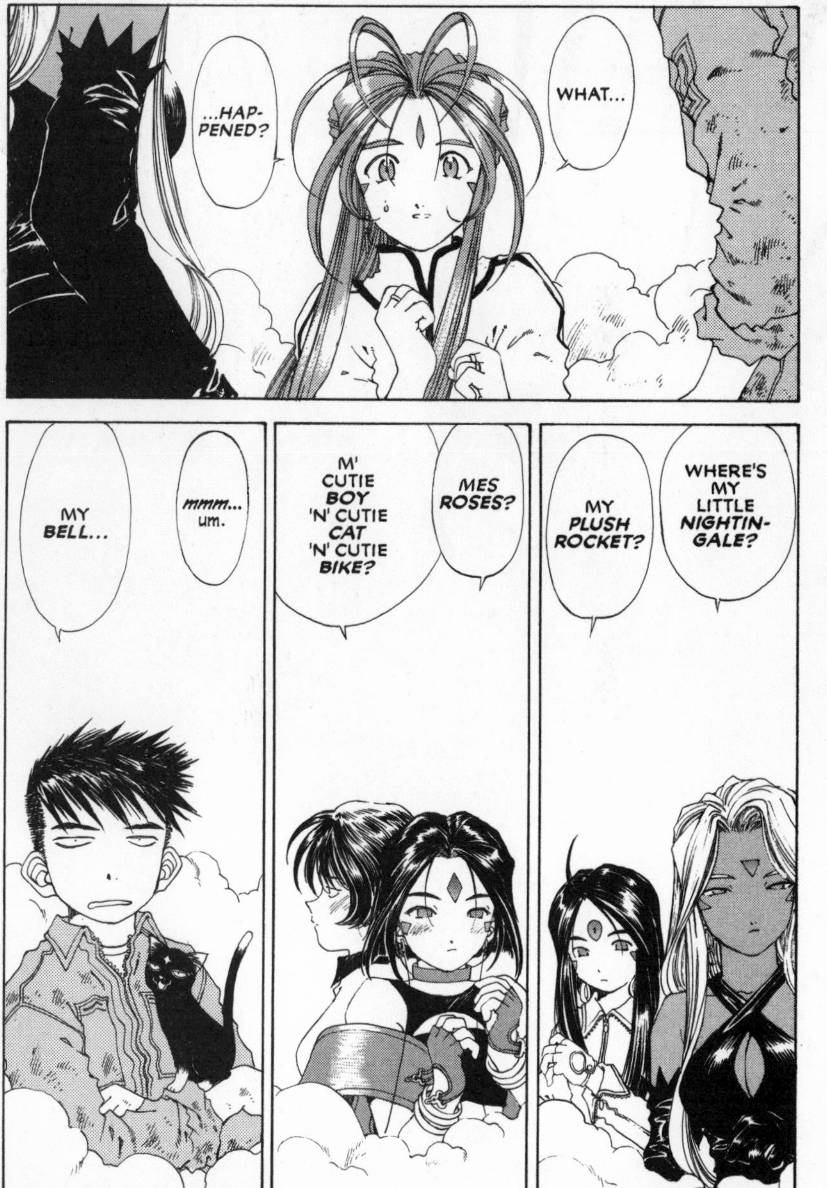
WHAT...
...HAP-PENED?
WHERE'S MY LITTLE NIGHTIN-GALE?
MY PLUSH ROCKET?
MES ROSES?
M' CUTIE BOY 'N' CUTIE CAT 'N' CUTIE BIKE?
mmm... um.
MY BELL...

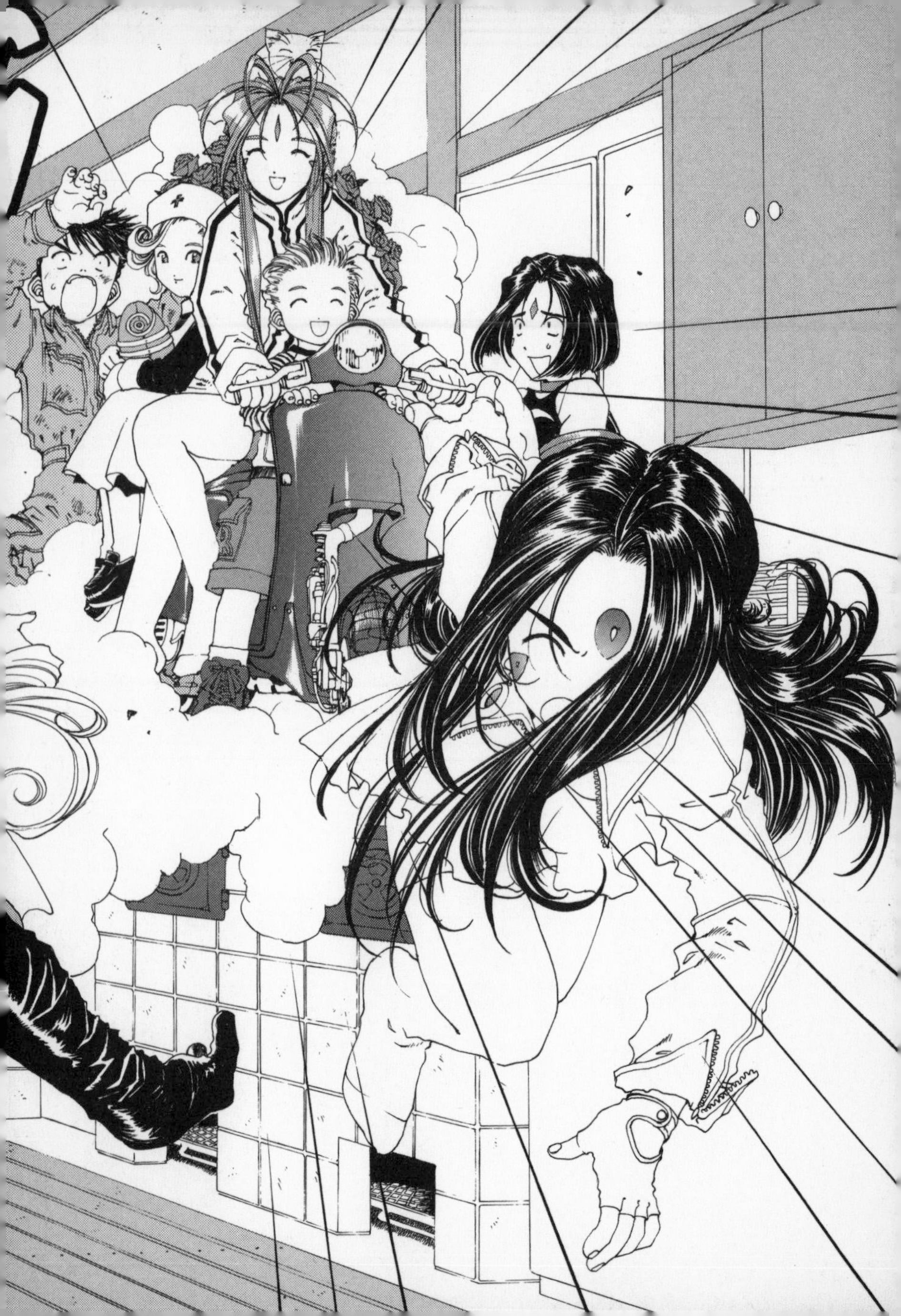

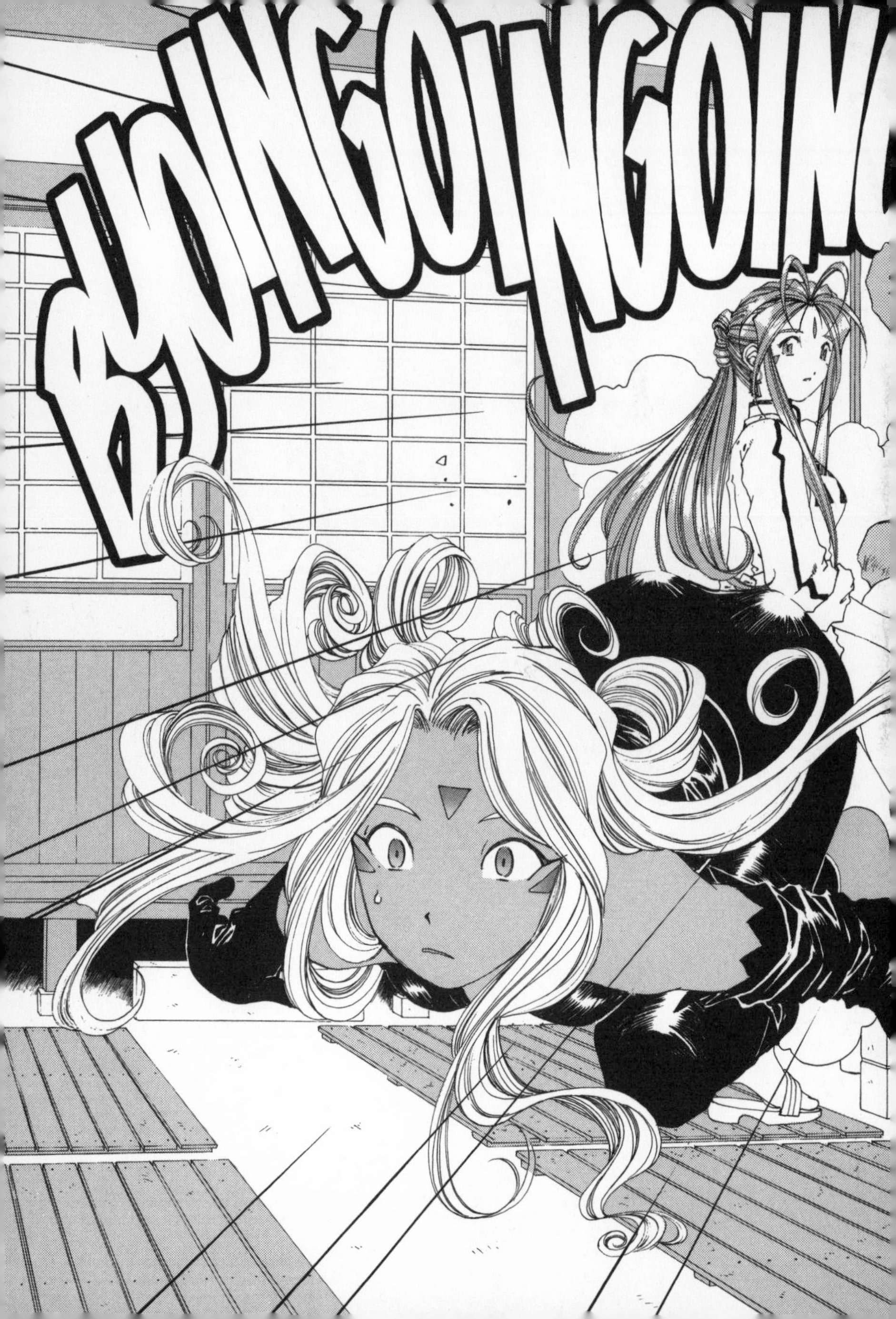
BOINGBOINGBOING

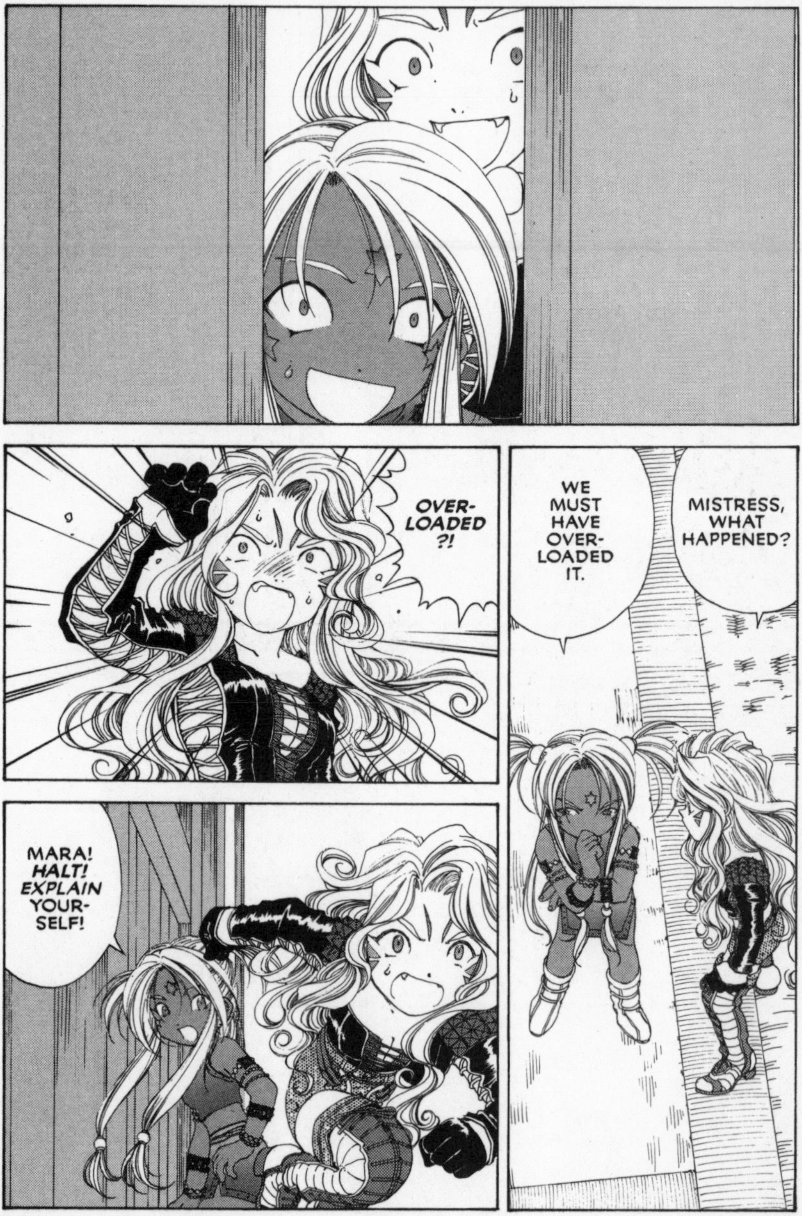
MISTRESS, WHAT HAPPENED?
WE MUST HAVE OVER-LOADED IT.
OVER-LOADED ?!
MARA! HALT! EXPLAIN YOUR-SELF!

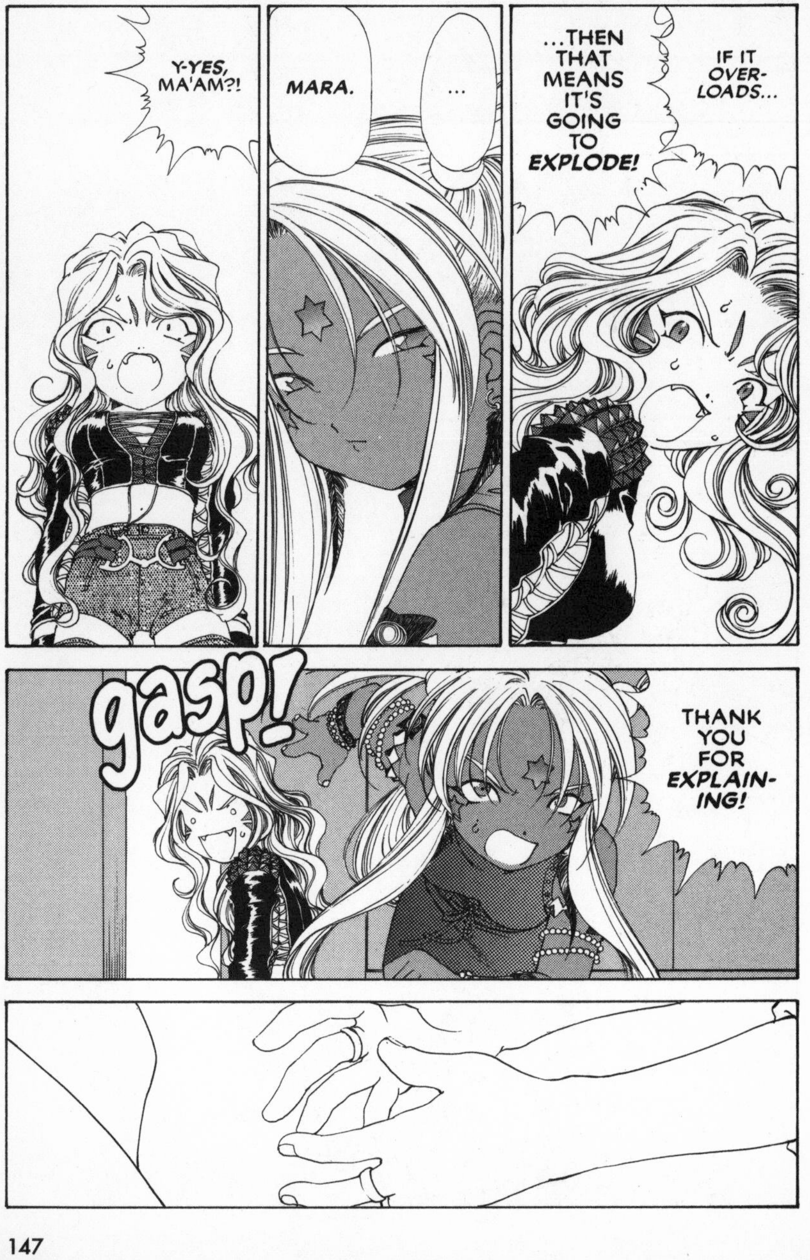
IF IT OVER-LOADS...
...THEN THAT MEANS IT'S GOING TO EXPLODE!
...
MARA.
Y-YES, MA'AM?!
THANK YOU FOR EXPLAIN-ING!
gasp!

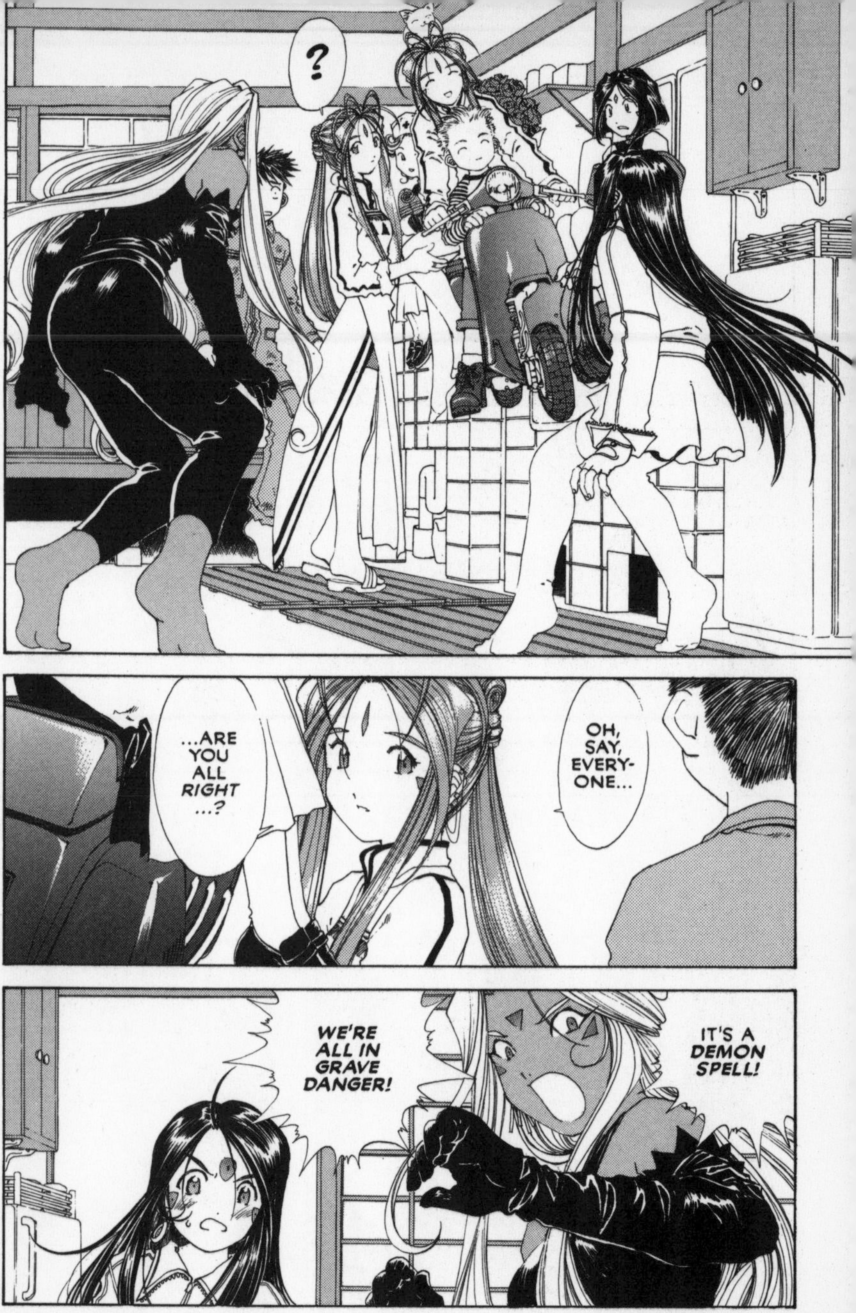
?
OH, SAY, EVERY-ONE...
...ARE YOU ALL RIGHT ...?
IT'S A DEMON SPELL!
WE'RE ALL IN GRAVE DANGER!

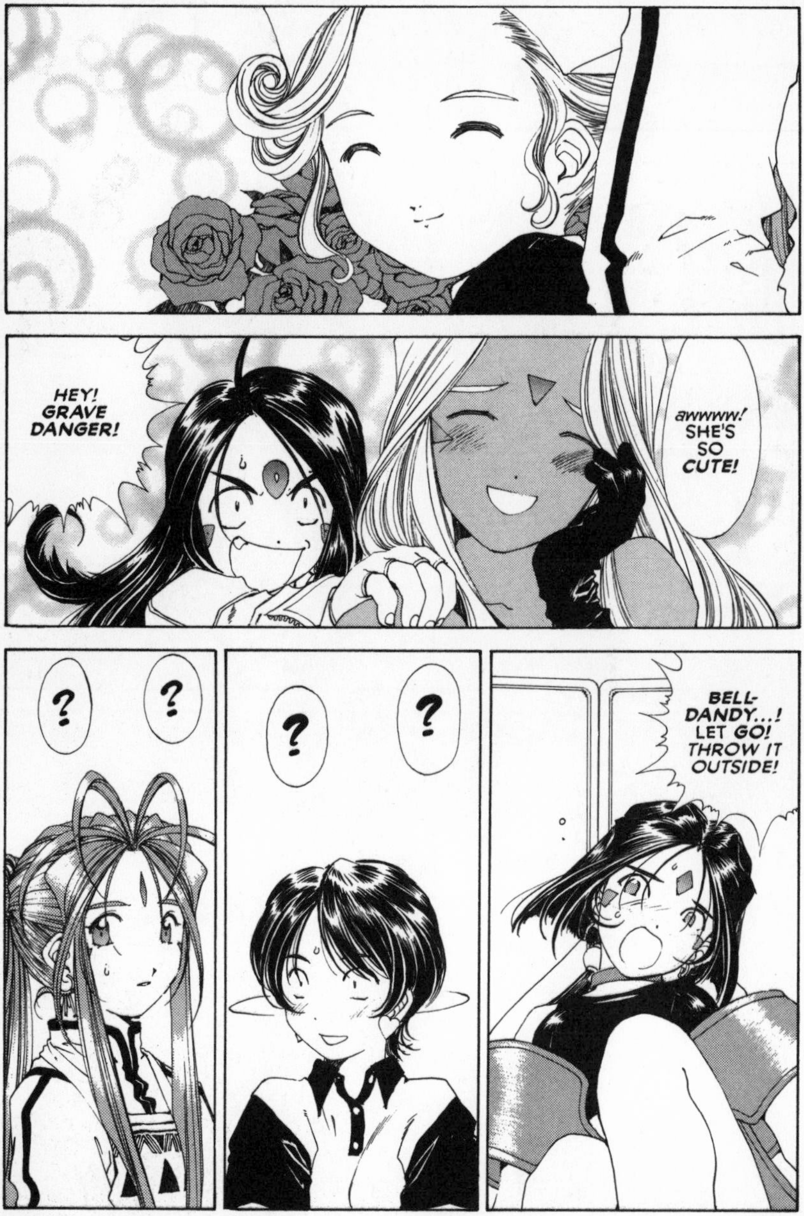
awwww! SHE'S SO CUTE!
HEY! GRAVE DANGER!
BELL-DANDY...! LET GO! THROW IT OUTSIDE!
?
?
?
?

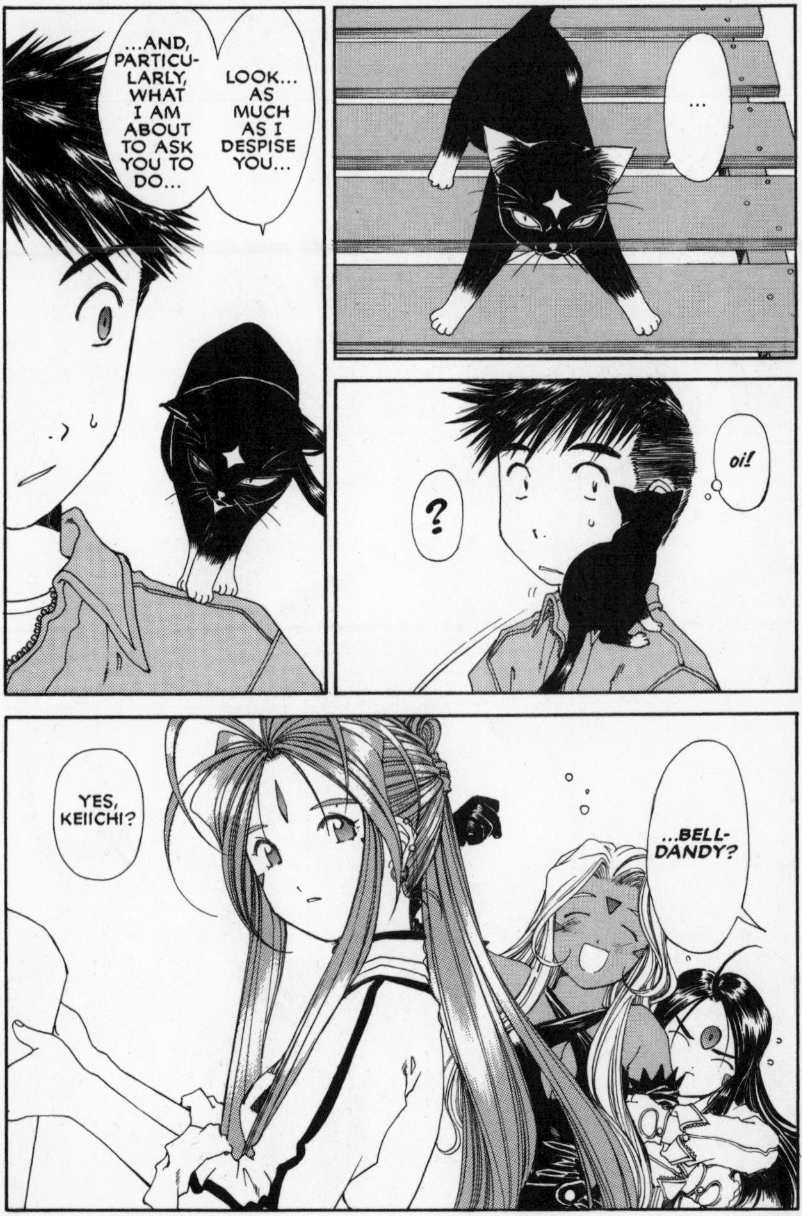
...
oi!
?
LOOK... AS MUCH AS I DESPISE YOU...
...AND, PARTICULARLY, WHAT I AM ABOUT TO ASK YOU TO DO...
...BELL-DANDY?
YES, KEIICHI?

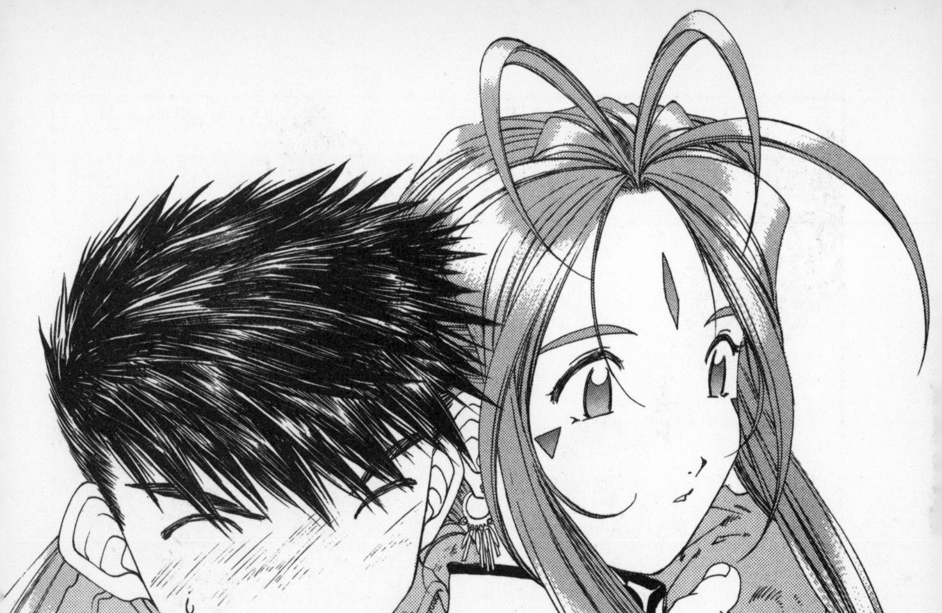

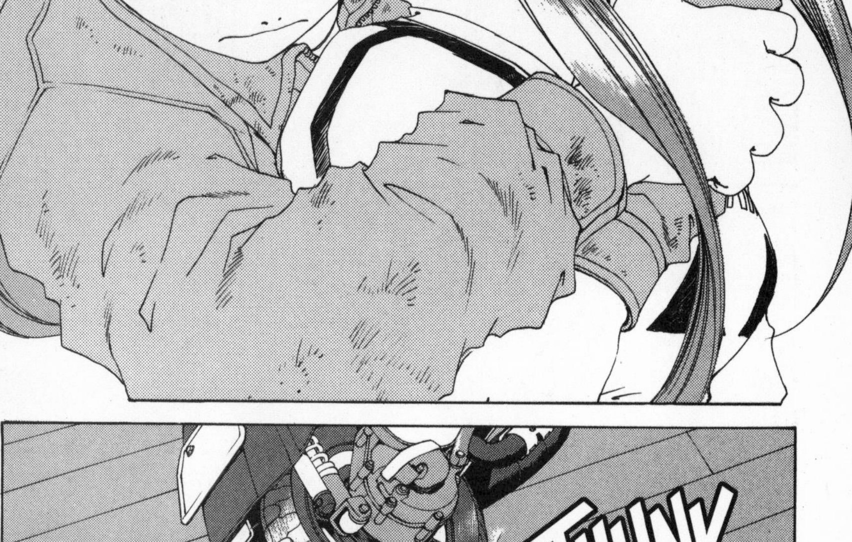
THUNK

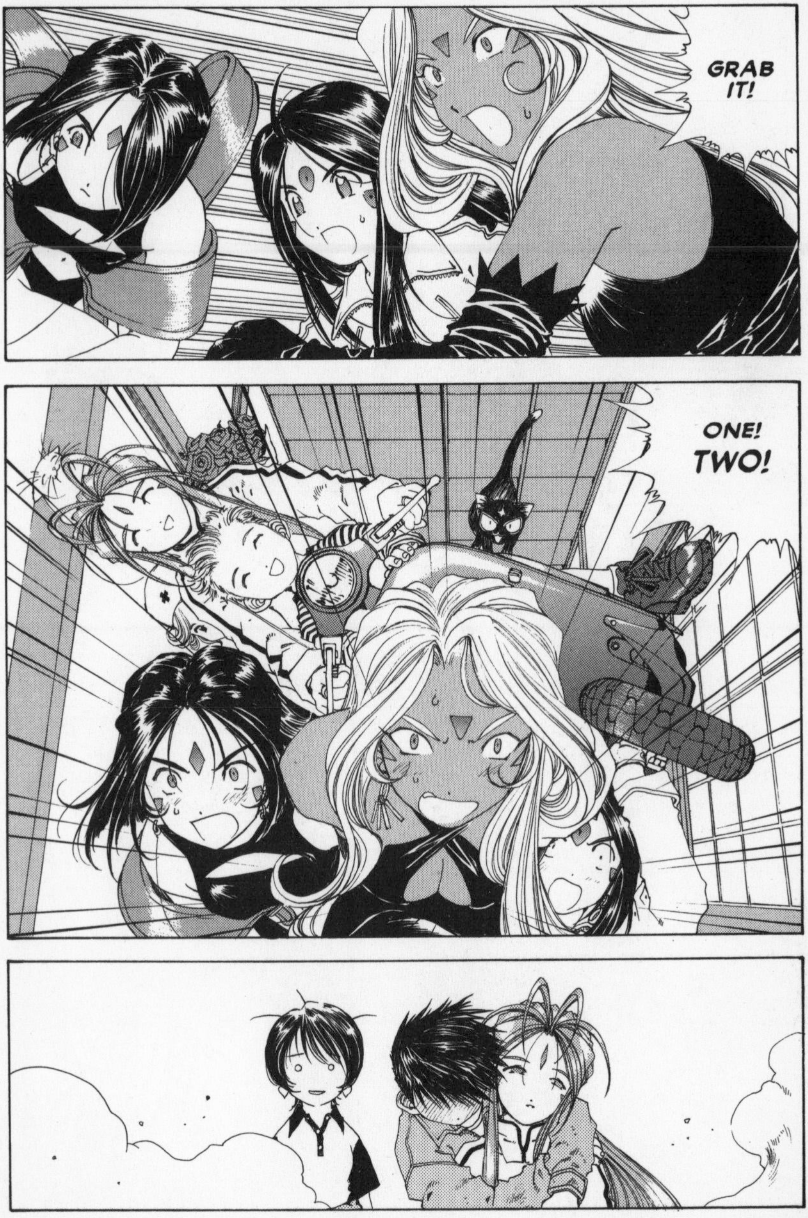
GRAB IT!
ONE! TWO!

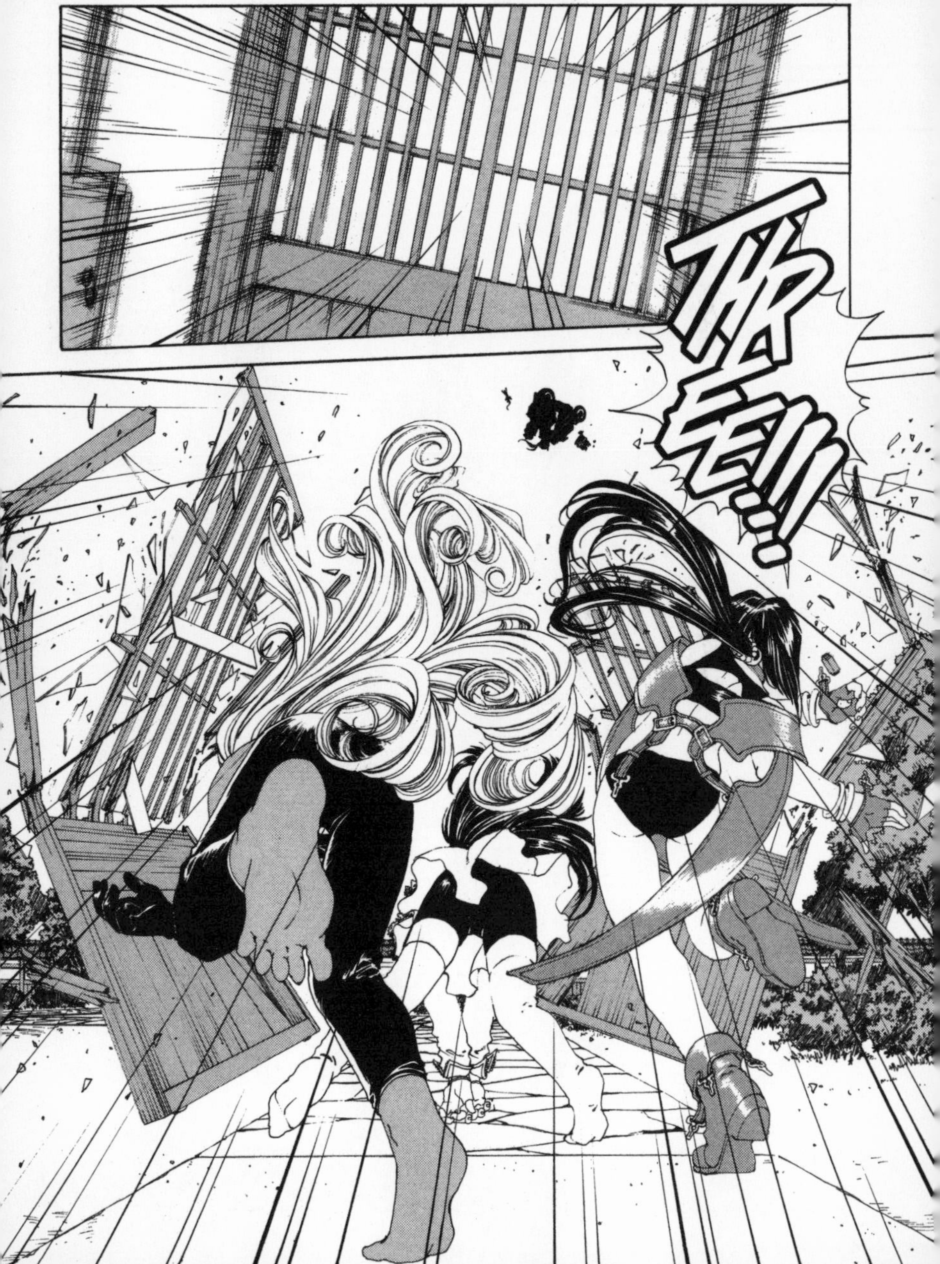
THREE!!...

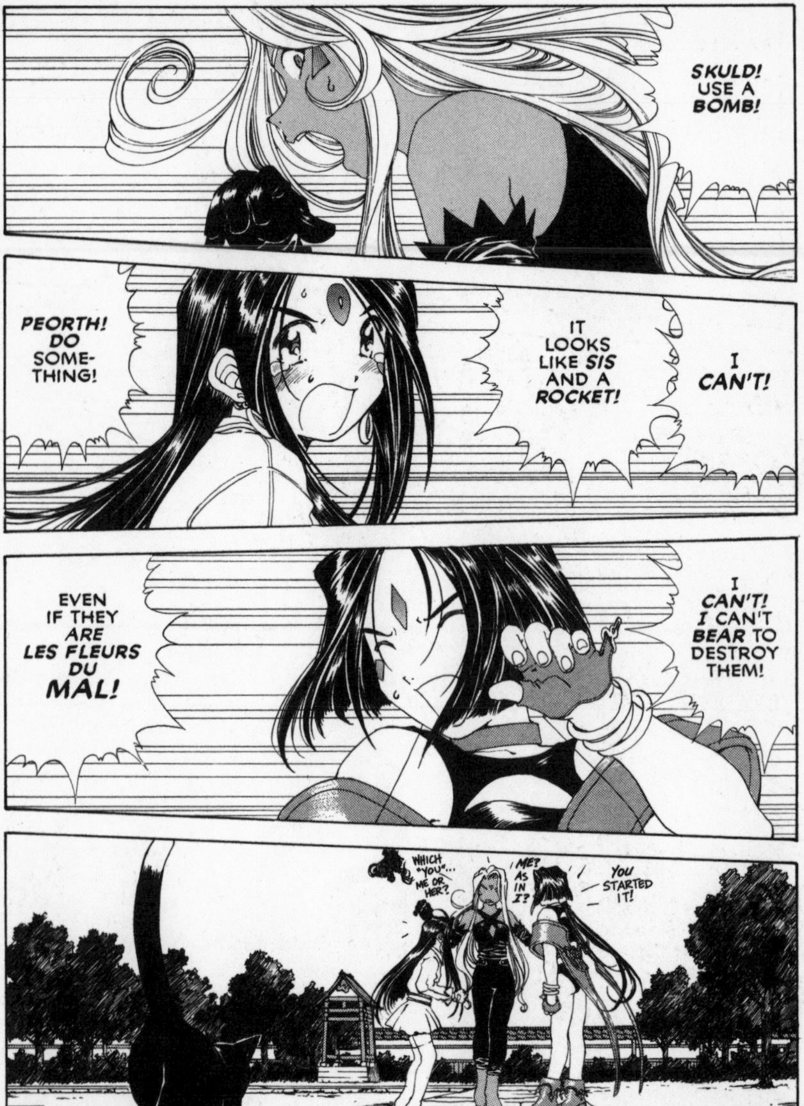
SKULD! USE A BOMB!
I CAN'T!
IT LOOKS LIKE SIS AND A ROCKET!
PEORTH! DO SOME-THING!
I CAN'T! I CAN'T BEAR TO DESTROY THEM!
EVEN IF THEY ARE LES FLEURS DU MAL!
YOU STARTED IT!
ME? AS IN I?
WHICH "YOU"... ME OR HER?

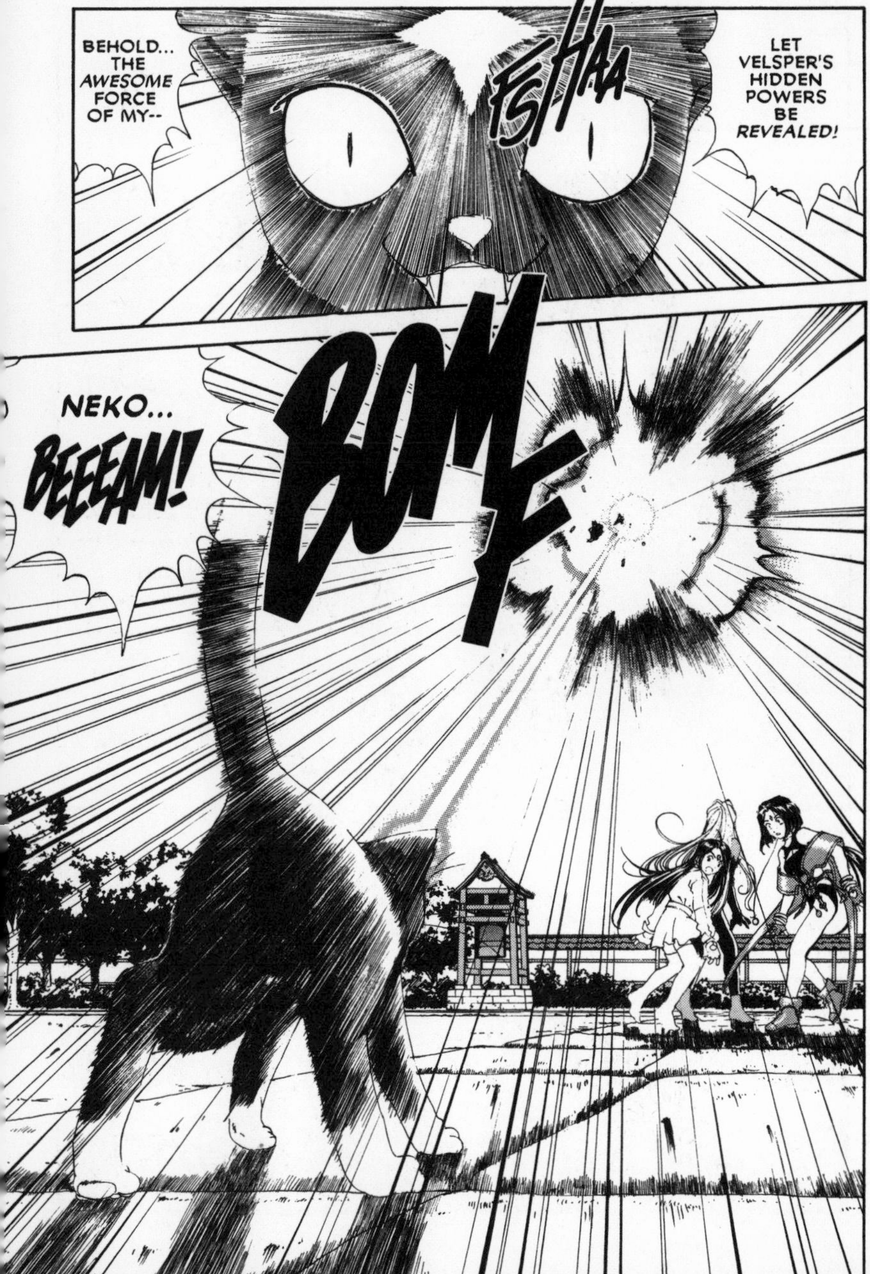
LET VELSPER'S HIDDEN POWERS BE REVEALED!
FSHAA
BEHOLD... THE AWESOME FORCE OF MY--
NEKO... BEEEAM!
BOM

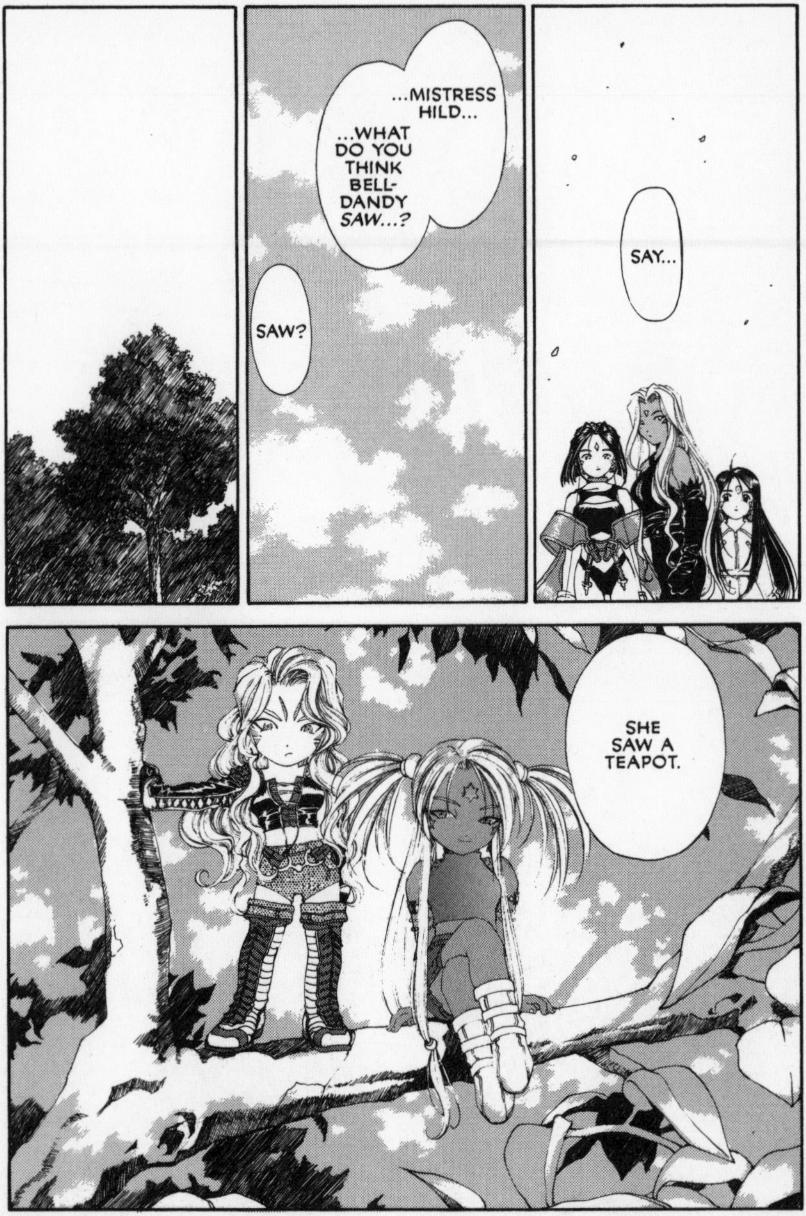
SAY...
...MISTRESS HILD... ...WHAT DO YOU THINK BELL-DANDY *SAW*...?
SAW?
SHE SAW A TEAPOT.

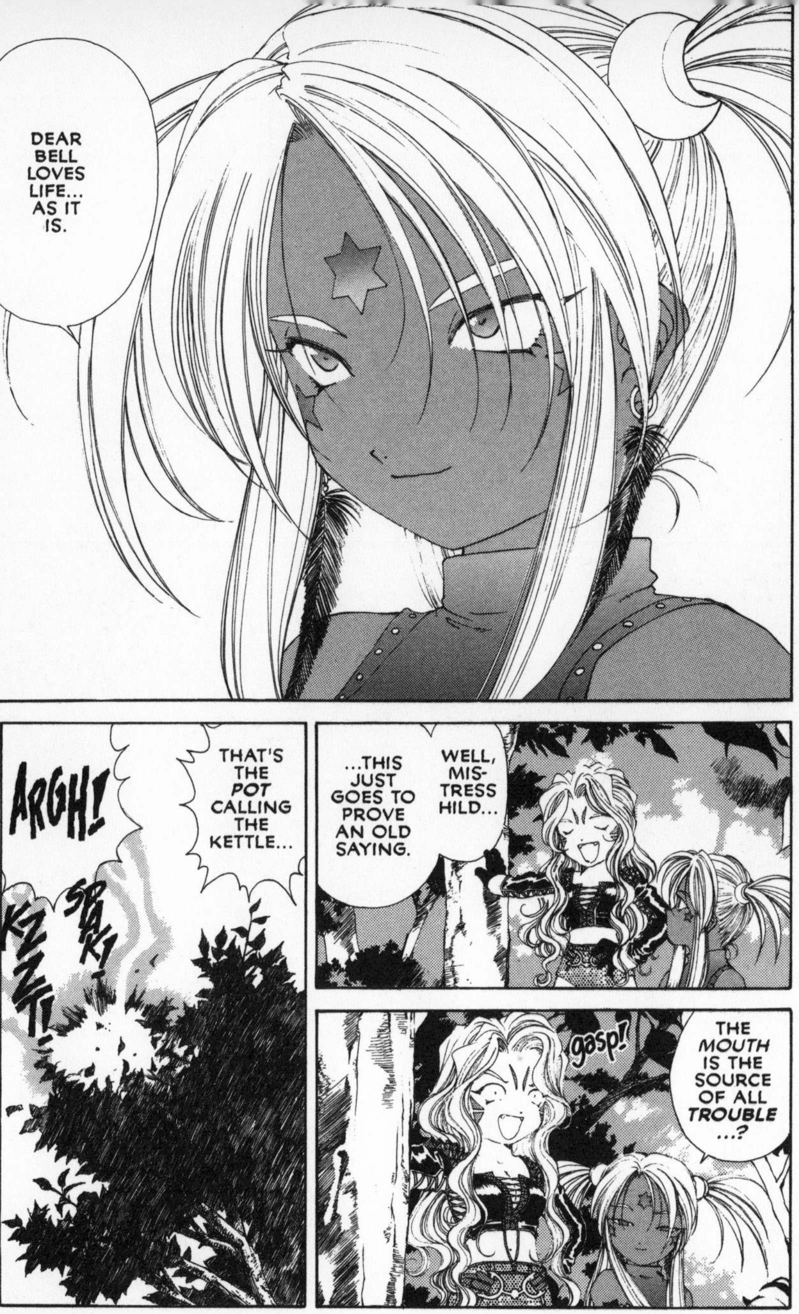
DEAR BELL LOVES LIFE... AS IT IS.
WELL, MISTRESS HILD...
...THIS JUST GOES TO PROVE AN OLD SAYING.
THE MOUTH IS THE SOURCE OF ALL TROUBLE ...?
gasp!
THAT'S THE POT CALLING THE KETTLE...
ARGH!

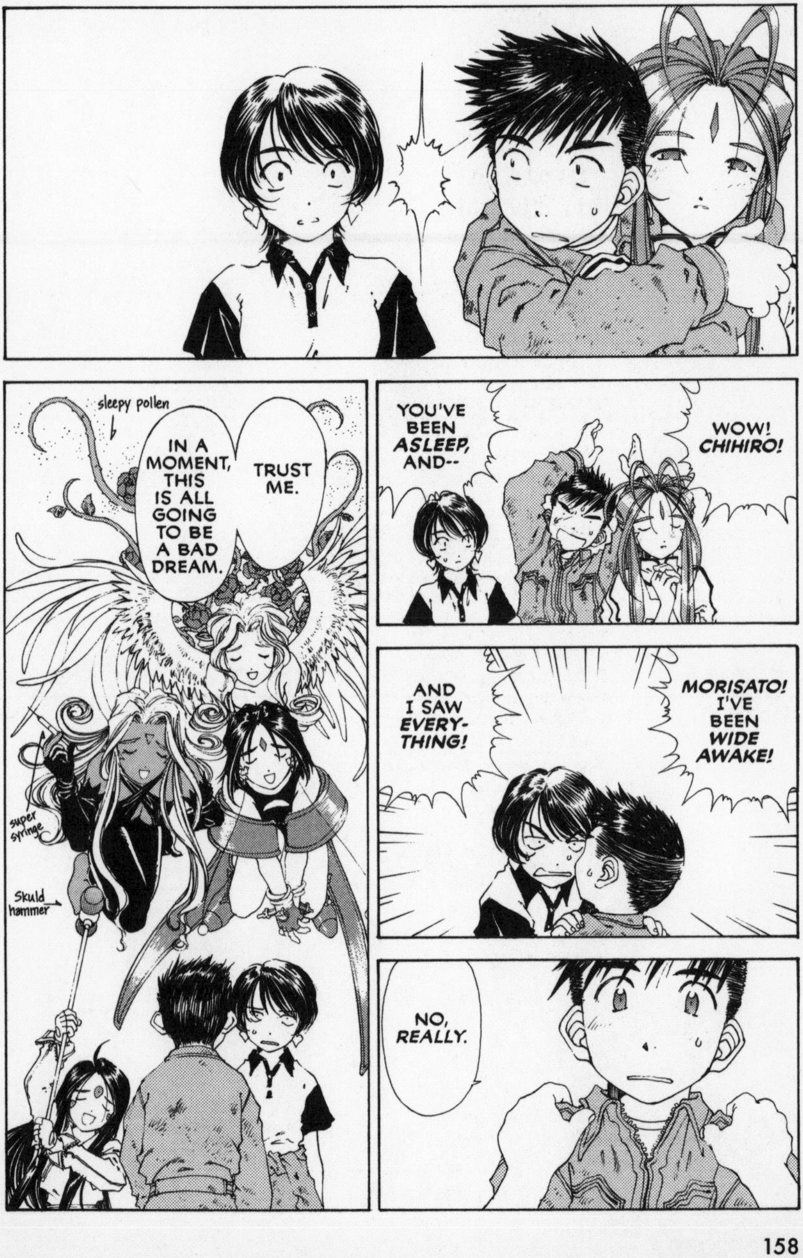
WOW! CHIHIRO!
YOU'VE BEEN ASLEEP, AND--
MORISATO! I'VE BEEN WIDE AWAKE!
AND I SAW EVERYTHING!
NO, REALLY.
TRUST ME.
IN A MOMENT, THIS IS ALL GOING TO BE A BAD DREAM.
sleepy pollen
super syringe
Skuld hammer

EDITOR
Carl Gustav Horn

DESIGNER
Debra Bailey

ART DIRECTOR
Lia Ribacchi

PUBLISHER
Mike Richardson

English-language version
produced by Dark Horse Comics

Published by Dark Horse Manga
A division of Dark Horse Comics, Inc.
10956 SE Main Street
Milwaukie, OR 97222
www.darkhorse.com

To find a comics shop in your area,
call the Comic Shop Locator Service
toll-free at 1-888-266-4226

First edition: December 2005
ISBN: 1-59307-400-X

1 3 5 7 9 10 8 6 4 2

Printed in Canada

letters to the
ENCHANTRESS

10956 SE Main Street, Milwaukie, Oregon 97222
omg@darkhorse.com • www.darkhorse.com

NOTE: Full addresses and e-mail addresses will not be printed, unless you ask! All fan artwork, letters, and e-mails submitted become the property of Dark Horse Comics.

First of all, thanks to all the readers for the positive reception of *Oh My Goddess!* Vol. 21 (see below). Before we get to the letters, just some quick notes from translator and editor on the volume you just completed (of course, if you're the type who jumps straight to the letters column, you're warned there may be spoilers ^_^).

9.2: In Norse mythology, Nidhogg was the serpent which gnawed the roots of Yggdrasil; to the Norse, the tree which underlaid the world, and, in the *Oh My Goddess!* cosmology, the computer system in the Goddess Realm that maintains and affects the realm of Earth.

18.1: The editor notes that Hild echoes the exact same offer (in Japanese, *sekai no hametsu nozomu nara*) made by Belldandy to Keiichi when she first met him in Vol. 1! This may explain the expression on his face . . .

25.4: Hild is switching from her usual referring to herself in the third person to just saying "I" and "me." This is to underscore there are certain confidences she might only share with Belldandy—whom even she seems to regard with some respect—and to specify that she is speaking about her personal life here, and not speaking corporately about herself as an executive representing the demon world.

36.1: Urd uses the term *mahojin*, which is traditionally translated as "magic square," although the kanji *jin* here (a different *jin* than the kanji meaning "person") by itself means a battle array or position taken up by a military force. The term "working" was used here, which, although somewhat vague, is strongly associated with ceremonial magic.

68.3: In the original Japanese, Hild did in fact ask Urd to say *okaa-san*, which is the normal, polite word for "mother," but Urd calls her *okachimenko* instead, which is an abnormal, impolite word for a woman whose features are aren't very symmetrical.

106.1: Nightingale, the little nurse of "Menzholatum," has her name taken from Florence Nightingale (1820-1910), the founder of modern nursing and a pioneer in epidemiology. Her appearance, however, is a satire of the mascot of "Mentholatum," the aromatic goop rubbed on ill children by generations of mothers to no very clear purpose. Although originally an American company, Mentholatum was bought in the 1970s by

Japan's Rohto Pharmaceutical Co., Ltd. More to the point, in 2004 Rohto Mentholatum also bought the Oxy line of skin care products, a purchase which caused their VP of Marketing & Sales to remark, "Mentholatum is acquiring a strong brand with immediate consumer recognition, 90 percent total brand awareness among the US teen target market, and a great tag line." Sounds a lot like manga.

First off, I want to say I love the series, and I love the new format. I'm looking forward to re-collecting the series again as you re-release them in the new right-to-left format.

However, this leads me to a question. The release schedule is one volume every two months, alternating new/old. With 20 volumes currently released, needing to be re-released, this means that it's going to take seven years (20/3 ~= 7) to re-release all the old volumes (thank the goddesses I have all of the old versions.) While this is semi-frustrating, it makes me wonder . . . is there enough material to provide NEW volumes for six more years? Because if there's that kind of assurance of longevity, well, then take as long as you like. The more OMG! we can get, the better place this world will be.

Thanks, and keep up
the wonderful work!
Ian Cyr
via e-mail

Thank you very much for your letter. I admit our program, simultaneously going both "backward" and "forward," is a bit awkward, but, of course, back in 1994 when OMG! began in English, no one ever imagined that one day the industry standard would become right-to-left.

As for new material, however, the most recent OMG! release in Japan is Vol. 31, so at three new volumes (along with three old volumes) per year, that would mean we would reach Vol. 31 in three years, that is, in December 2008. I think. However, a new OMG! volume comes out in Japan about every six months. So three years from now (assuming the series keeps going; so far it shows no sign of an imminent conclusion) we'll have another six to release.

This calculation gives us five years' worth of new volumes. At that point, we'd face what has happened to a fair amount of manga in the U.S. with quick releases—you get the initial volumes quickly, but then you reach a point where you've caught up with the Japanese release. So once we reach that theoretical point (and if Fujishima-san is still doing OMG!, which is, of course, ultimately up to him) then in December 2010—the year we make contact—we'll have to switch from one new volume every four months to one new volume every six months.

Thanks again, and please be on the lookout for another OMG! book we're doing, Oh My Goddess! Colors, to be released near the end of this year. It's basically a retrospective of all the OMG! we've done this far in the left-to-right edition, and is thus especially meant for the established fan. I personally don't hesitate to recommend our "old" volumes to anyone new to the series who doesn't want to wait for the unflopped re-release; after all, the new editions are based directly on those old editions, with the same basic translation, lettering style, etc.—the main difference, of course, is that we're switching to right-to-left.

Hi,

Thanks for the wonderful *OMG!* series. Finally the series continues. Man that was a long wait until the new TPB came out. Unfortunately wrong-sided now, I was never a big fan of the Japanese way of reading but I guess I'm now in a minority :-(

Anyways I have a question about the series. Since the *OMG!* movie we know that Belldandy and K1 come together, not that there was any doubt they will but it is good to know. What about Skuld and Sentaro? She is my absolute favorite although she is a brat ;-) but she deserves some love too, will they have some adventures together? Sentaro was absent for a while.

MARA!!!!! I love this hideous demon, will she ever strike back again? I hope we get some stories about her relationship with the goddesses.

Thanks for all the answers
Michael Ritter
via e-mail

Although Mr. Ritter doesn't come right out and say it, I gather he is writing in from Germany, judging by e-mail header, which promises *"DSL-Flatrates mit Tempo-Garantie!"* for only *"4,99 Euro/Monat."* Actually, "Ritter" is an old German word for "Knight," so in theory his name could be "Michael Knight." And everyone knows David Hasselhoff is very big in Germany, so I have to wonder.

Well, actually Sentaro going MIA is an interesting issue; Yoshitoh Asari also brings this up in his *OMG!* fan manga that introduced *Oh My Goddess! Colors.* But Mara's absence is a mystery no longer, as in Vol. 22 she and Hild show they are not to be underestimated due to size. As Bushwick Bill would say, "First of all I laugh."

Dear Mr. Horn,

First, allow me to express my appreciation for your long overdue switch from flipped art to the un-flipped Japanese style. Also matching the Japanese *tankobon* volumes has been long overdue, so I am very grateful you are doing this.

That said, I have a couple of related problems. First, Peorth and French. While I don't yet own the original *tankobon* where Peorth appears, I am fairly sure she doesn't speak French. I believe I read that this was an addition by the English translators to give some flair to the character for which Fujishima-sensei agreed. Is this true?

Whether true or not, I'm led to my second point. If it is okay to have untranslated French in an English-translated manga, why is it not okay to have ALL of the Japanese honorifics included (to include title/honorifics like "senpai'" "sensei." "oneesama," etc.)? I know the translators have worked to accommodate this ("Keiichi-dear" rather than "Keiichi-san" as an example), but this isn't the 80's or the 90's.

If you would follow Del Rey's example and include the honorifics, translator notes, etc., this *Oh My Goddess!* fan would happily re-purchase all of the old volumes from Dark Horse. Not only that, I'd be out there singing your praises everywhere I could.

If adding French to a character gives her flair, how much more would adding honorifics deepen the Western view of the characters?

Thanks for your time.
Earl "AstroNerdBoy" Commander
via e-mail

This letter actually is two letters, as there was a brief exchange of correspondence. The first reply was:

Thank you very much for your letter to "Letters to the Enchantress." I am generally relying on the good judgment of the team which has adapted the manga into English for eleven years. Specifically, the translator of *OMG!* is no lightweight; she is a columnist for *Newsweek's* Japan bureau—you understand why I would respect her opinions in this matter, including Peorth dropping phrases in French, a style introduced as you describe. My favorite is her exclamation in "Are You Being Served?," "*Ça me soulève le* **coeur**!"

OMG! may, in fact, be the longest continuously-published manga in the U.S. (note: as Toshi Yoshida was good enough to point out, it's only #2; *Ranma 1/2* is the longest ^_^), which must, I believe, be counted as some evidence of the quality of its adaptation.

I sincerely believe that the achievements of the Studio Proteus/Dark Horse version of *OMG!* far outweigh any individual criticisms people may have of it. I'm not saying that of my work, but of the work of Studio Proteus, from whom I inherited the title. Flopped or unflopped, I would have no hesitation in recommending the "classic" version to new readers. After all, it is the one which kept people reading for eleven years.

On the other hand, I also believe your point is very well taken about how readership (or the perception of readership) has changed since *OMG!* began. I am in fact restoring a number of specifically Japanese references beginning with the unflopped re-release of Vol. 1, and there will also be a section of notes.

I'm not sure about putting back in *all* the honorifics. As you note, the translator already made an effort to reflect the relations between the characters in their speech (arguably, a task which required more work on her part than simply marking names with "kun," "chan," etc.) and to put them all back in without also rewriting the speech back to its "base state" would, it seems to me, risk muddying the waters rather than making them more clear.

Earl wrote back:

Dear Mr. Horn (or I can call you Carl if you like),

Thanks so much for your rapid response. I'm sorry my own work schedule interfered with my getting back to you, but converting from a contractor to a regular employee at a large company can be an "interesting" experience (worth it in the end, I hope). ^_^;;;

Anyway, if you'll allow me to bore you for a few more minutes, allow me to tell a small story. Back when I found myself unemployed due to WorldCom's activities, I had a lot of free time and investigated how anime was doing in America. You see, back in 1989-1991, I was stationed at Yokota AB in Japan and my roommate/best friend told me that anime/manga was going to be big in the U.S. in ten years. As the year was now 2002, I thought I'd see if his prediction had come true. Lo and behold, he'd been right.

So I thought I'd sample a few small anime titles, one being *Oh My Goddess!* as released by AnimEigo. I watched it in English and loved it. I soon discovered that the OAV was based on a manga. So when I was once again gainfully employed, I purchased all of the then-released graphic novels from Dark Horse. Again, I loved it.

As time went on and I began sampling the Japanese versions (with subtitles) of anime, I discovered (thanks in great part to FUNimation) how changed an English version could be over the original script. I was not pleased by this. Somewhere during this time, I also became annoyed with the flipping of the art in the manga *Oh My Goddess!*, especially when it became so very obvious (Skuld's or Urd's hair-part flipping sides on different pages).

It was then that I did some investigation and discovered things like how the characters really addressed each other (Japanese honorifics) and the like. After that, I became a strong anti-domestication person, desirous to have the Japanese honorifics left in the translations (subtitles for anime, text for manga) as well as certain Japanese cultural things (to be fair, it wasn't just *Oh My Goddess!* that led me to this on the anime side, but it was on the manga side).

See, I'm in favor OF re-writing the text. After all, if some of the original Japanese references are being placed back in, why not re-write the script to include the honorifics? To me it seems simple, yet I know that this would cost a little extra money. To me, it would be money well-spent because the "hardcore" fans like myself would not only repurchase the series, but would be out there telling everyone they SHOULD re-purchase the series. I do this for FUNimation and their taking over the license to the Slayers TV series (all three). ^_^

Anyway, I don't want to harp so I'll wrap this up now. I do appreciate your consideration of these matters and listening to a hardcore (and money-spending) fan rant a bit.

Earl

Yokota AB, of course, was the setting of Hiroyuki Kitakubo's amazing film *Blood: The Last Vampire*. It's good to know what went down there back in 1966 didn't put them off anime. I should note that in the days before either the Web or a commercial anime home video industry in the U.S. (which was only getting started here in 1989), fans stationed at bases in Japan were an important source of information, tapes, and goods on anime. We never asked what they handed off from the PX in exchange.

Of course, I look at the Japanese originals in editing the unflopped old versions, so I can note something about how people are speaking. "San," being relatively neutral, will probably remain "invisible," but you'll see some chans in Vol. 1 and we'll bust with a kun in Vol. 2. The general *principle* of re-

storing Japanese cultural references will be very much there, however, both in the script and in the notes section.

As you say, these days, people want to know about these things, although, again, I would argue that Studio Proteus's adaptations were optimal for *OMG!*'s original market (monthly comics readers) and it's precisely because they built such an audience for this title that I now have the opportunity to go back and comment on such original Japanese references.

Now, it may *sound* completely obvious that the goal of re-releasing the "old" *OMG!* volumes is to get previous fans to buy them a second time, but it actually surprised me when people brought this up. In my own mind, because people now reading *OMG!* Vol. 22 presumably got this far with the flopped versions, the unflopped *OMG!* Vol. 1 is instead directed at the brand-new reader, the person in the bookstores (remember *OMG!* began here in the comics stores) who wants to discover the story for the first time.

Of course, if you *want* to buy it, cool, and hopefully you'll find the new material there (cover, interior color pages, notes section, Fujishima's introduction) to be worth your while. But this honestly wasn't intended to get established readers to buy something twice. Instead I want a bunch of new *OMG!* fans to join the throng, fans who will now realize how much has been ripped off since 1989 from Fujishima-san ^_^

Hi there Enchantress!

This is Alicia. I love the *Oh/Ah! My Goddess* comic books! I love the story and the characters that are thought up. It all seems to fall together into a real lifestyle. I can relate to many things I've read in these amazing stories it seems. And all my friends that know of the series have told me I kinda look like and act like Belldandy. Which is really awesome because she is my favorite character!

I would love to learn more about the one who created my favorite series! And I think Belldandy's angel's name should be Holy Bell instead of Blessed Bell. I love both names but I think Holy Bell seems to go together better with Belldandy. I'm not exactly sure why at the moment but yeah. Well, I hope to see more great things happening with the series. Which I know there will be. I have seen and read nothing that I thought was bad for a second! If that made any sense.

Sincerely,
Alicia aka Ashiyama
Ashiyama1@aol.com

Yeah, that made sense ^_^ You wouldn't happen to be the person who cos-played as Bell for Hidenori Matsubara (character designer of the three *OMG!* anime versions) at Anime Central? He really liked that fan. Belldandy is pretty difficult to equal, as everyone in the *Oh My Goddess!* story is always discovering.

If you do check out the unflopped re-release of *Oh My Goddess!* Vol. 1 (which should be out by the time you read this), we've included Kosuke Fujishima's original messages to readers from that time, to show what was on his mind as the story developed. By the way, Belldandy's angel will definitely be called Holy Bell. Just in time for Christmas!

Mr. Horn,

First of all, I would like to say that I'm glad that you're the new editor for *Oh My Goddess!* It's rare for me to see an editor who puts so much into his work, because I know from word of mouth that you're working very hard to fix mistakes and trying to get everything in order. I'm sure others have contacted you about the use of Peorth's French,

Urd referring to Hild as "mother," and a few other things in Vol. 21. I trust that you will be able to handle things better with time, especially since you're so willingly working with the fans.

I wish you the best of luck with this series, and I do hope that you stay with it. I can't say I understand how hard it is, but I do respect that you're trying very hard.

If this gets printed, feel free to print my e-mail/website.

Jonathan Sieng Chua
love.a.riddle@gmail.com
AIM: Love a Riddle
http://www.1up-mushroom.net

Thank you for your support ^_^. I do have my own way of going about things, which may not be the way others would.

As I say, this is only the Dark Horse version of *Oh My Goddess!* It happens to also be the officially licensed English version, and I think it's a pretty good one—but I would never say that this version is the only way it could be done. That's a silly thing to say, especially in this day and age, and I think you all know what I'm talking about. I do try to explain some of the reasoning behind the adaptation process, however. Please keep writing—and don't forget to cough up some of that fan art.

THE LEGEND OF MOTHER SARAH
Katsuhiro Otomo
Tunnel Town
B&W / 1-56971-145-3 / $18.95

LONE WOLF AND CUB
Kazuo Koike and Goseki Kojima
Volume 1: The Assassin's Road
296-page B&W / 1-56971-502-5 / $9.95

Volume 2: The Gateless Barrier
296-page B&W / 1-56971-503-3 / $9.95

Volume 3: The Flute of the Fallen Tiger
304-page B&W / 1-56971-504-1 / $9.95

Volume 4: The Bell Warden
304-page B&W / 1-56971-505-X / $9.95

Volume 5: Black Wind
288-page B&W / 1-56971-506-8 / $9.95

Volume 6: Lanterns for the Dead
288-page B&W / 1-56971-507-6 / $9.95

Volume 7: Cloud Dragon, Wind Tiger
320-page B&W / 1-56971-508-4 / $9.95

Volume 8: Chains of Death
304-page B&W / 1-56971-509-2 / $9.95

Volume 9: Echo of the Assassin
288-page B&W / 1-56971-510-6 / $9.95

Volume 10: Hostage Child
320-page B&W / 1-56971-511-4 / $9.95

Volume 11: Talisman of Hades
320-page B&W / 1-56971-512-2 / $9.95

Volume 12: Shattered Stones
304-page B&W / 1-56971-513-0 / $9.95

**Volume 13: The Moon in the East,
The Sun in the West**
320-page B&W / 1-56971-585-8 / $9.95

Volume 14: The Day of the Demons
320-page B&W / 1-56971-586-6 / $9.95

Volume 15: Brothers of the Grass
352-page B&W / 1-56971-587-4 / $9.95

Volume 16: The Gateway into Winter
320-page B&W / 1-56971-588-2 / $9.95

Volume 17: Will of the Fang
320-page B&W / 1-56971-589-0 / $9.95

Volume 18: Twilight of the Kurokuwa
320-page B&W / 1-56971-590-4 / $9.95

Volume 19: The Moon in Our Hearts
320-page B&W / 1-56971-591-2 / $9.95

Volume 20: A Taste of Poison
320-page B&W / 1-56971-592-0 / $9.95

Volume 21: Fragrance of Death
320-page B&W / 1-56971-593-9 / $9.95

Volume 22: Heaven and Earth
288-page B&W / 1-56971-594-7 / $9.95

Volume 23: Tears of Ice
320-page B&W / 1-56971-595-5 / $9.95

Volume 24: In These Small Hands
320-page B&W / 1-56971-596-3 / $9.95

Volume 25: Perhaps in Death
320-page B&W / 1-56971-597-1 / $9.95

Volume 26: Struggle in the Dark
312-page B&W / 1-56971-598-X / $9.95

Volume 27: Battle's Eve
300-page B&W / 1-56971-599-8 / $9.95

Volume 28: The Lotus Throne
320-page B&W / 1-56971-600-5 / $9.95

LOST WORLD
Osamu Tezuka
248-page B&W / 1-56971-865-2 / $14.95

METROPOLIS
Osamu Tezuka
168-page B&W / 1-56971-864-4 / $13.95

NEXTWORLD
Osamu Tezuka
Volume 1
160-page B&W / 1-56971-866-0 / $13.95

Volume 2
168-page B&W / 1-56971-867-9 / $13.95

ORION
Masamune Shirow
272-page B&W / 1-56971-572-6 / $19.95

OUTLANDERS
Johji Manabe
Volume 2
192-page B&W / 1-56971-162-3 / $13.95

Volume 3
160-page B&W / 1-56971-163-1 / $13.95

Volume 4
168-page B&W / 1-56971-069-4 / $12.95

Volume 5
216-page B&W / 1-56971-275-1 / $14.95

Volume 6
200-page B&W / 1-56971-423-1 / $14.95

Volume 7
184-page B&W / 1-56971-424-X / $14.95

Volume 8
176-page B&W / 1-56971-425-8 / $14.95

SERAPHIC FEATHER
*Hiroyuki Utatane, Toshiya Takeda,
Yo Morimoto*
Volume 1: Crimson Angel
232-page B&W / 1-56971-555-6 / $17.95

Volume 2: Seeds of Chaos
240-page B&W / 1-56971-739-7 / $17.95

Volume 3: Target Zone
240-page B&W / 1-56971-912-8 / $17.95

Volume 4: Dark Angel
240-page B&W / 1-56971-913-6 / $17.95

SHADOW LADY
Masakazu Katsura
Volume 1: Dangerous Love
200-page B&W / 1-56971-408-8 / $17.95

Volume 2: The Awakening
184-page B&W / 1-56971-446-0 / $15.95

Volume 3: Sudden Death
176-page B&W / 1-56971-477-0 / $14.95

SHADOW STAR
Mohiro Kitoh
Volume 1: Shadow Star
192-page B&W / 1-56971-548-3 / $15.95

Volume 2: Darkness Visible
182-page B&W / 1-56971-740-0 / $14.95

Volume 3: Shadows of the Past
144-page B&W / 1-56971-743-5 / $13.95

Volume 4: Nothing but the Truth
160-page B&W / 1-56971-920-9 / $14.95

Volume 5: A Flower's Fragrance
208-page B&W / 1-56971-990-X / $15.95

3X3 EYES
Yuzo Takada

Volume 1: House of Demons
160-page B&W / 1-56971-930-6 / $14.95

Volume 2: Curse of the Gesu
152-page B&W / 1-56971-931-X / $14.95

Volume 3: Flight of the Demon
208-page B&W / 1-56971-553-X / $15.95

Volume 4: Blood of the Sacred Demon
144-page B&W / 1-56971-735-4 / $13.95

Volume 5: Summoning of the Beast
152-page B&W / 1-56971-747-8 / $14.95

Volume 6: Key to the Sacred Land
136-page B&W / 1-56971-881-4 / $13.95

Volume 7: The Shadow of the Kunlun
224-page B&W / 1-56971-981-0 / $17.95

STOP! This is the back of the book!

This manga collection is translated into English, but arranged in right-to-left reading format to maintain the artwork's visual orientation as originally drawn and published in Japan. If you've never read comics this way before, take a look at the diagram below to give yourself an idea of how to go about it. Basically, you'll be starting in the upper right-hand corner, and will read each word balloon and panel moving right-to-left. It may take a little getting used to, but you should get the hang of it very quickly. Have fun! If this is the millionth manga you've read this way, never mind.

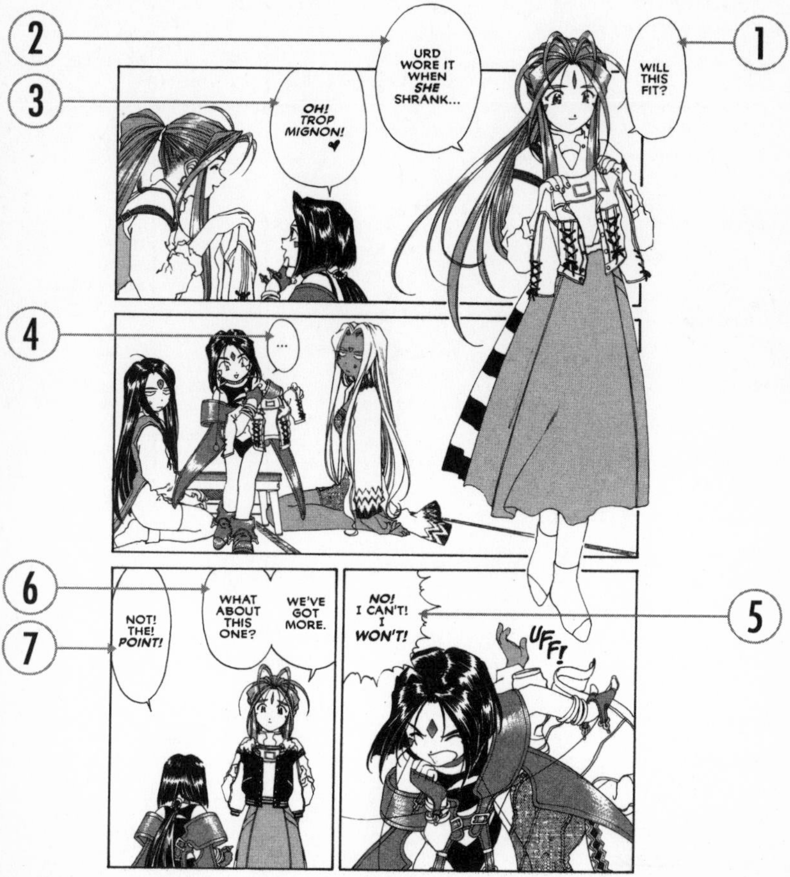

1
WILL THIS FIT?
2
URD WORE IT WHEN *SHE* SHRANK...
3
OH! TROP MIGNON!
4
...
5
NO! I CAN'T! I WON'T!
UFF!
WE'VE GOT MORE.
6
WHAT ABOUT THIS ONE?
7
NOT! THE! *POINT!*